SPELL CHECKERS™

VOLUME 2

An Oni Press Publication

D1472982

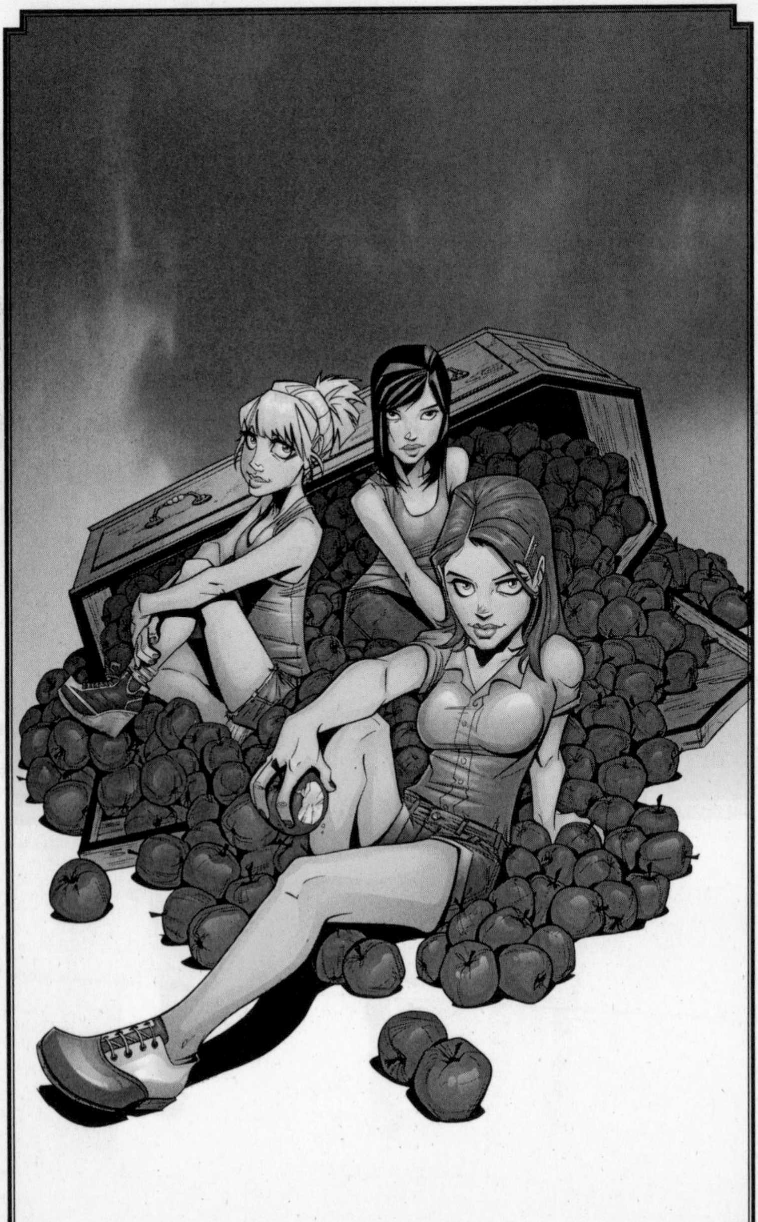

SPELL CHECKERS ™

VOLUME 2: SONS OF A PREACHER MAN

written by
JAMIE S. RICH

illustrated by
NICOLAS HITORI DE

flashbacks and cover
illustrated by
JOËLLE JONES

cover colored by
KIMBALL DAVIS

lettered by
DOUGLAS E. SHERWOOD

design by
KEITH WOOD

edited by
JILL BEATON

Oni Press, Inc.

publisher Joe Nozemack

editor in chief James Lucas Jones

marketing director Cory Casoni

art director Keith Wood

operations director George Rohac

editor Jill Beaton

editor Charlie Chu

production assistant Douglas E. Sherwood

Spell Checkers, Volume 2, September 2011. Published by Oni Press, Inc.
1305 SE Martin Luther King Jr. Blvd., Suite A, Portland, OR 97214. Spell Checkers
is ™ & © 2011 Jamie S. Rich, Joëlle Jones and Nicholas Louchez. All rights reserved.
Unless otherwise specified, all other material © 2011 Oni Press, Inc. Oni Press logo
and icon ™ & © 2011 Oni Press, Inc. All rights reserved. Oni Press logo and icon
artwork created by Dave Gibbons. The events, institutions, and characters presented
in this book are fictional. Any resemblance to actual persons, living or dead, is purely
coincidental. No portion of this publication may be reproduced, by any means, with-
out the express written permission of the copyright holders.

Oni Press Inc.
1305 SE Martin Luther King Jr. Blvd.
Suite A
Portland, OR 97214

www.onipress.com

First Edition: September 2011

ISBN: 978-1-934964-72-9
Library of Congress Control Number: 2011906141

1 3 5 7 9 10 8 6 4 2

Printed in the U.S.A.

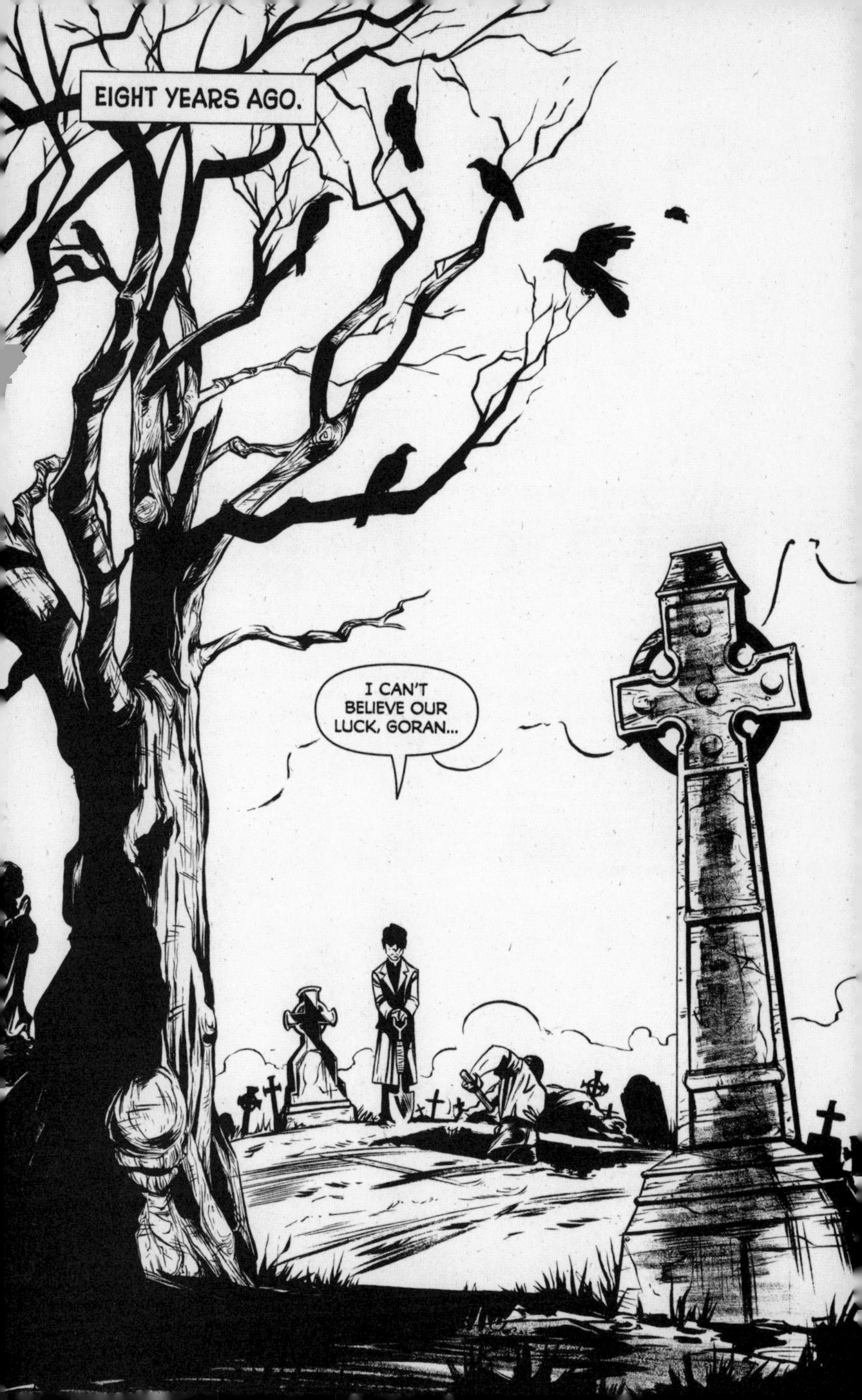
EIGHT YEARS AGO.
I CAN'T BELIEVE OUR LUCK, GORAN...

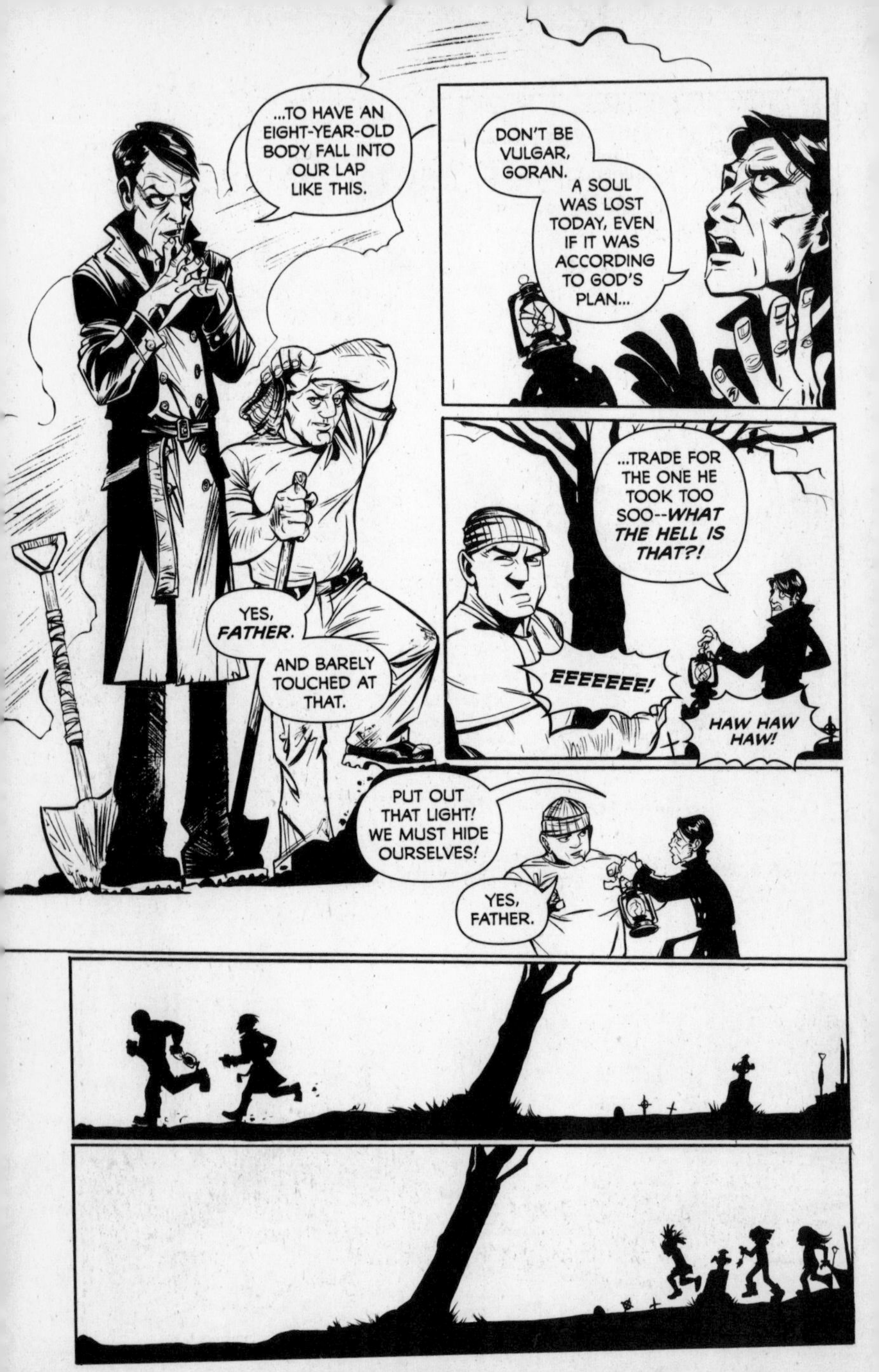
...TO HAVE AN EIGHT-YEAR-OLD BODY FALL INTO OUR LAP LIKE THIS.
DON'T BE VULGAR, GORAN.
A SOUL WAS LOST TODAY, EVEN IF IT WAS ACCORDING TO GOD'S PLAN...
YES, *FATHER*.
AND BARELY TOUCHED AT THAT.
...TRADE FOR THE ONE HE TOOK TOO SOO--*WHAT THE HELL IS THAT?!*
EEEEEEE!
HAW HAW HAW!
PUT OUT THAT LIGHT! WE MUST HIDE OURSELVES!
YES, FATHER.

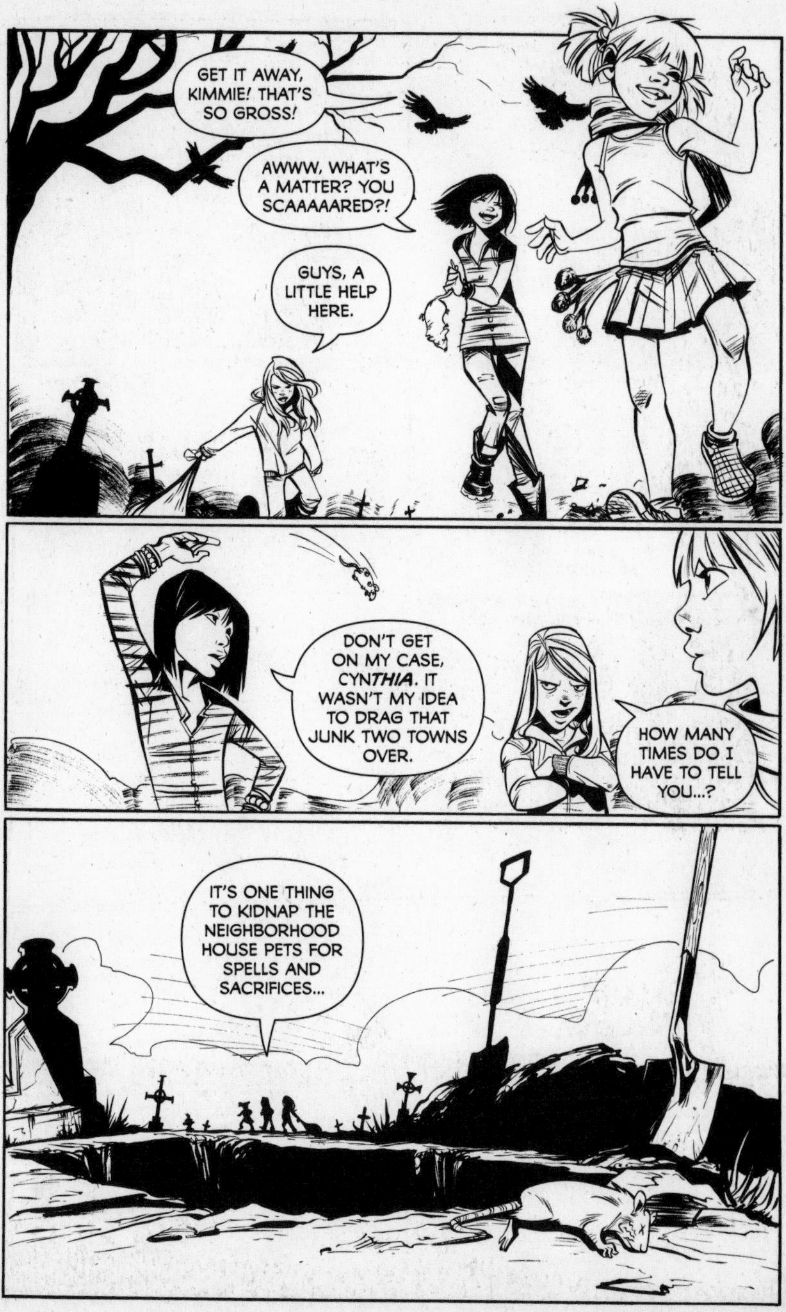
GET IT AWAY, KIMMIE! THAT'S SO GROSS!
AWWW, WHAT'S A MATTER? YOU SCAAAAARED?!
GUYS, A LITTLE HELP HERE.
DON'T GET ON MY CASE, CYN*THIA*. IT WASN'T MY IDEA TO DRAG THAT JUNK TWO TOWNS OVER.
HOW MANY TIMES DO I HAVE TO TELL YOU...?
IT'S ONE THING TO KIDNAP THE NEIGHBORHOOD HOUSE PETS FOR SPELLS AND SACRIFICES...

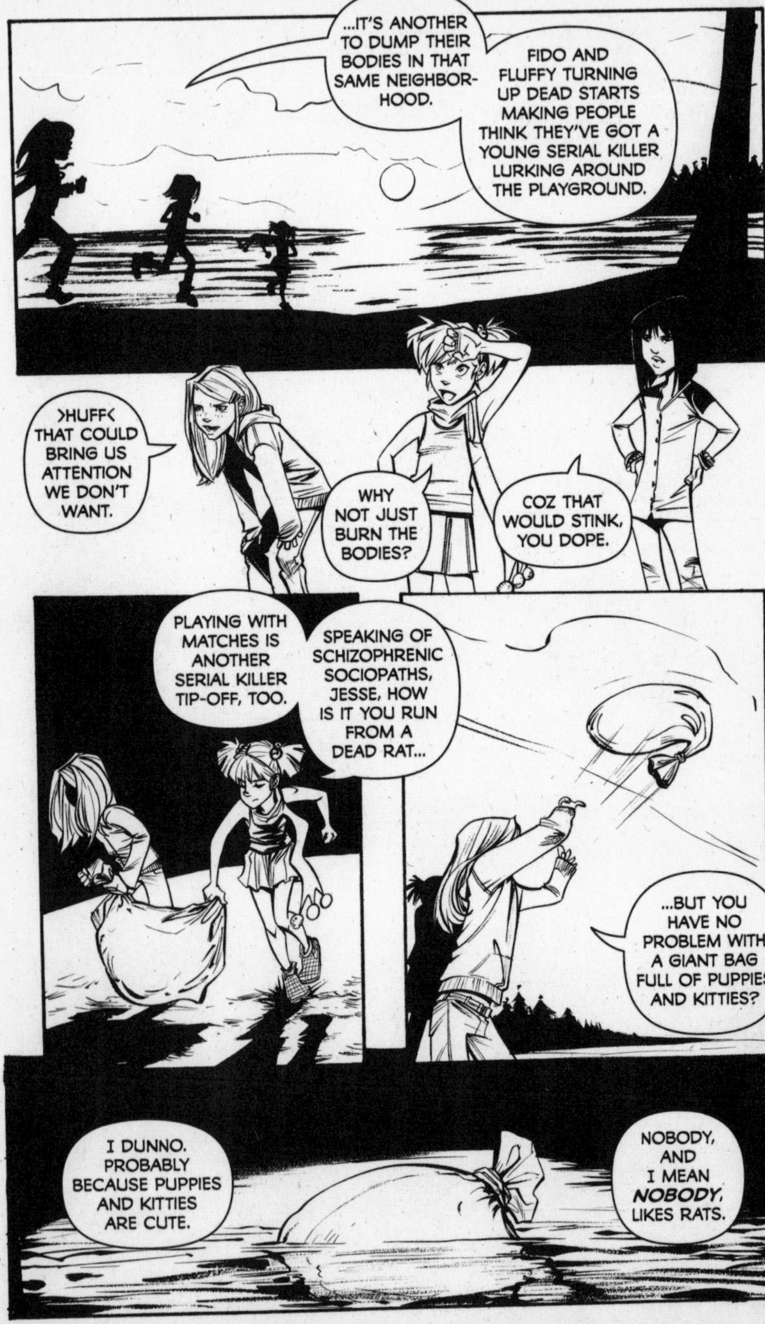
...IT'S ANOTHER TO DUMP THEIR BODIES IN THAT SAME NEIGHBOR-HOOD.
FIDO AND FLUFFY TURNING UP DEAD STARTS MAKING PEOPLE THINK THEY'VE GOT A YOUNG SERIAL KILLER LURKING AROUND THE PLAYGROUND.
>HUFF< THAT COULD BRING US ATTENTION WE DON'T WANT.
WHY NOT JUST BURN THE BODIES?
COZ THAT WOULD STINK, YOU DOPE.
PLAYING WITH MATCHES IS ANOTHER SERIAL KILLER TIP-OFF, TOO.
SPEAKING OF SCHIZOPHRENIC SOCIOPATHS, JESSE, HOW IS IT YOU RUN FROM A DEAD RAT...
...BUT YOU HAVE NO PROBLEM WITH A GIANT BAG FULL OF PUPPIES AND KITTIES?
I DUNNO. PROBABLY BECAUSE PUPPIES AND KITTIES ARE CUTE.
NOBODY, AND I MEAN ***NOBODY***, LIKES RATS.

Chapter 1
"Do The Double Bump"

I

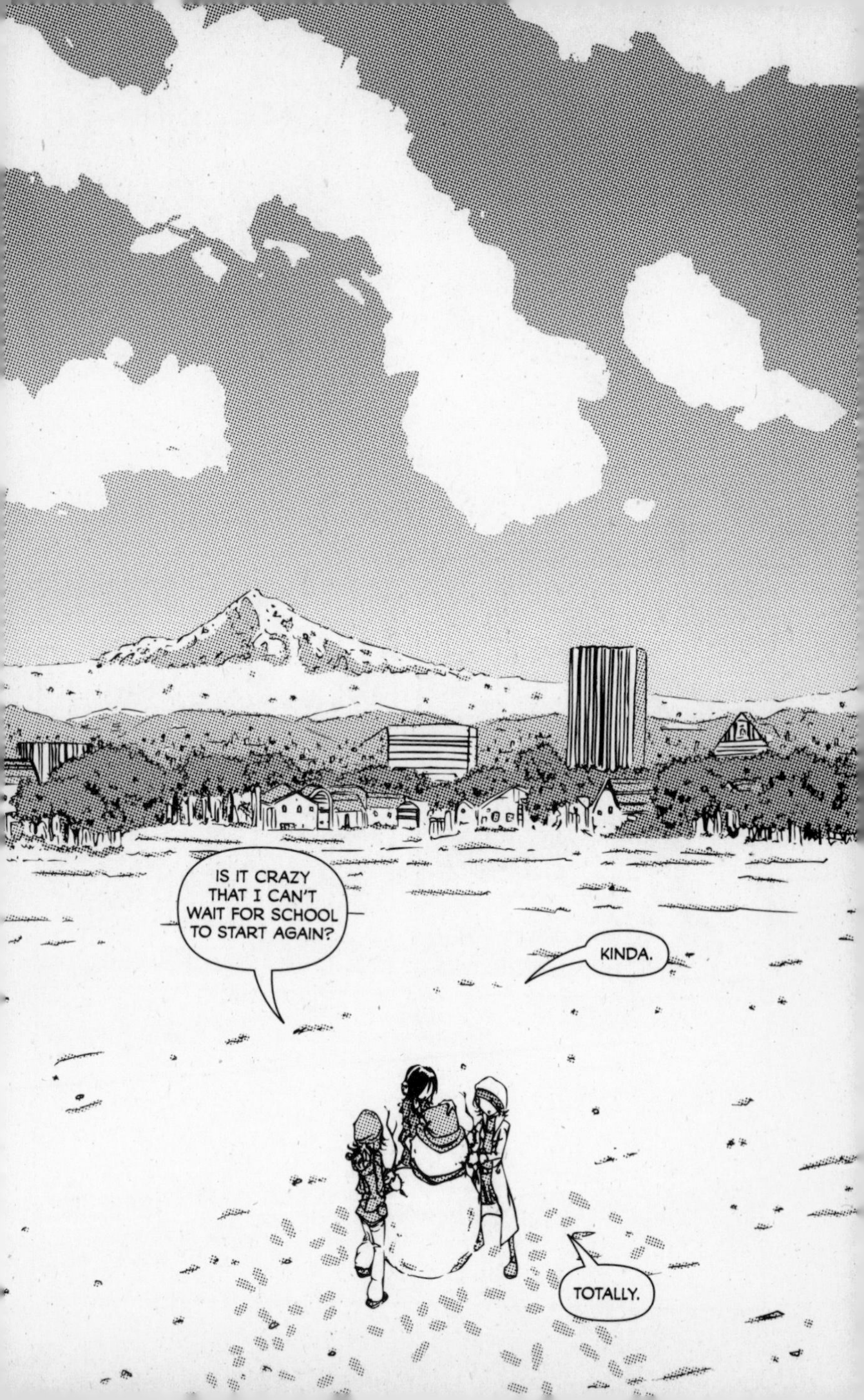
IS IT CRAZY THAT I CAN'T WAIT FOR SCHOOL TO START AGAIN?
KINDA.
TOTALLY.

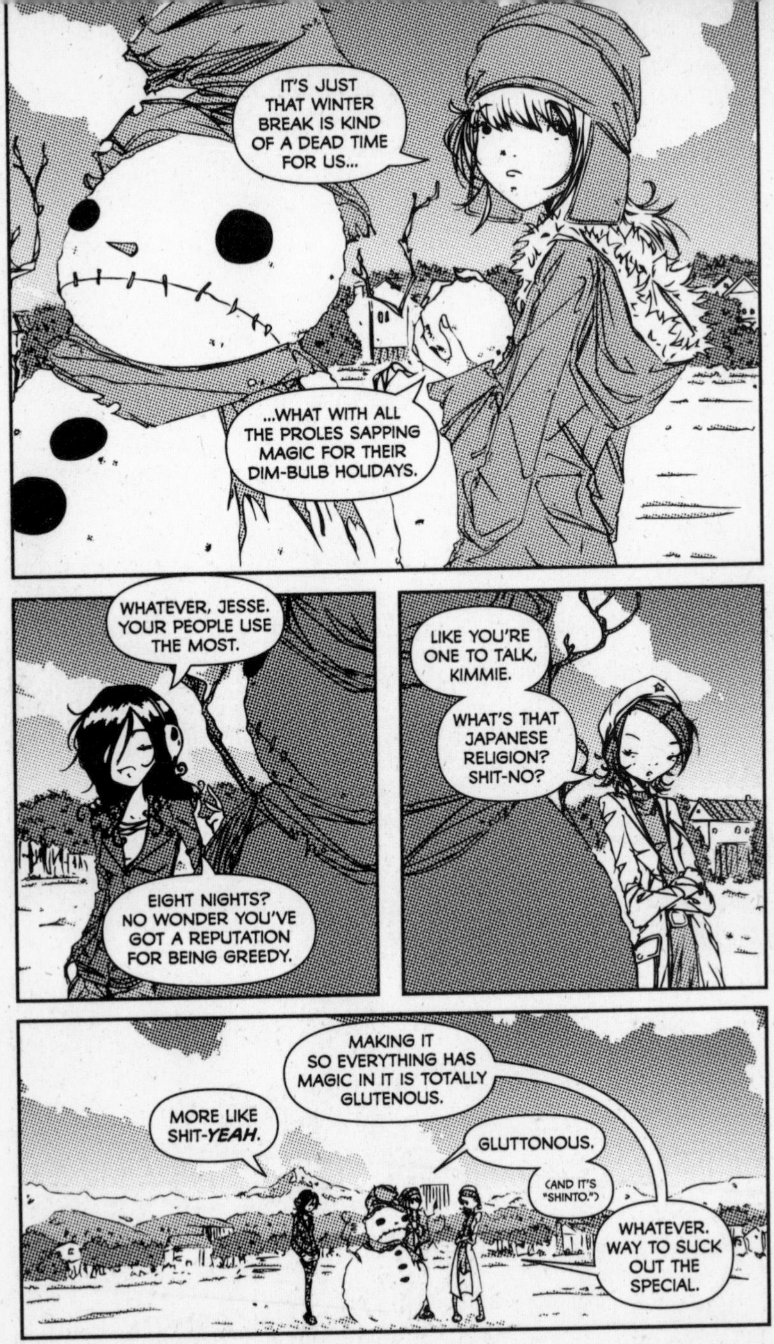
IT'S JUST THAT WINTER BREAK IS KIND OF A DEAD TIME FOR US...
...WHAT WITH ALL THE PROLES SAPPING MAGIC FOR THEIR DIM-BULB HOLIDAYS.
WHATEVER, JESSE. YOUR PEOPLE USE THE MOST.
EIGHT NIGHTS? NO WONDER YOU'VE GOT A REPUTATION FOR BEING GREEDY.
LIKE YOU'RE ONE TO TALK, KIMMIE.
WHAT'S THAT JAPANESE RELIGION? SHIT-NO?
MAKING IT SO EVERYTHING HAS MAGIC IN IT IS TOTALLY GLUTENOUS.
MORE LIKE SHIT-*YEAH*.
GLUTTONOUS.
(AND IT'S "SHINTO.")
WHATEVER. WAY TO SUCK OUT THE SPECIAL.

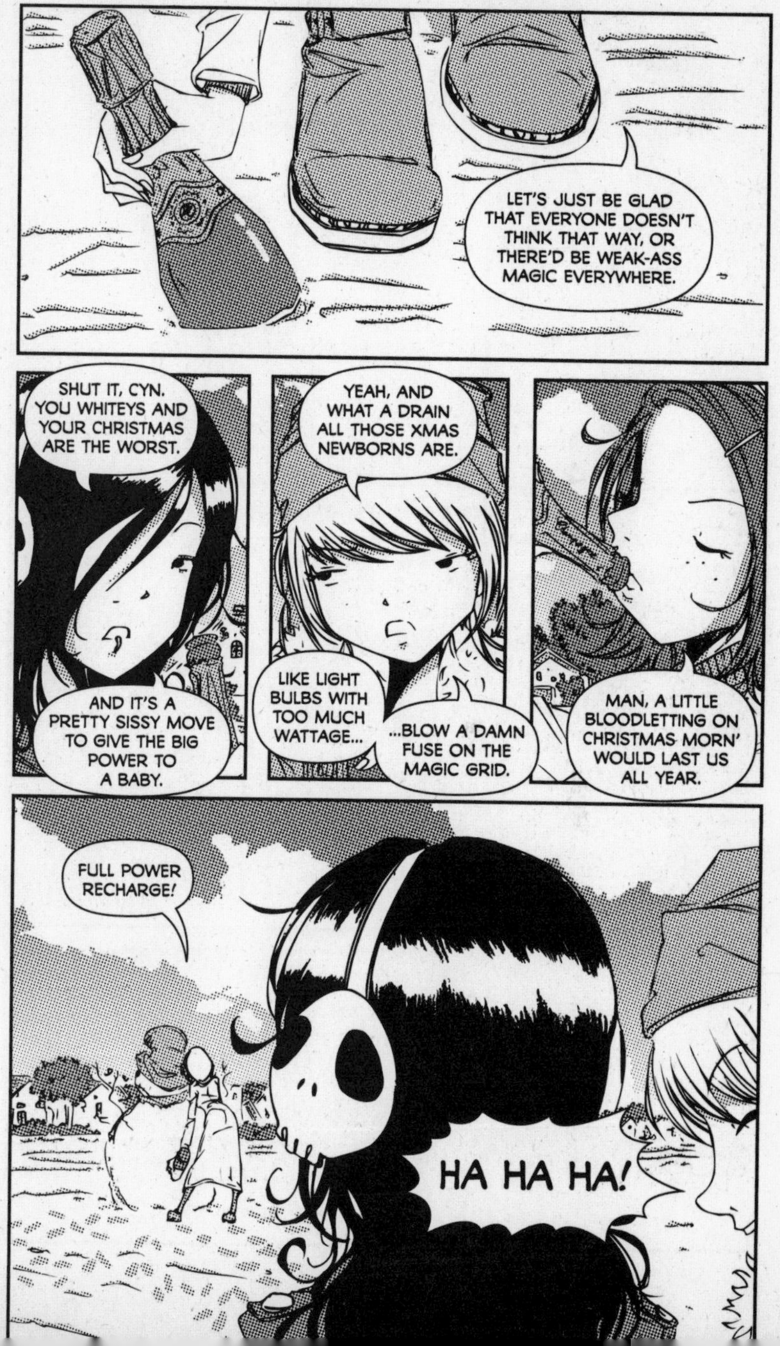
LET'S JUST BE GLAD THAT EVERYONE DOESN'T THINK THAT WAY, OR THERE'D BE WEAK-ASS MAGIC EVERYWHERE.
SHUT IT, CYN. YOU WHITEYS AND YOUR CHRISTMAS ARE THE WORST.
AND IT'S A PRETTY SISSY MOVE TO GIVE THE BIG POWER TO A BABY.
YEAH, AND WHAT A DRAIN ALL THOSE XMAS NEWBORNS ARE.
LIKE LIGHT BULBS WITH TOO MUCH WATTAGE...
...BLOW A DAMN FUSE ON THE MAGIC GRID.
MAN, A LITTLE BLOODLETTING ON CHRISTMAS MORN' WOULD LAST US ALL YEAR.
FULL POWER RECHARGE!
HA HA HA!

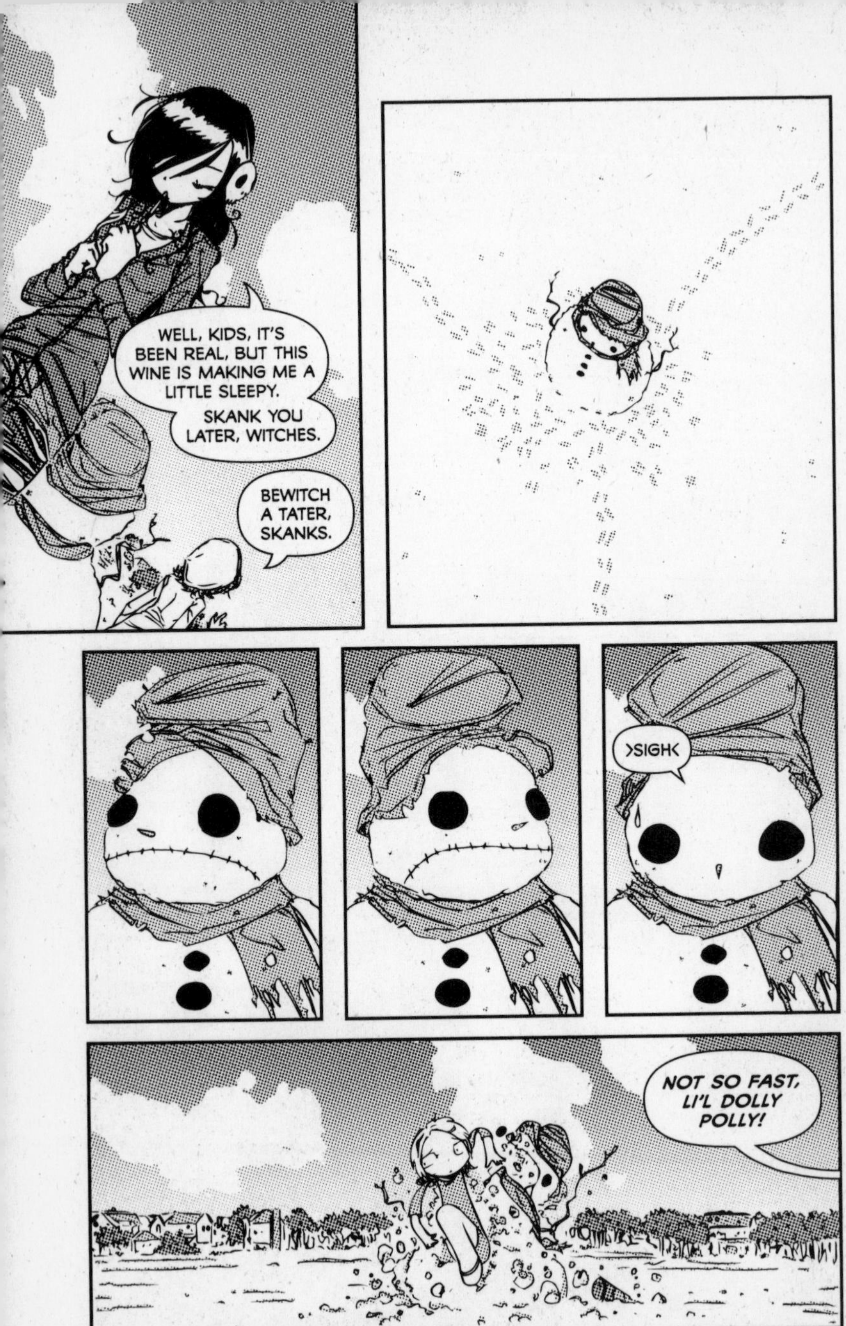
WELL, KIDS, IT'S BEEN REAL, BUT THIS WINE IS MAKING ME A LITTLE SLEEPY.
SKANK YOU LATER, WITCHES.
BEWITCH A TATER, SKANKS.
>SIGH<
NOT SO FAST, LI'L DOLLY POLLY!

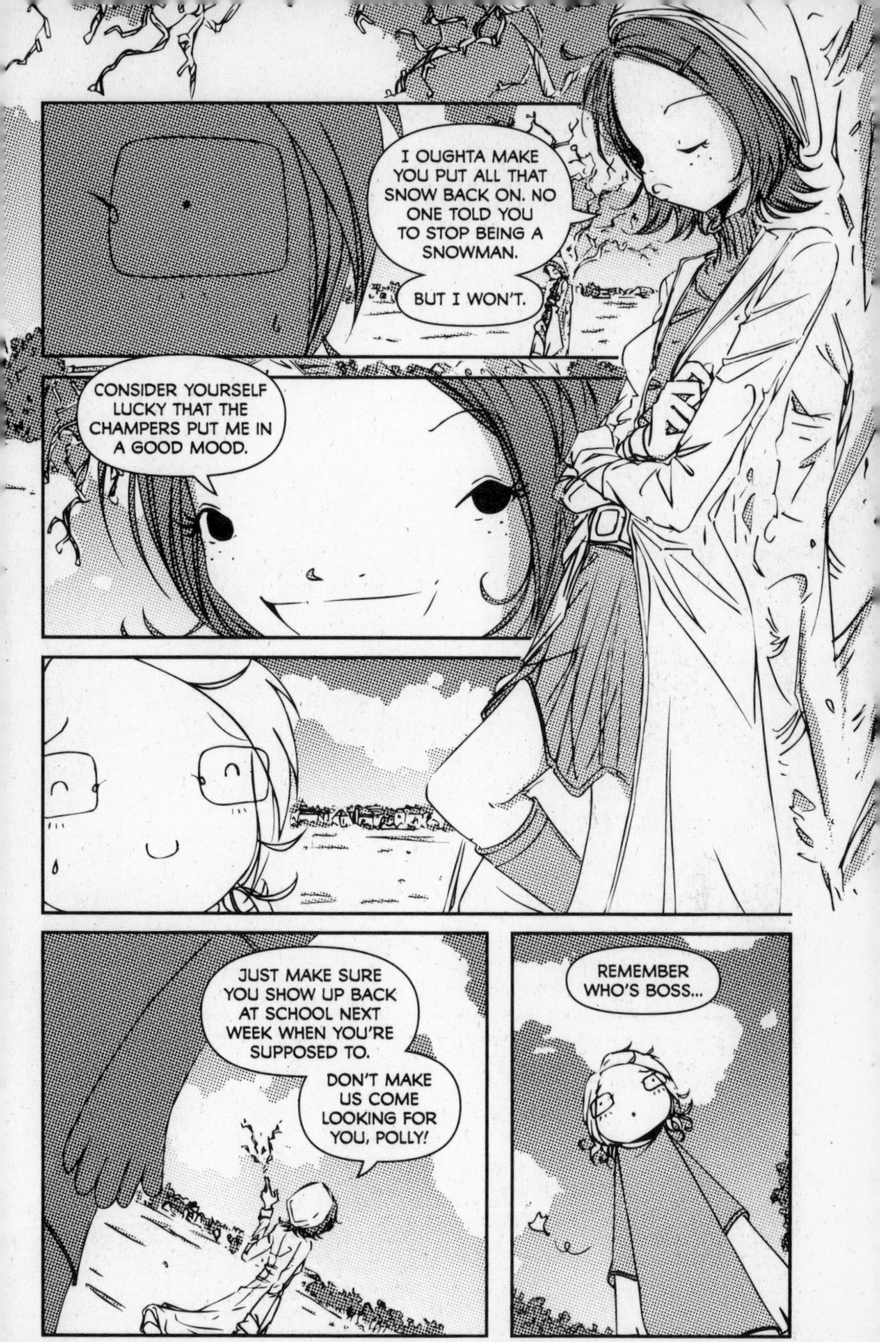
I OUGHTA MAKE YOU PUT ALL THAT SNOW BACK ON. NO ONE TOLD YOU TO STOP BEING A SNOWMAN.
BUT I WON'T.
CONSIDER YOURSELF LUCKY THAT THE CHAMPERS PUT ME IN A GOOD MOOD.
JUST MAKE SURE YOU SHOW UP BACK AT SCHOOL NEXT WEEK WHEN YOU'RE SUPPOSED TO.
DON'T MAKE US COME LOOKING FOR YOU, POLLY!
REMEMBER WHO'S BOSS...

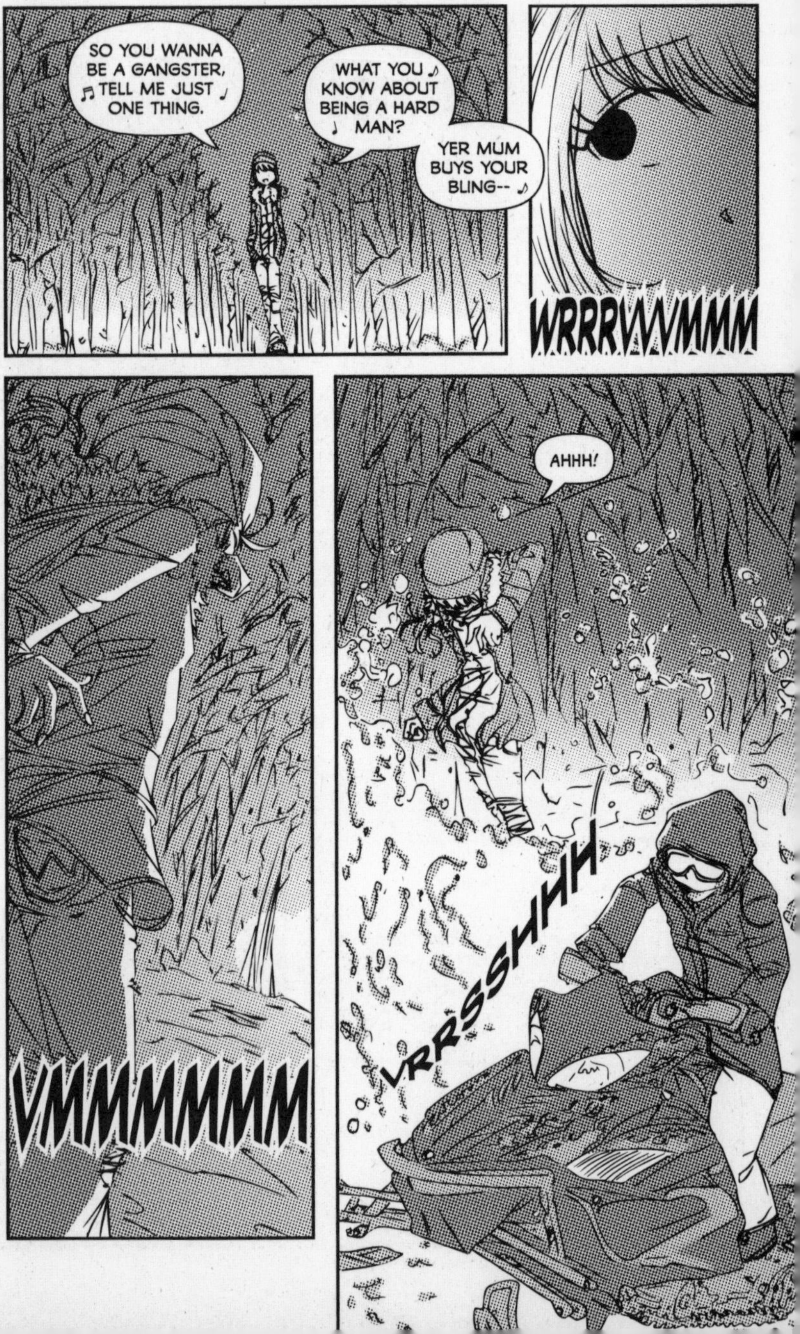
SO YOU WANNA BE A GANGSTER, ♫ TELL ME JUST ♪ ONE THING.
WHAT YOU ♪ KNOW ABOUT BEING A HARD ♪ MAN?
YER MUM BUYS YOUR BLING-- ♪
WRRRVVVMMM
VMMMMMMM
AHHH!
VRRSSHHH

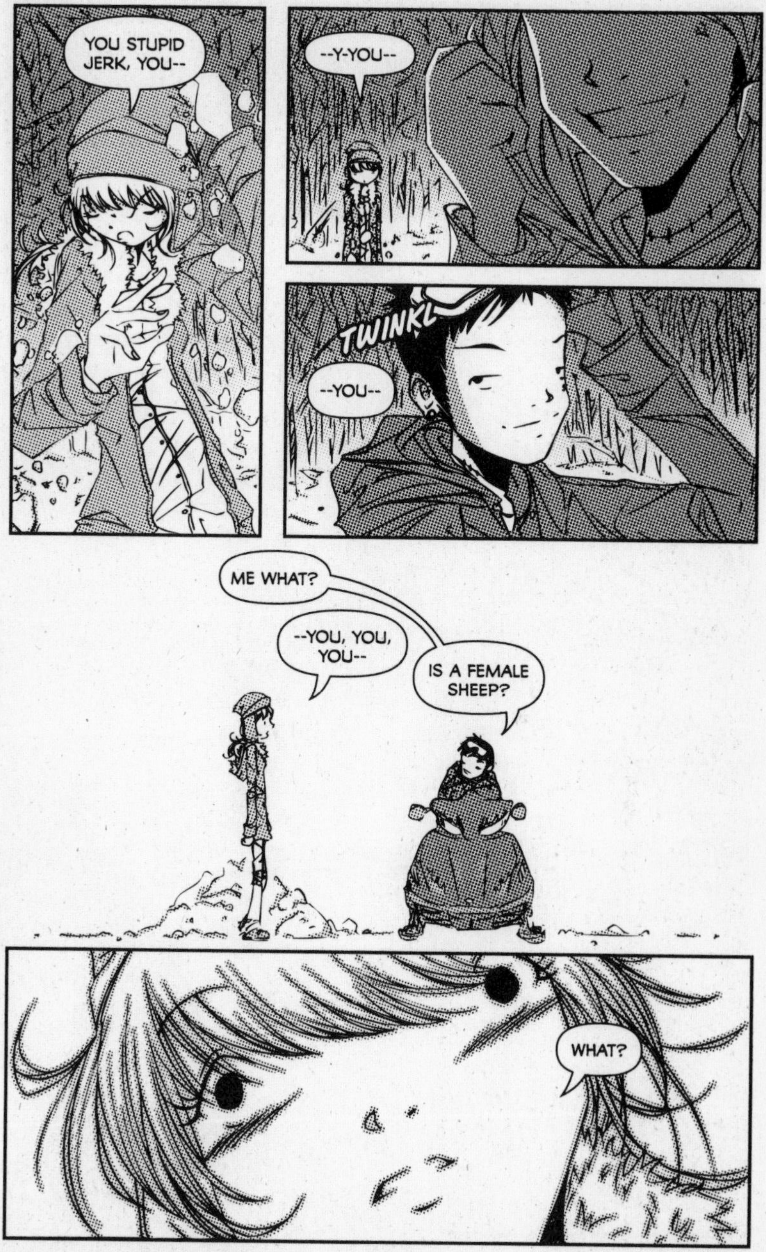
YOU STUPID JERK, YOU--
--Y-YOU--
TWINKL
--YOU--
ME WHAT?
--YOU, YOU, YOU--
IS A FEMALE SHEEP?
WHAT?

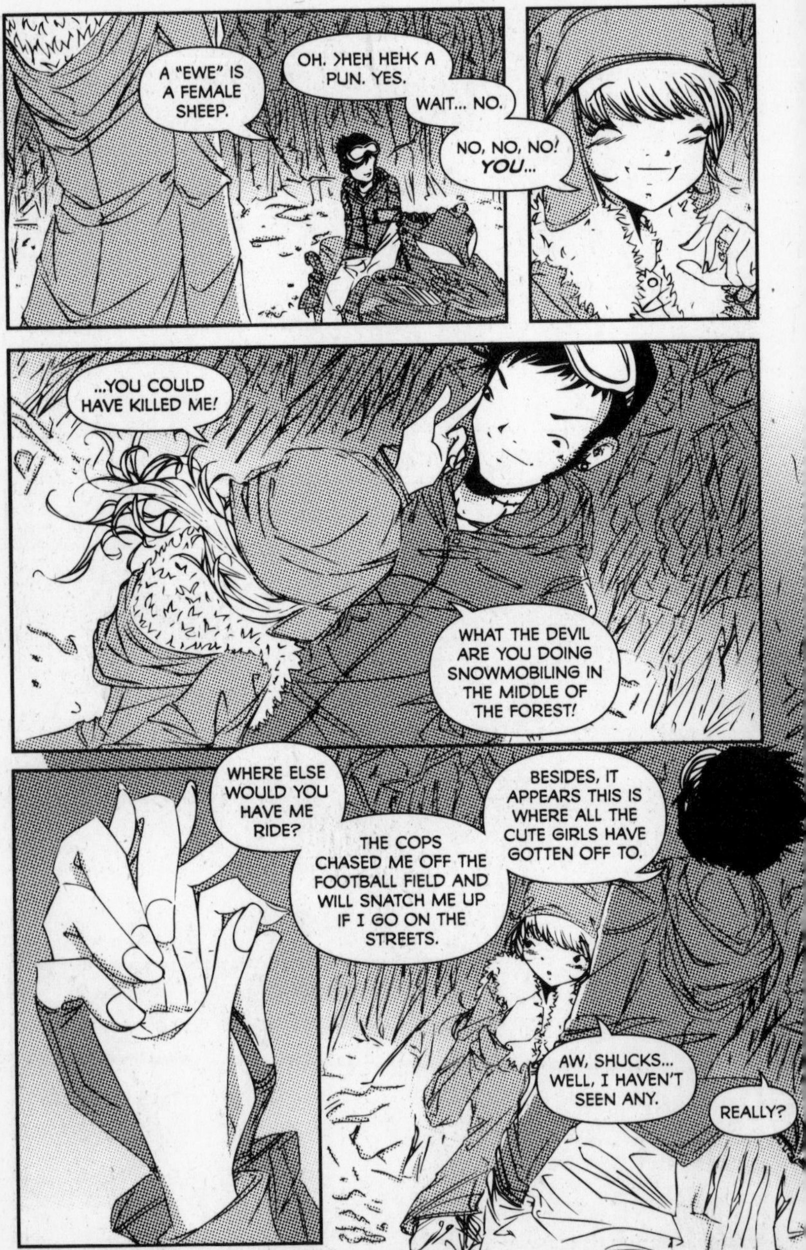
A "EWE" IS A FEMALE SHEEP.
OH. >HEH HEH< A PUN. YES.
WAIT... NO.
NO, NO, NO! ***YOU...***
...YOU COULD HAVE KILLED ME!
WHAT THE DEVIL ARE YOU DOING SNOWMOBILING IN THE MIDDLE OF THE FOREST!
WHERE ELSE WOULD YOU HAVE ME RIDE?
THE COPS CHASED ME OFF THE FOOTBALL FIELD AND WILL SNATCH ME UP IF I GO ON THE STREETS.
BESIDES, IT APPEARS THIS IS WHERE ALL THE CUTE GIRLS HAVE GOTTEN OFF TO.
AW, SHUCKS... WELL, I HAVEN'T SEEN ANY.
REALLY?

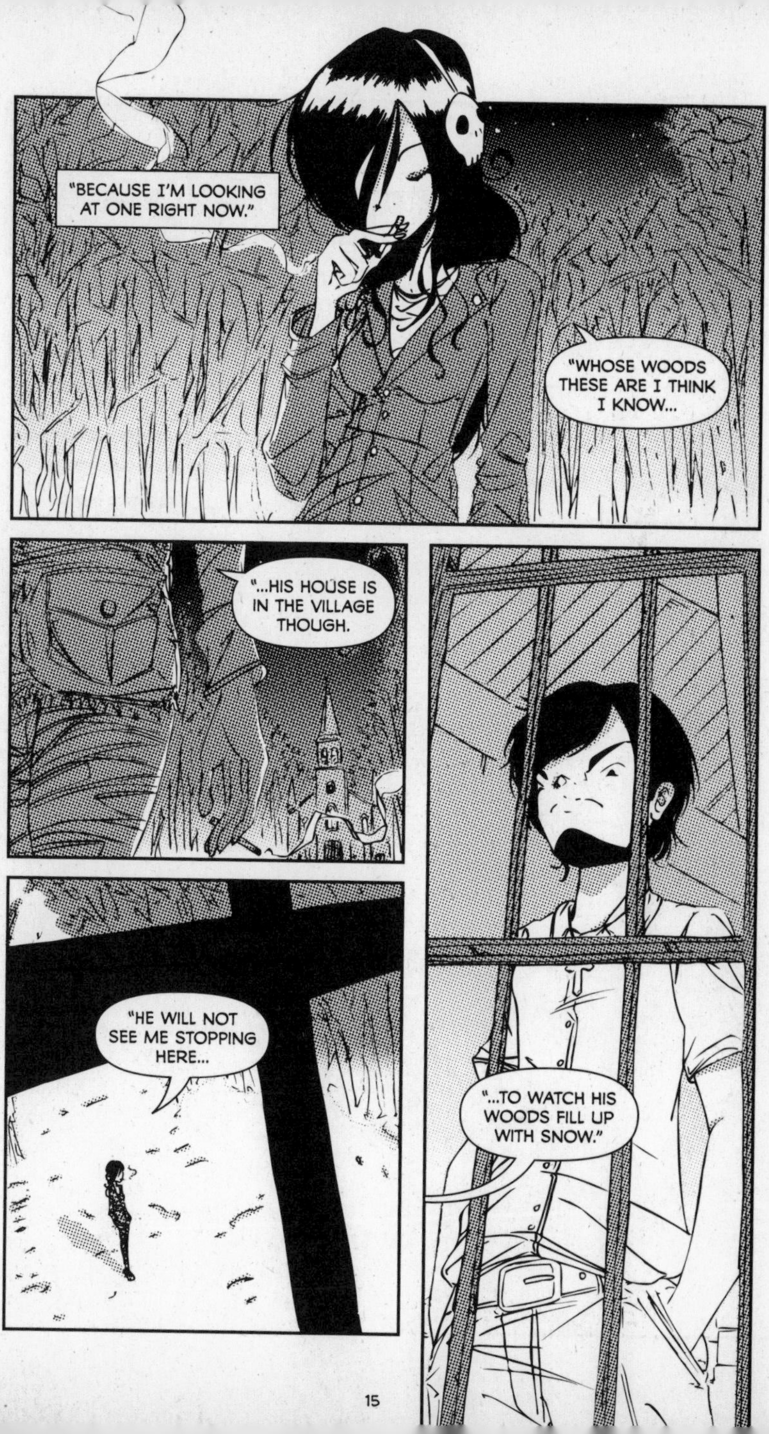
"BECAUSE I'M LOOKING AT ONE RIGHT NOW."
"WHOSE WOODS THESE ARE I THINK I KNOW...
"...HIS HOUSE IS IN THE VILLAGE THOUGH.
"HE WILL NOT SEE ME STOPPING HERE...
"...TO WATCH HIS WOODS FILL UP WITH SNOW."

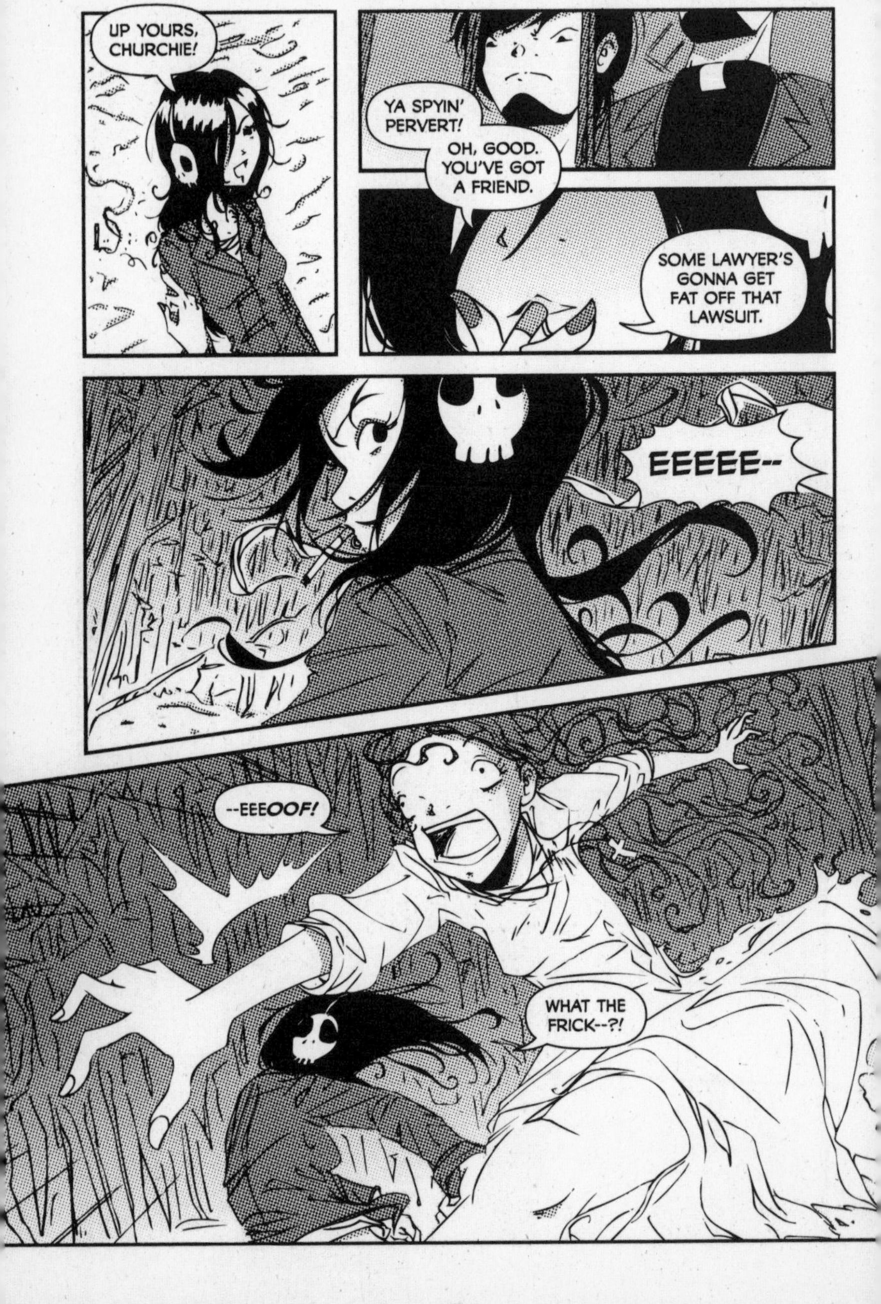
UP YOURS, CHURCHIE!
YA SPYIN' PERVERT!
OH, GOOD. YOU'VE GOT A FRIEND.
SOME LAWYER'S GONNA GET FAT OFF THAT LAWSUIT.
EEEEE--
--EEEOOF!
WHAT THE FRICK--?!

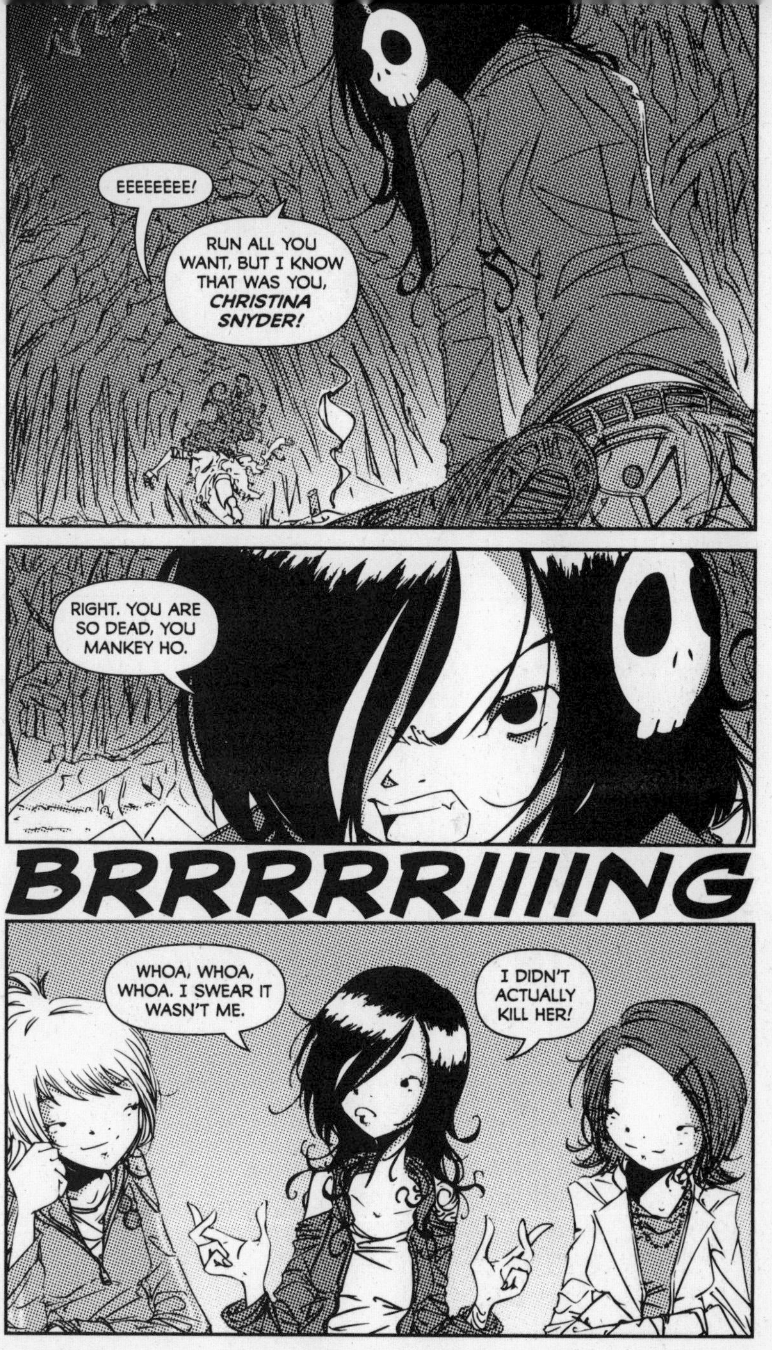
EEEEEEEE!
RUN ALL YOU WANT, BUT I KNOW THAT WAS YOU, CHRISTINA SNYDER!
RIGHT. YOU ARE SO DEAD, YOU MANKEY HO.
BRRRRRIIIING
WHOA, WHOA, WHOA. I SWEAR IT WASN'T ME.
I DIDN'T ACTUALLY KILL HER!

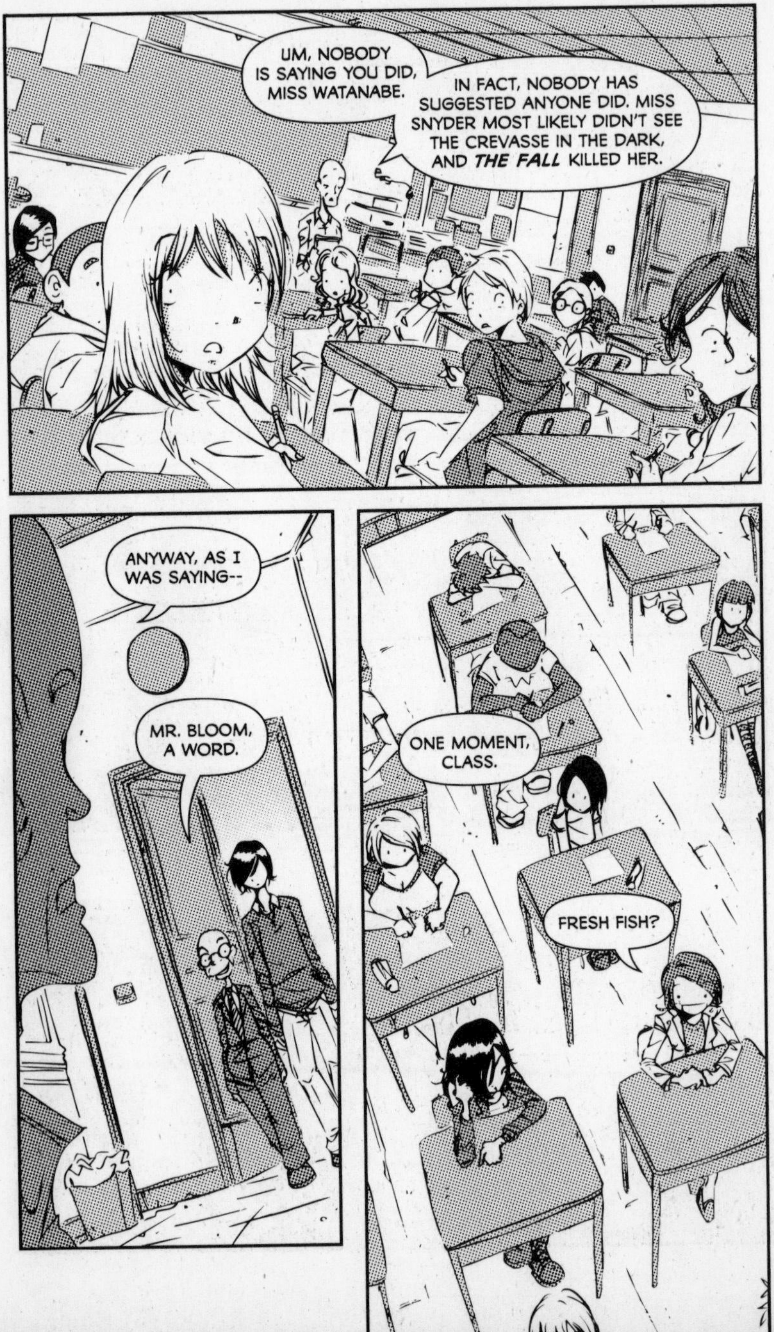
UM, NOBODY IS SAYING YOU DID, MISS WATANABE.
IN FACT, NOBODY HAS SUGGESTED ANYONE DID. MISS SNYDER MOST LIKELY DIDN'T SEE THE CREVASSE IN THE DARK, AND *THE FALL* KILLED HER.
ANYWAY, AS I WAS SAYING--
MR. BLOOM, A WORD.
ONE MOMENT, CLASS.
FRESH FISH?

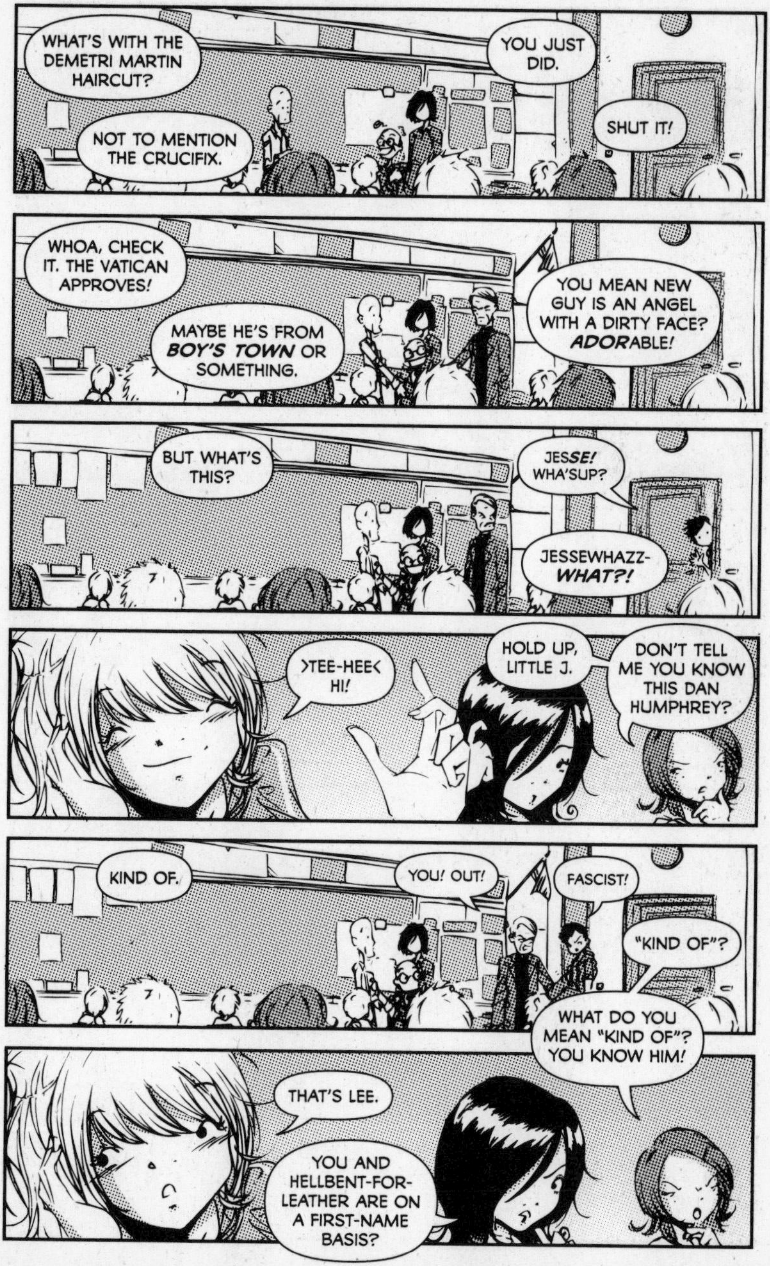
WHAT'S WITH THE DEMETRI MARTIN HAIRCUT?
NOT TO MENTION THE CRUCIFIX.
YOU JUST DID.
SHUT IT!
WHOA, CHECK IT. THE VATICAN APPROVES!
MAYBE HE'S FROM *BOY'S TOWN* OR SOMETHING.
YOU MEAN NEW GUY IS AN ANGEL WITH A DIRTY FACE? *ADOR*ABLE!
BUT WHAT'S THIS?
JES*SE!* WHA'SUP?
JESSEWHAZZ-*WHAT?!*
>TEE-HEE< HI!
HOLD UP, LITTLE J.
DON'T TELL ME YOU KNOW THIS DAN HUMPHREY?
KIND OF.
YOU! OUT!
FASCIST!
"KIND OF"?
WHAT DO YOU MEAN "KIND OF"? YOU KNOW HIM!
THAT'S LEE.
YOU AND HELLBENT-FOR-LEATHER ARE ON A FIRST-NAME BASIS?

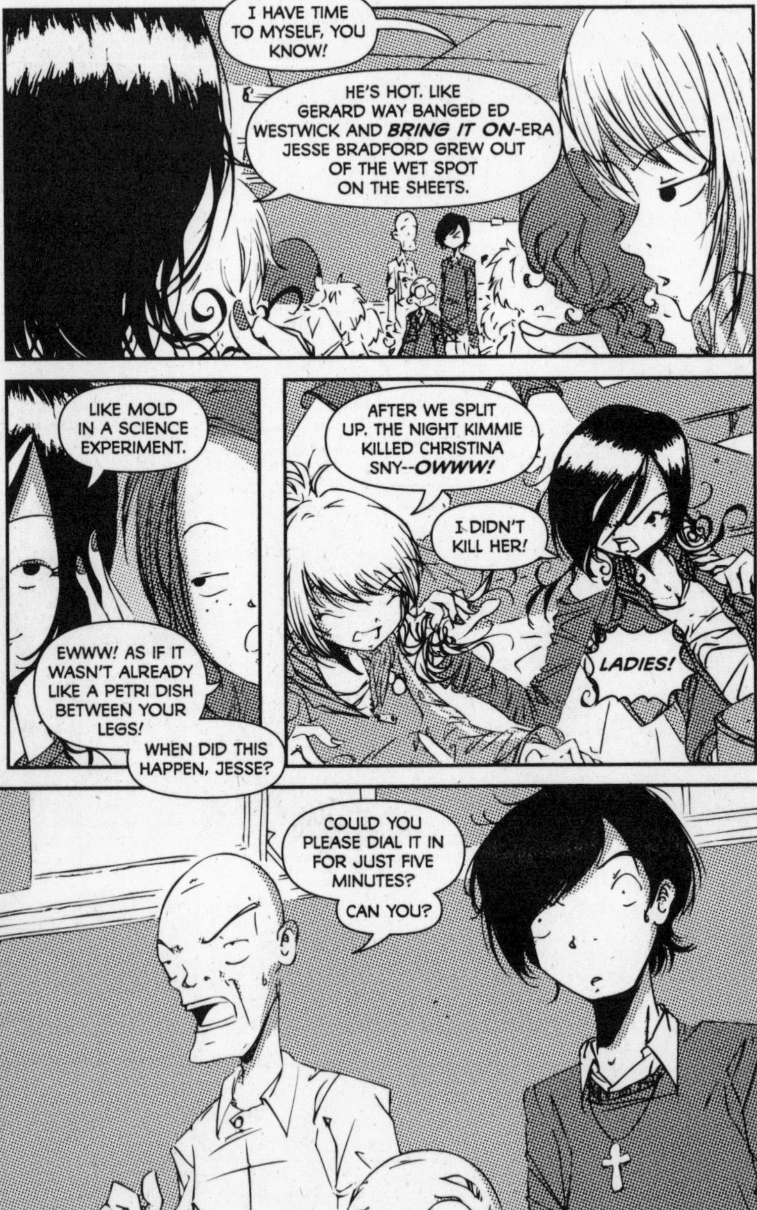
I HAVE TIME TO MYSELF, YOU KNOW!
HE'S HOT. LIKE GERARD WAY BANGED ED WESTWICK AND *BRING IT ON*-ERA JESSE BRADFORD GREW OUT OF THE WET SPOT ON THE SHEETS.
LIKE MOLD IN A SCIENCE EXPERIMENT.
EWWW! AS IF IT WASN'T ALREADY LIKE A PETRI DISH BETWEEN YOUR LEGS!
WHEN DID THIS HAPPEN, JESSE?
AFTER WE SPLIT UP. THE NIGHT KIMMIE KILLED CHRISTINA SNY--*OWWW!*
I DIDN'T KILL HER!
LADIES!
COULD YOU PLEASE DIAL IT IN FOR JUST FIVE MINUTES?
CAN YOU?

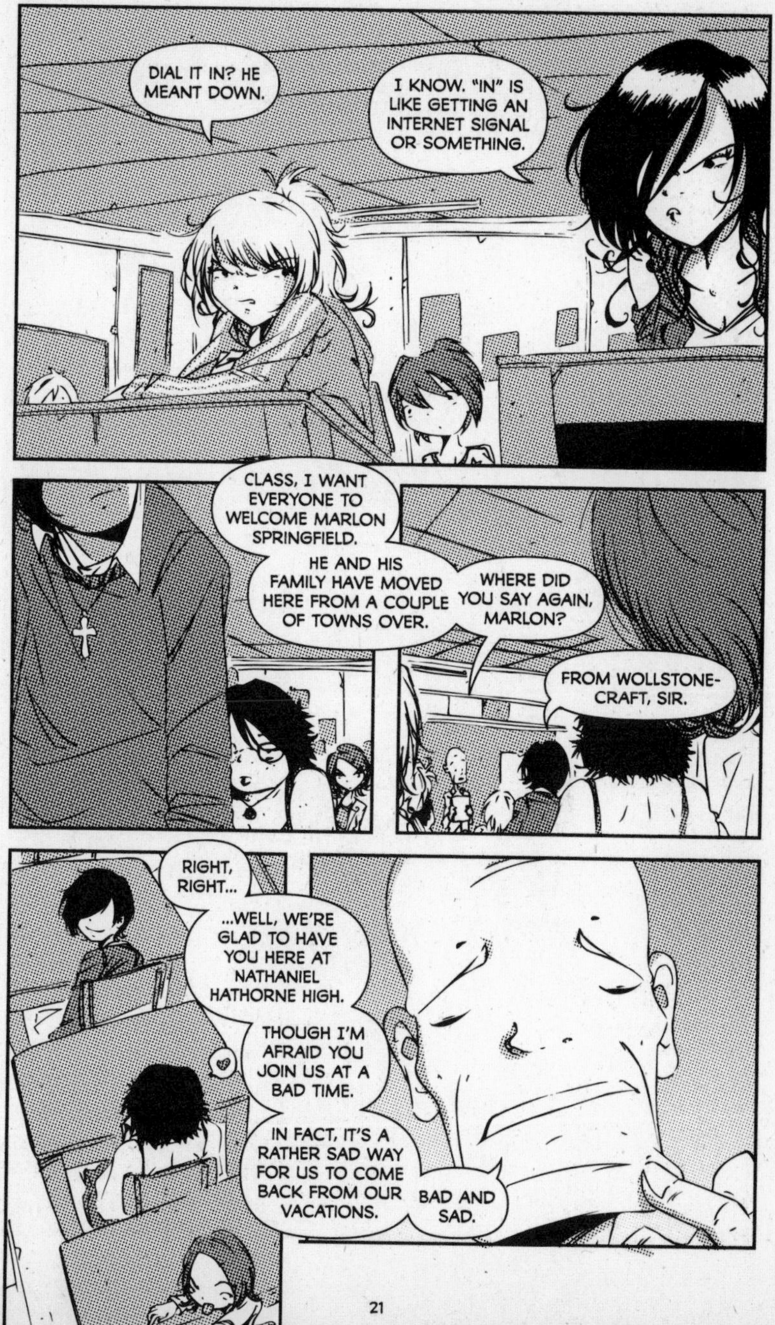
DIAL IT IN? HE MEANT DOWN.
I KNOW. "IN" IS LIKE GETTING AN INTERNET SIGNAL OR SOMETHING.
CLASS, I WANT EVERYONE TO WELCOME MARLON SPRINGFIELD.
HE AND HIS FAMILY HAVE MOVED HERE FROM A COUPLE OF TOWNS OVER.
WHERE DID YOU SAY AGAIN, MARLON?
FROM WOLLSTONE-CRAFT, SIR.
RIGHT, RIGHT...
...WELL, WE'RE GLAD TO HAVE YOU HERE AT NATHANIEL HATHORNE HIGH.
THOUGH I'M AFRAID YOU JOIN US AT A BAD TIME.
IN FACT, IT'S A RATHER SAD WAY FOR US TO COME BACK FROM OUR VACATIONS.
BAD AND SAD.

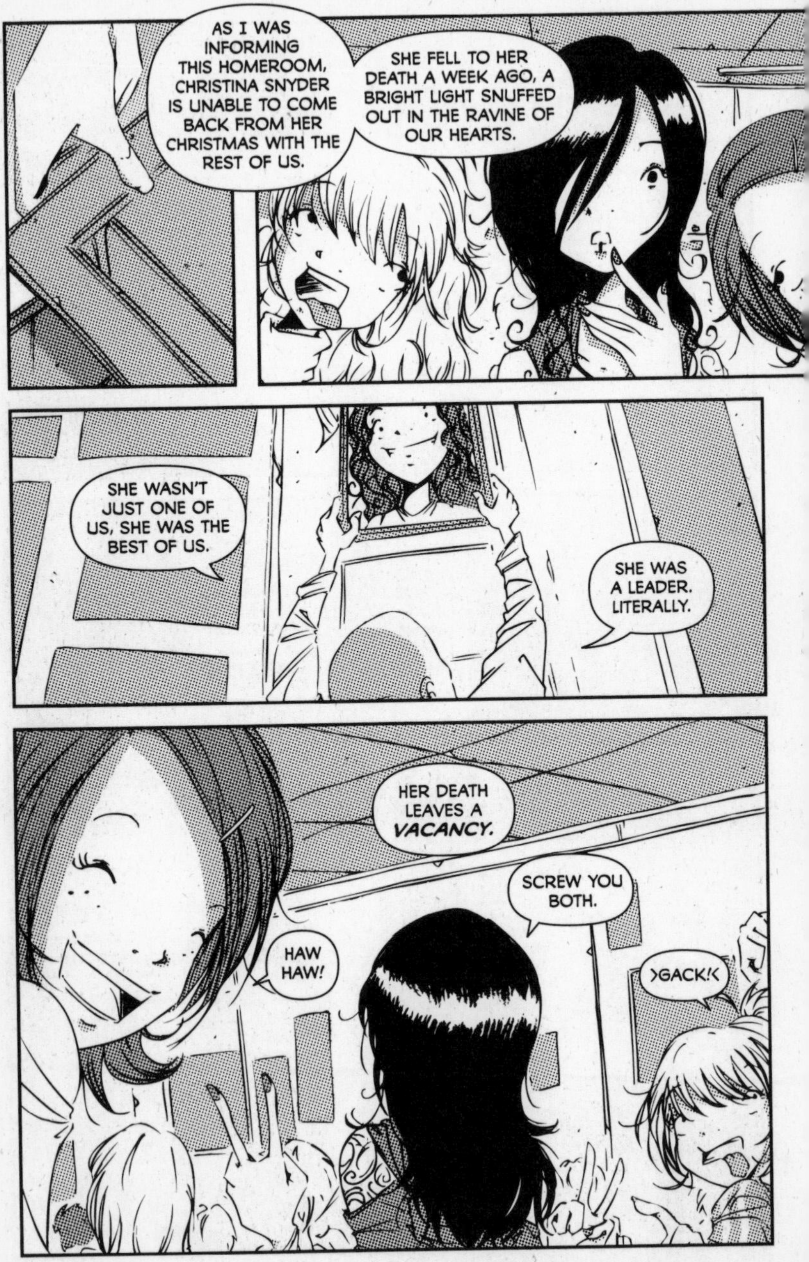
AS I WAS INFORMING THIS HOMEROOM, CHRISTINA SNYDER IS UNABLE TO COME BACK FROM HER CHRISTMAS WITH THE REST OF US.
SHE FELL TO HER DEATH A WEEK AGO, A BRIGHT LIGHT SNUFFED OUT IN THE RAVINE OF OUR HEARTS.
SHE WASN'T JUST ONE OF US, SHE WAS THE BEST OF US.
SHE WAS A LEADER. LITERALLY.
HER DEATH LEAVES A *VACANCY.*
SCREW YOU BOTH.
HAW HAW!
>GACK!<

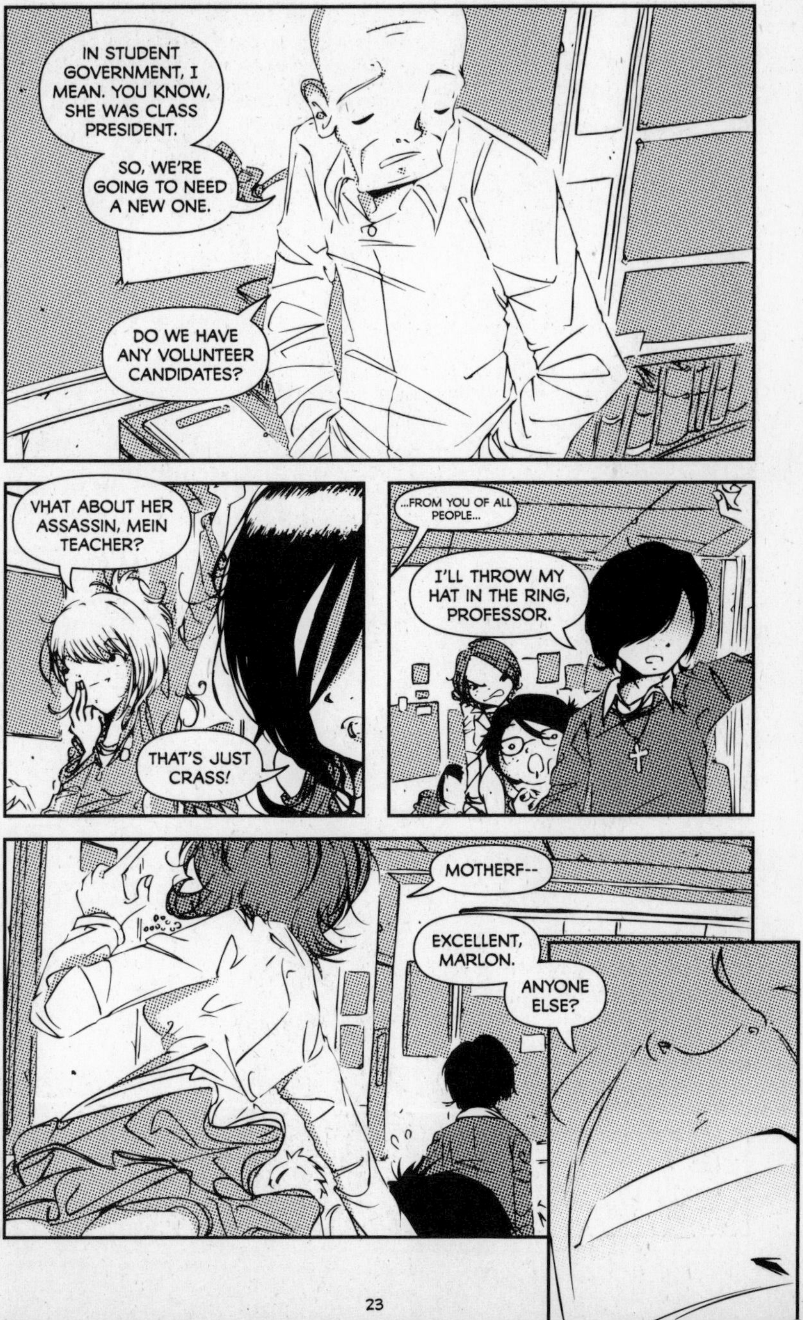
IN STUDENT GOVERNMENT, I MEAN. YOU KNOW, SHE WAS CLASS PRESIDENT.
SO, WE'RE GOING TO NEED A NEW ONE.
DO WE HAVE ANY VOLUNTEER CANDIDATES?
VHAT ABOUT HER ASSASSIN, MEIN TEACHER?
THAT'S JUST CRASS!
...FROM YOU OF ALL PEOPLE...
I'LL THROW MY HAT IN THE RING, PROFESSOR.
MOTHERF--
EXCELLENT, MARLON.
ANYONE ELSE?

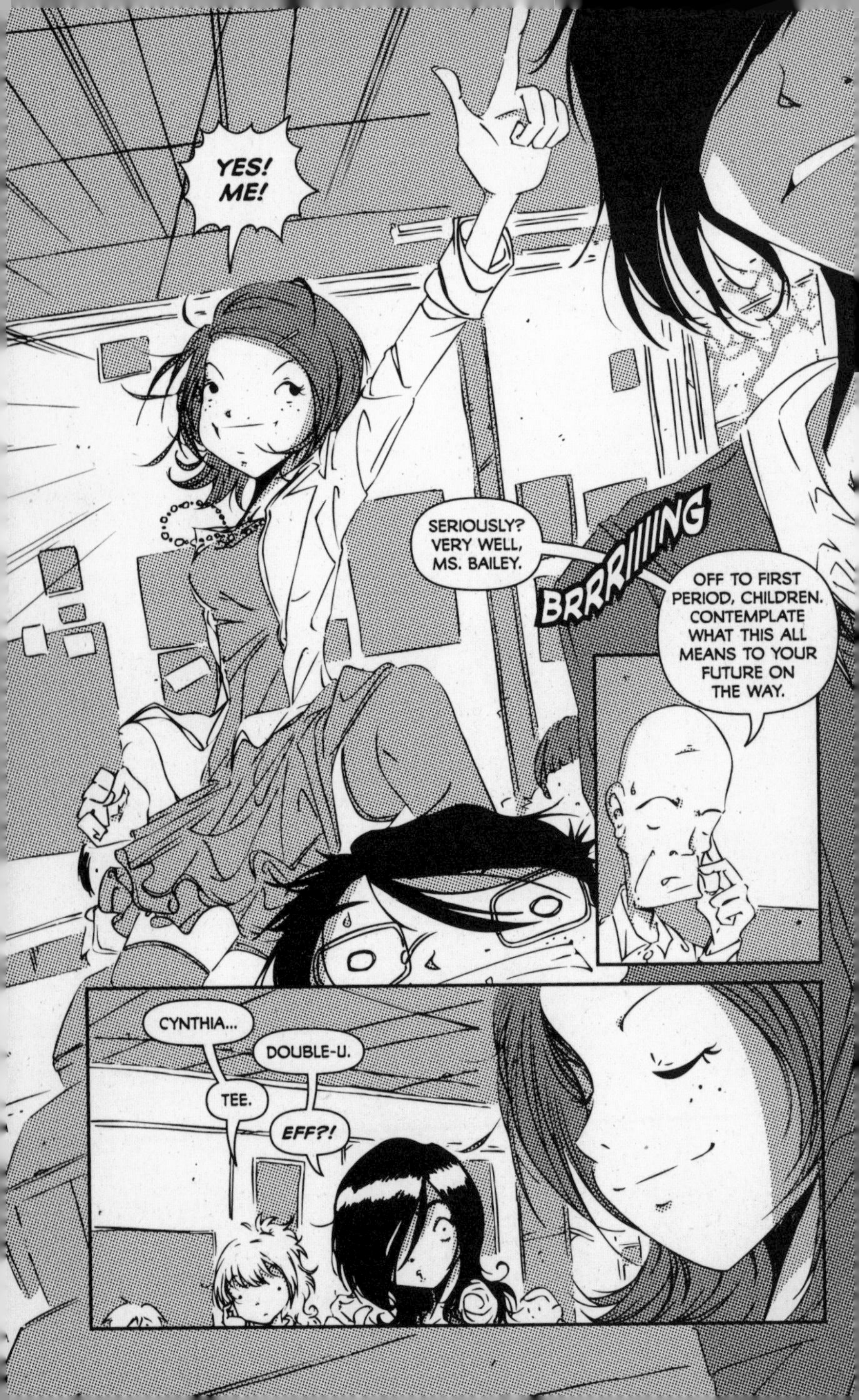
YES! ME!
SERIOUSLY? VERY WELL, MS. BAILEY.
BRRRIIIING
OFF TO FIRST PERIOD, CHILDREN. CONTEMPLATE WHAT THIS ALL MEANS TO YOUR FUTURE ON THE WAY.
CYNTHIA...
DOUBLE-U.
TEE.
EFF?!

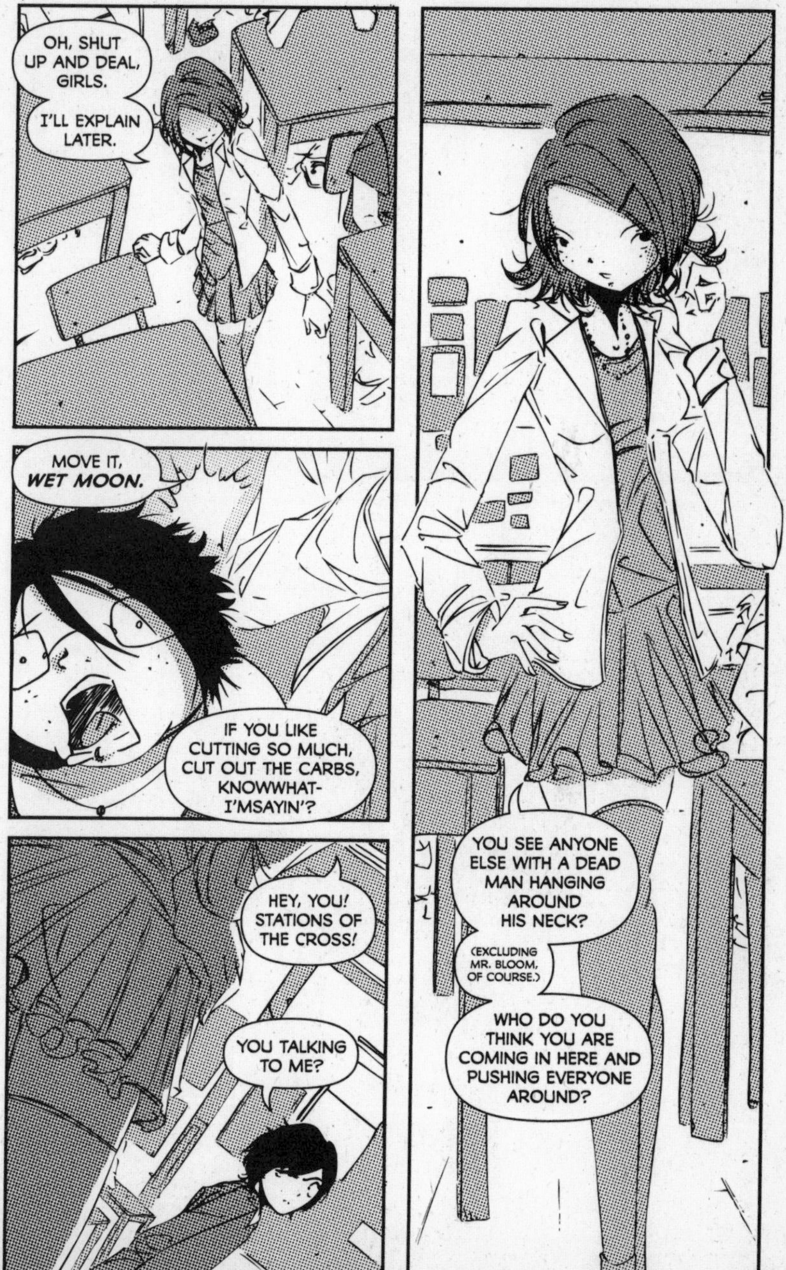
OH, SHUT UP AND DEAL, GIRLS.
I'LL EXPLAIN LATER.
MOVE IT, ***WET MOON.***
IF YOU LIKE CUTTING SO MUCH, CUT OUT THE CARBS, KNOWWHAT-I'MSAYIN'?
HEY, YOU! STATIONS OF THE CROSS!
YOU TALKING TO ME?
YOU SEE ANYONE ELSE WITH A DEAD MAN HANGING AROUND HIS NECK?
(EXCLUDING MR. BLOOM, OF COURSE.)
WHO DO YOU THINK YOU ARE COMING IN HERE AND PUSHING EVERYONE AROUND?

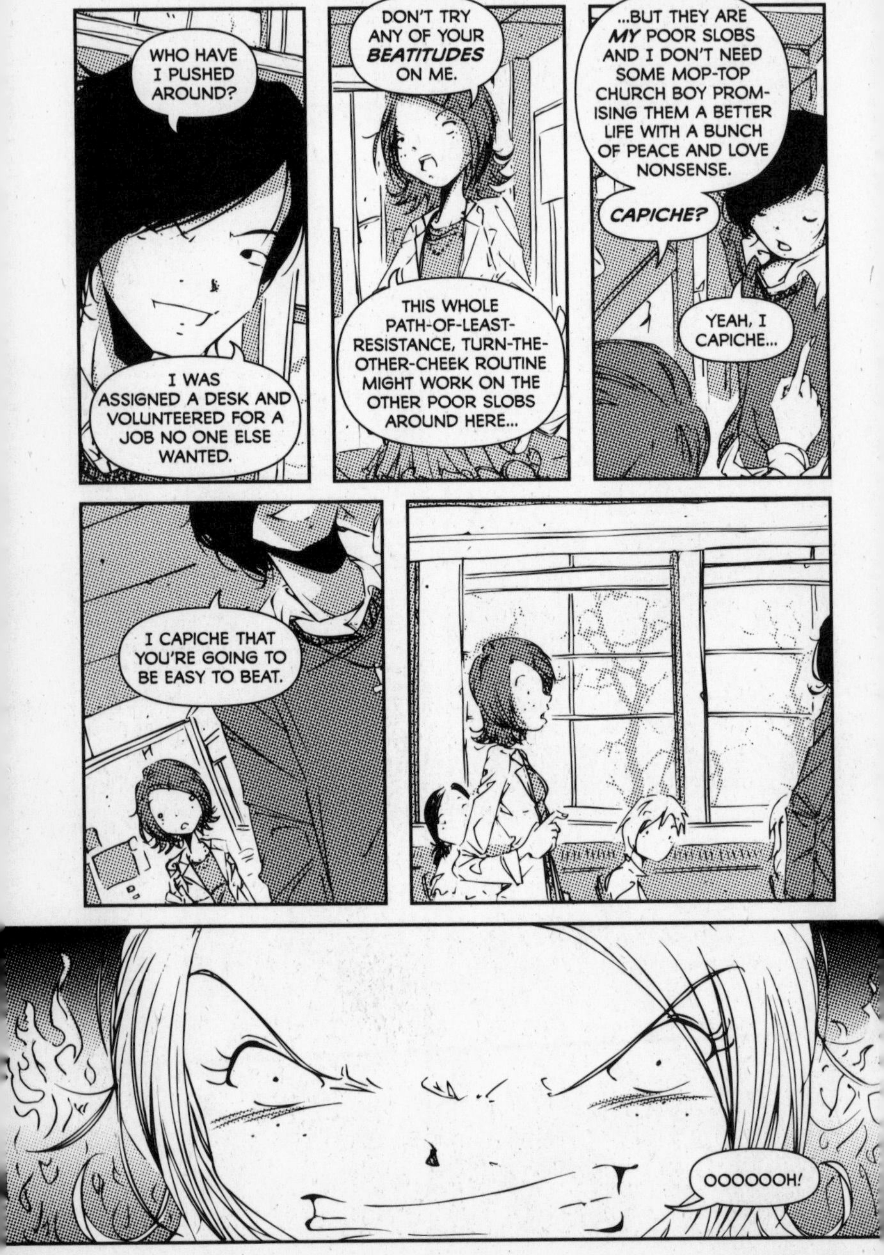
WHO HAVE I PUSHED AROUND?
I WAS ASSIGNED A DESK AND VOLUNTEERED FOR A JOB NO ONE ELSE WANTED.
DON'T TRY ANY OF YOUR *BEATITUDES* ON ME.
THIS WHOLE PATH-OF-LEAST-RESISTANCE, TURN-THE-OTHER-CHEEK ROUTINE MIGHT WORK ON THE OTHER POOR SLOBS AROUND HERE...
...BUT THEY ARE *MY* POOR SLOBS AND I DON'T NEED SOME MOP-TOP CHURCH BOY PROMISING THEM A BETTER LIFE WITH A BUNCH OF PEACE AND LOVE NONSENSE.
CAPICHE?
YEAH, I CAPICHE...
I CAPICHE THAT YOU'RE GOING TO BE EASY TO BEAT.
OOOOOOH!

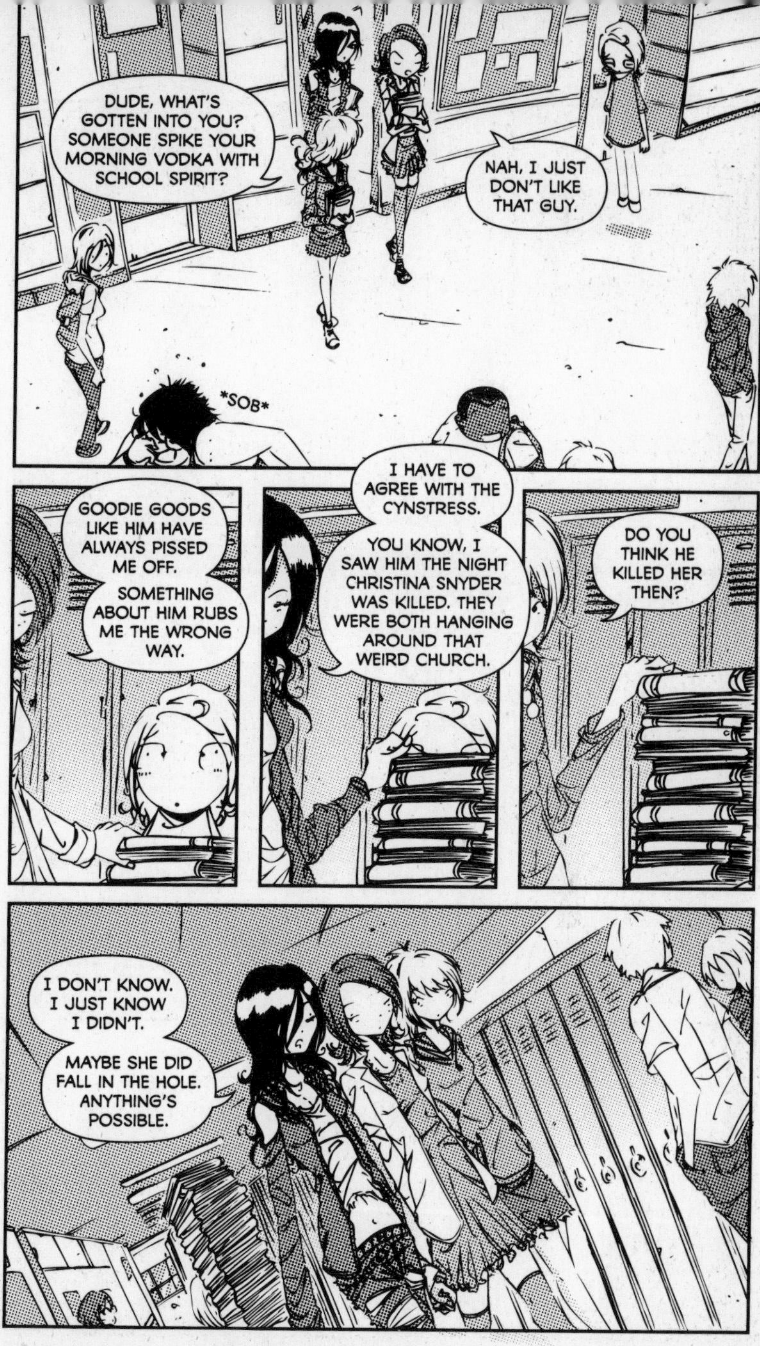
DUDE, WHAT'S GOTTEN INTO YOU? SOMEONE SPIKE YOUR MORNING VODKA WITH SCHOOL SPIRIT?
NAH, I JUST DON'T LIKE THAT GUY.
SOB
GOODIE GOODS LIKE HIM HAVE ALWAYS PISSED ME OFF.
SOMETHING ABOUT HIM RUBS ME THE WRONG WAY.
I HAVE TO AGREE WITH THE CYNSTRESS.
YOU KNOW, I SAW HIM THE NIGHT CHRISTINA SNYDER WAS KILLED. THEY WERE BOTH HANGING AROUND THAT WEIRD CHURCH.
DO YOU THINK HE KILLED HER THEN?
I DON'T KNOW. I JUST KNOW I DIDN'T.
MAYBE SHE DID FALL IN THE HOLE. ANYTHING'S POSSIBLE.

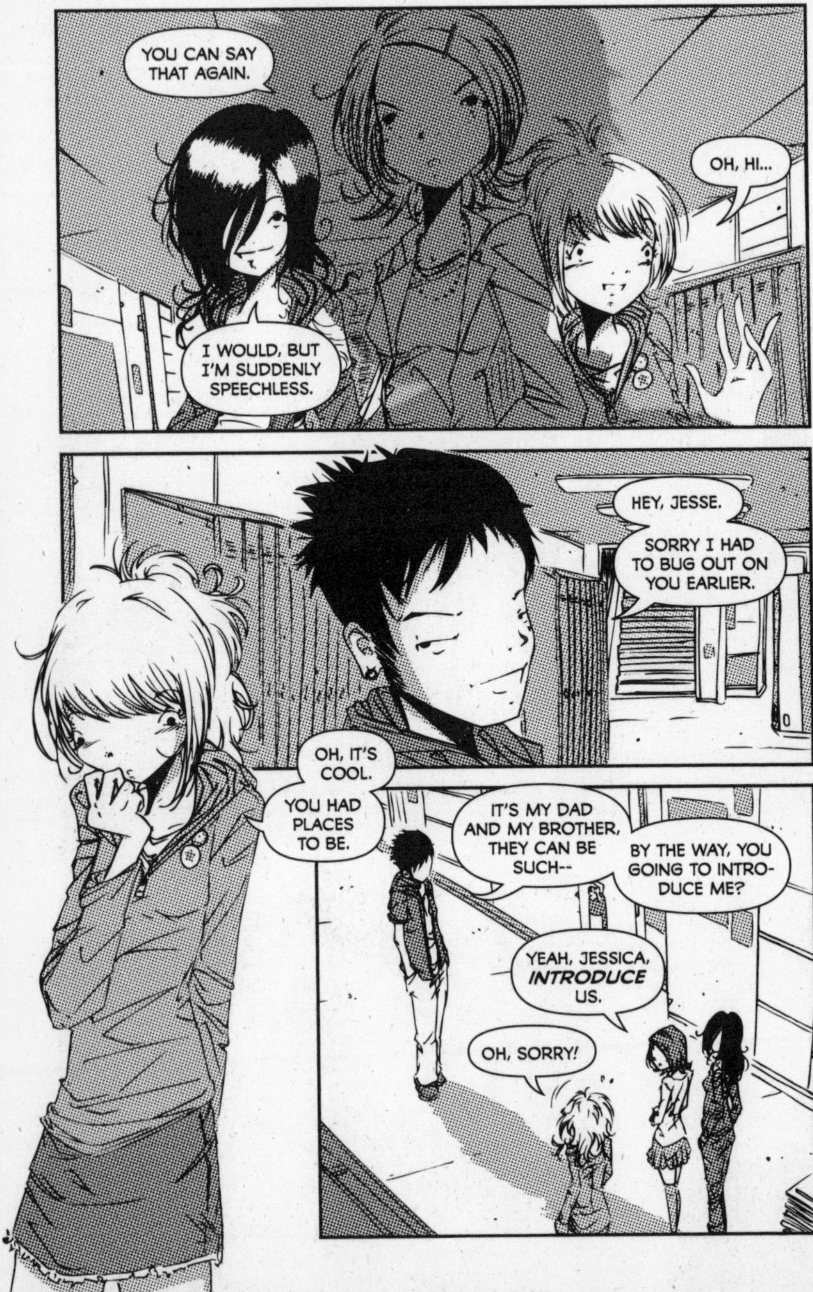
YOU CAN SAY THAT AGAIN.
I WOULD, BUT I'M SUDDENLY SPEECHLESS.
OH, HI...
HEY, JESSE.
SORRY I HAD TO BUG OUT ON YOU EARLIER.
OH, IT'S COOL.
YOU HAD PLACES TO BE.
IT'S MY DAD AND MY BROTHER, THEY CAN BE SUCH--
BY THE WAY, YOU GOING TO INTRO-DUCE ME?
YEAH, JESSICA, *INTRODUCE* US.
OH, SORRY!

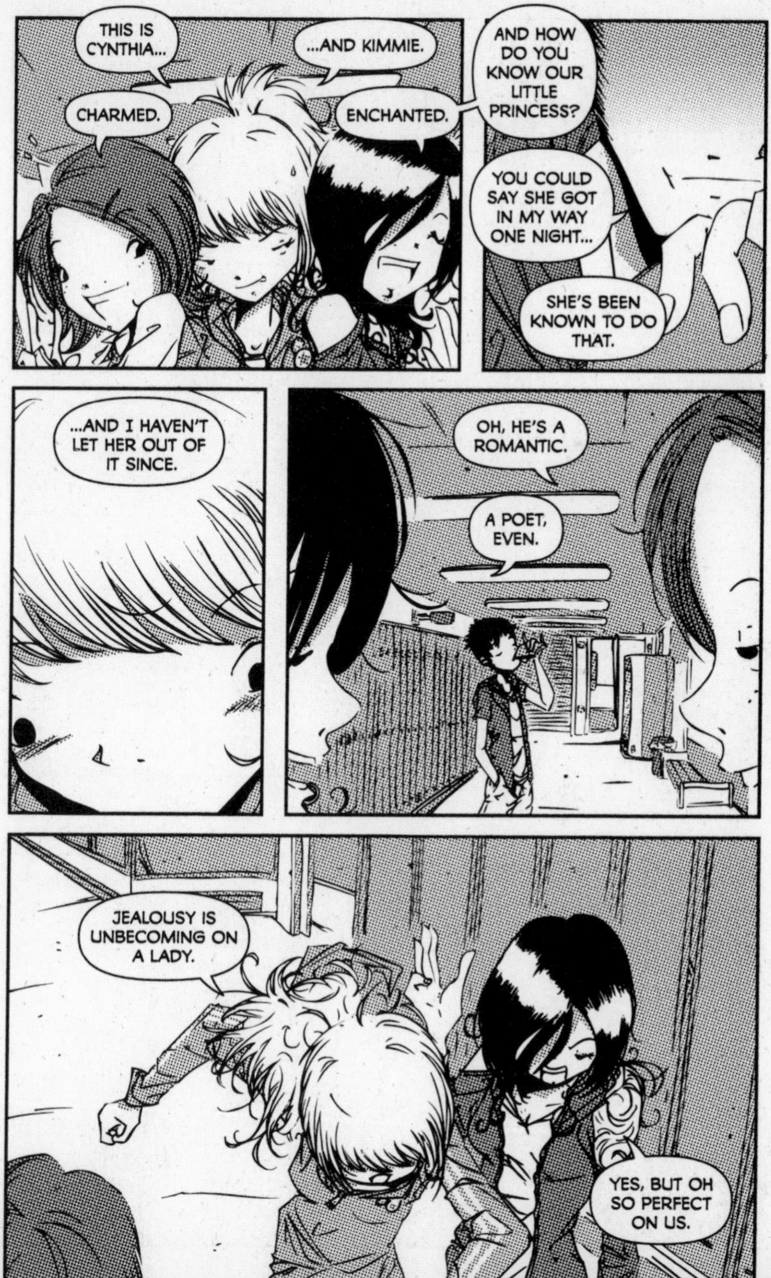
THIS IS CYNTHIA...
...AND KIMMIE.
CHARMED.
ENCHANTED.
AND HOW DO YOU KNOW OUR LITTLE PRINCESS?
YOU COULD SAY SHE GOT IN MY WAY ONE NIGHT...
SHE'S BEEN KNOWN TO DO THAT.
...AND I HAVEN'T LET HER OUT OF IT SINCE.
OH, HE'S A ROMANTIC.
A POET, EVEN.
JEALOUSY IS UNBECOMING ON A LADY.
YES, BUT OH SO PERFECT ON US.

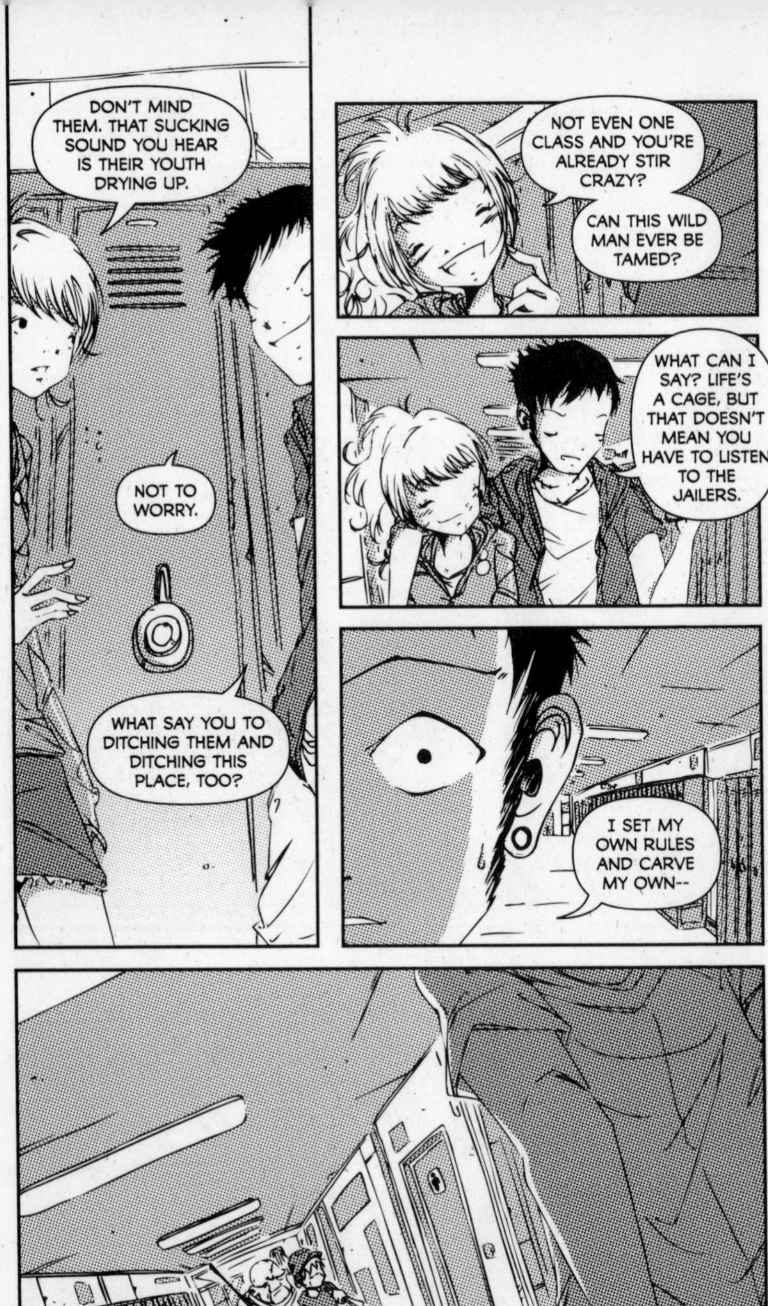
DON'T MIND THEM. THAT SUCKING SOUND YOU HEAR IS THEIR YOUTH DRYING UP.
NOT TO WORRY.
WHAT SAY YOU TO DITCHING THEM AND DITCHING THIS PLACE, TOO?
NOT EVEN ONE CLASS AND YOU'RE ALREADY STIR CRAZY?
CAN THIS WILD MAN EVER BE TAMED?
WHAT CAN I SAY? LIFE'S A CAGE, BUT THAT DOESN'T MEAN YOU HAVE TO LISTEN TO THE JAILERS.
I SET MY OWN RULES AND CARVE MY OWN--

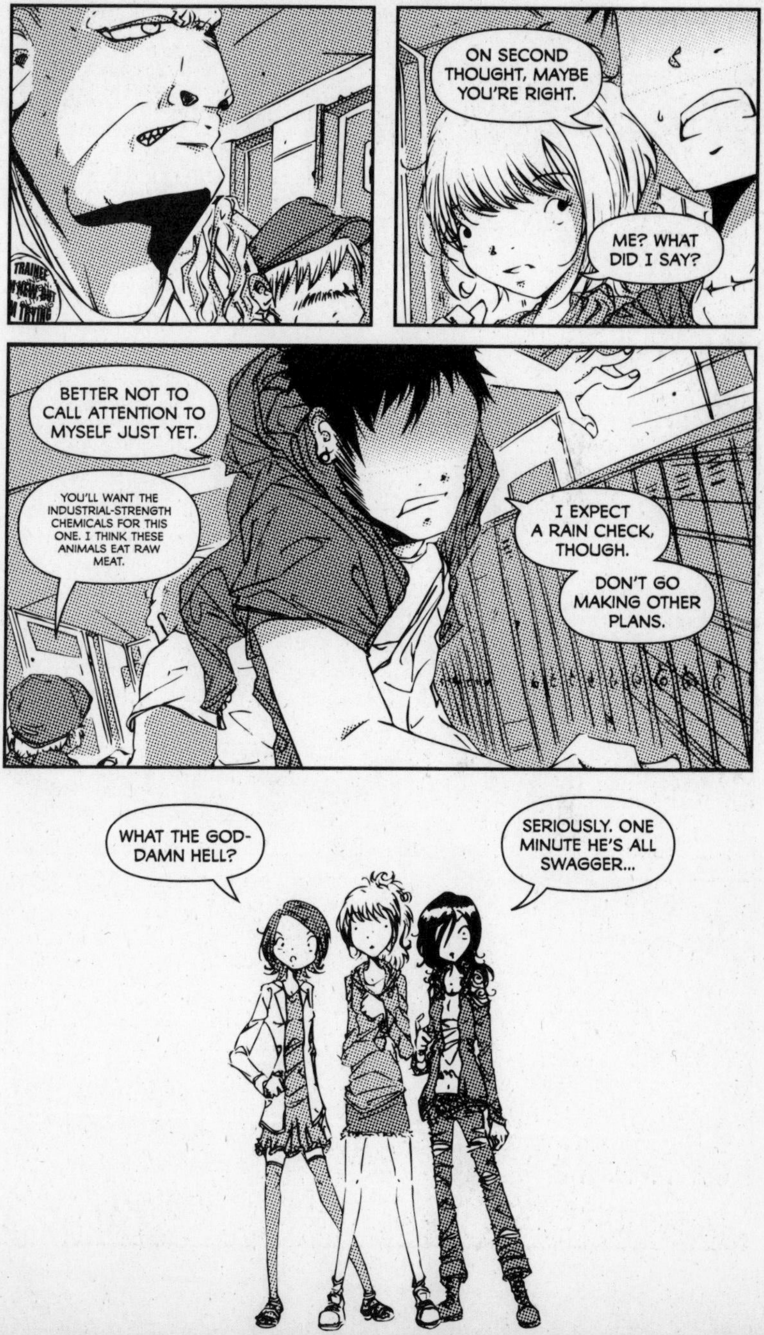
ON SECOND THOUGHT, MAYBE YOU'RE RIGHT.
ME? WHAT DID I SAY?
BETTER NOT TO CALL ATTENTION TO MYSELF JUST YET.
YOU'LL WANT THE INDUSTRIAL-STRENGTH CHEMICALS FOR THIS ONE. I THINK THESE ANIMALS EAT RAW MEAT.
I EXPECT A RAIN CHECK, THOUGH.
DON'T GO MAKING OTHER PLANS.
WHAT THE GOD-DAMN HELL?
SERIOUSLY. ONE MINUTE HE'S ALL SWAGGER...

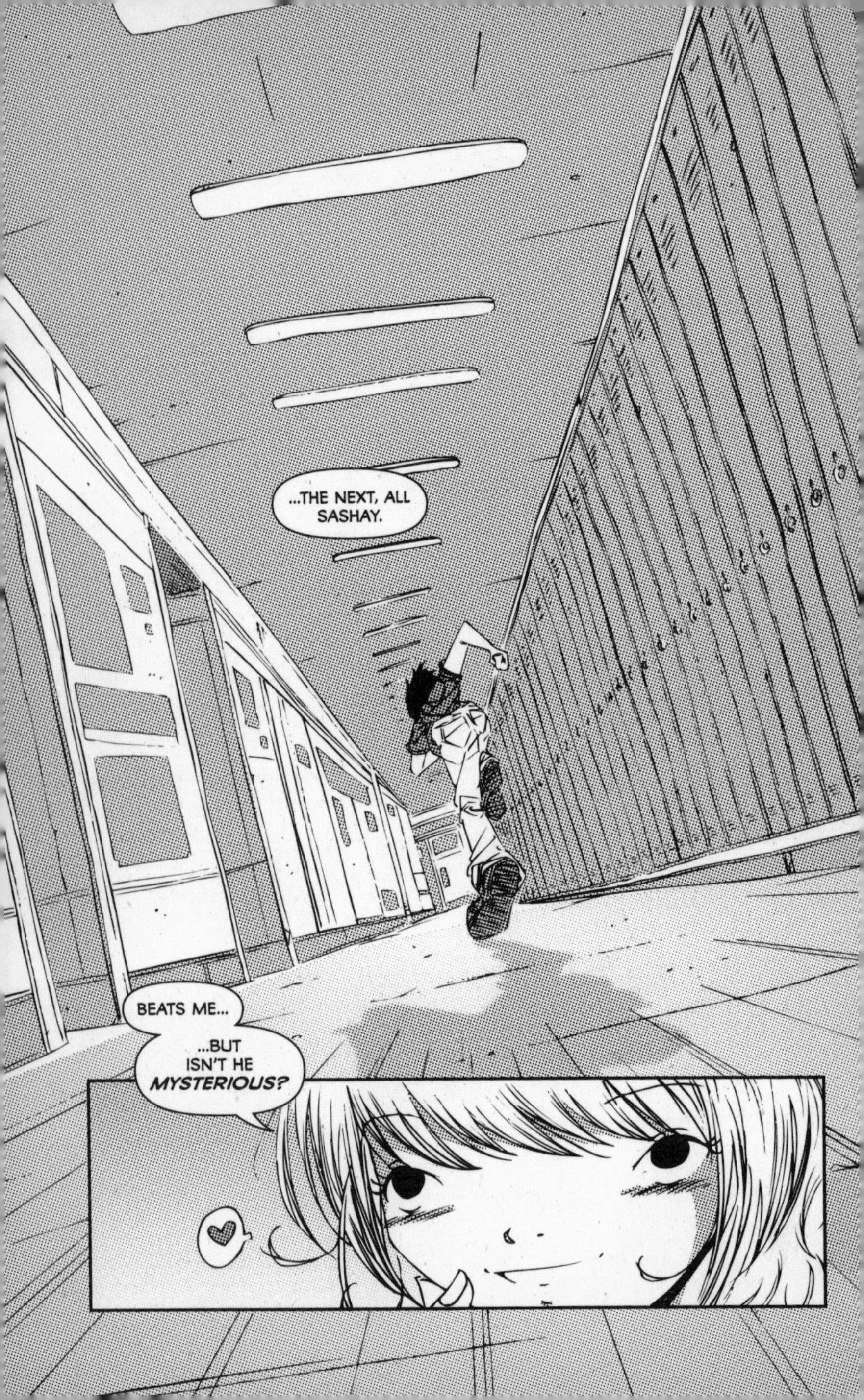
...THE NEXT, ALL SASHAY.
BEATS ME...
...BUT ISN'T HE *MYSTERIOUS?*

Chapter 2
"Sexy! No No No..."

2

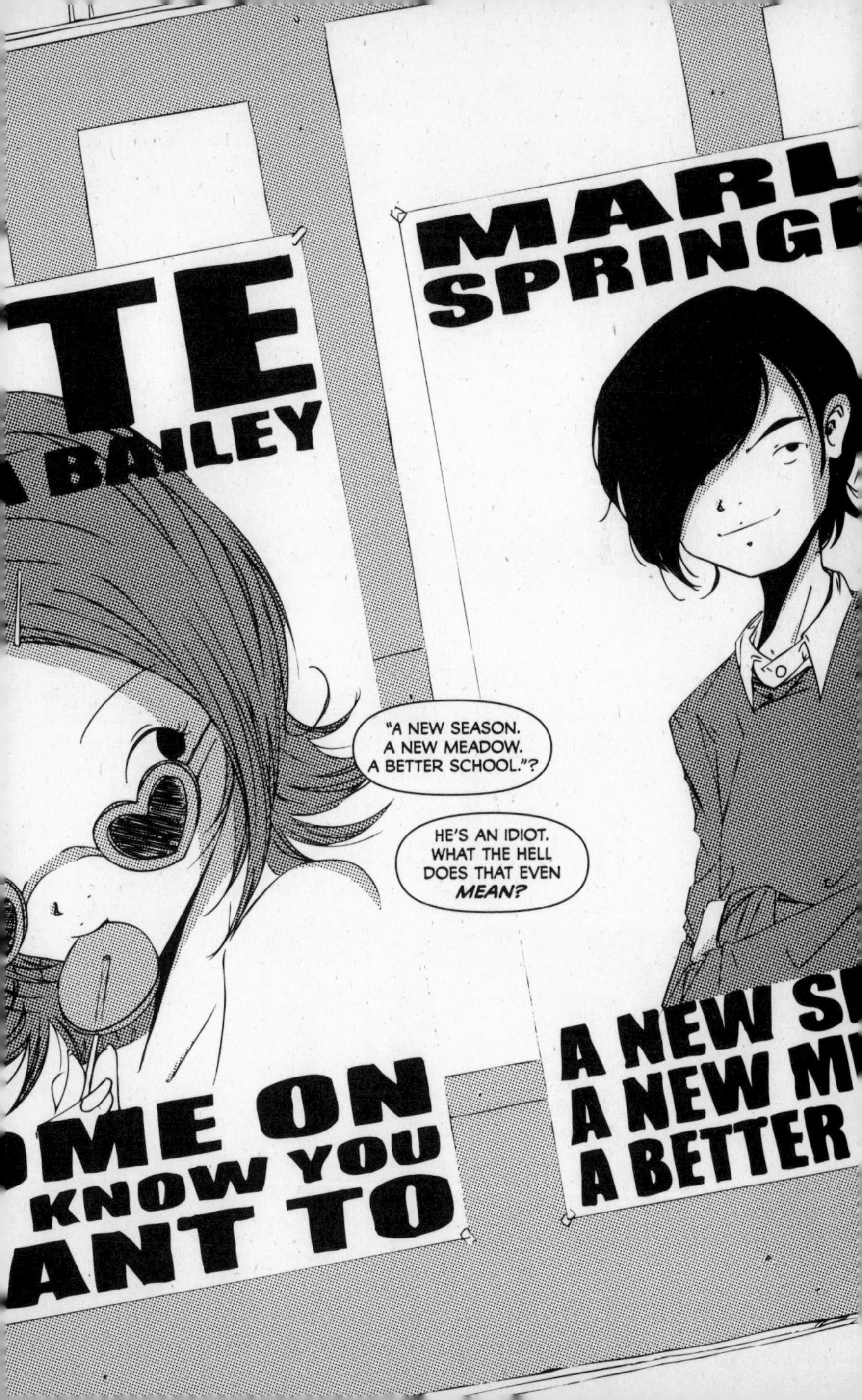
BAILEY
KNOW YOU
A BETTER
"A NEW SEASON. A NEW MEADOW. A BETTER SCHOOL."?
HE'S AN IDIOT. WHAT THE HELL DOES THAT EVEN *MEAN?*

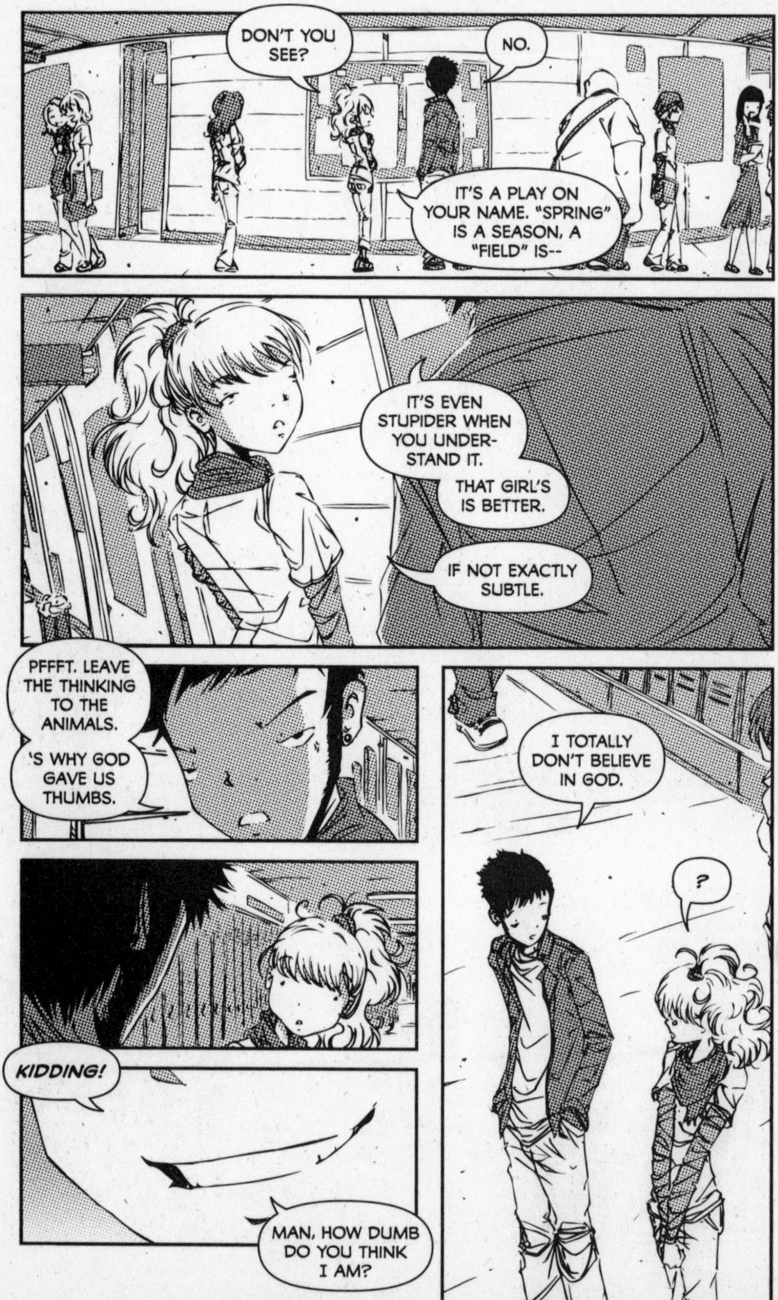
DON'T YOU SEE?
NO.
IT'S A PLAY ON YOUR NAME. "SPRING" IS A SEASON, A "FIELD" IS--
IT'S EVEN STUPIDER WHEN YOU UNDER-STAND IT.
THAT GIRL'S IS BETTER.
IF NOT EXACTLY SUBTLE.
PFFFT. LEAVE THE THINKING TO THE ANIMALS.
'S WHY GOD GAVE US THUMBS.
I TOTALLY DON'T BELIEVE IN GOD.
?
KIDDING!
MAN, HOW DUMB DO YOU THINK I AM?

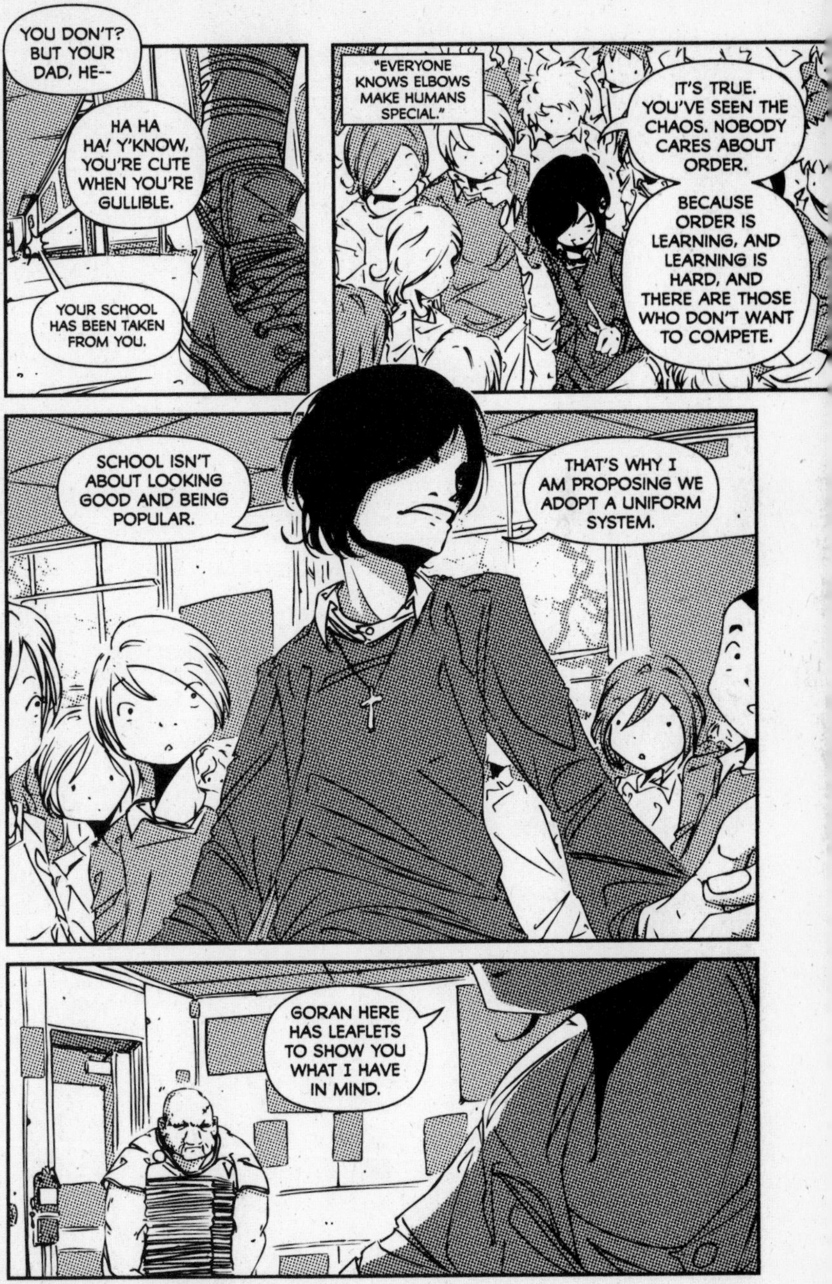
YOU DON'T? BUT YOUR DAD, HE--
HA HA HA! Y'KNOW, YOU'RE CUTE WHEN YOU'RE GULLIBLE.
YOUR SCHOOL HAS BEEN TAKEN FROM YOU.
"EVERYONE KNOWS ELBOWS MAKE HUMANS SPECIAL."
IT'S TRUE. YOU'VE SEEN THE CHAOS. NOBODY CARES ABOUT ORDER.
BECAUSE ORDER IS LEARNING, AND LEARNING IS HARD, AND THERE ARE THOSE WHO DON'T WANT TO COMPETE.
SCHOOL ISN'T ABOUT LOOKING GOOD AND BEING POPULAR.
THAT'S WHY I AM PROPOSING WE ADOPT A UNIFORM SYSTEM.
GORAN HERE HAS LEAFLETS TO SHOW YOU WHAT I HAVE IN MIND.

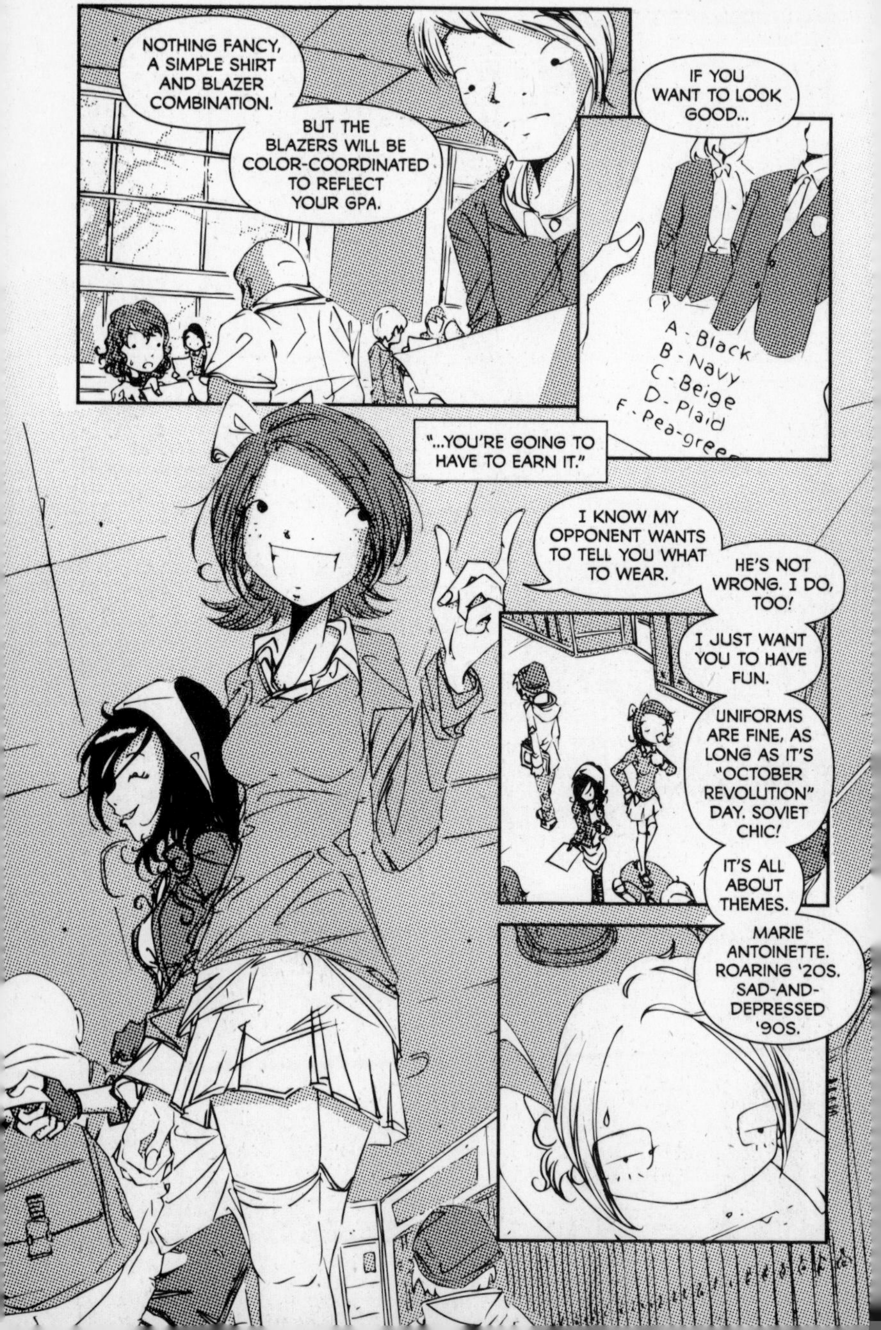
NOTHING FANCY, A SIMPLE SHIRT AND BLAZER COMBINATION.
BUT THE BLAZERS WILL BE COLOR-COORDINATED TO REFLECT YOUR GPA.
IF YOU WANT TO LOOK GOOD...
A - Black
B - Navy
C - Beige
D - Plaid
F - Pea-green
"...YOU'RE GOING TO HAVE TO EARN IT."
I KNOW MY OPPONENT WANTS TO TELL YOU WHAT TO WEAR.
HE'S NOT WRONG. I DO, TOO!
I JUST WANT YOU TO HAVE FUN.
UNIFORMS ARE FINE, AS LONG AS IT'S "OCTOBER REVOLUTION" DAY. SOVIET CHIC!
IT'S ALL ABOUT THEMES.
MARIE ANTOINETTE. ROARING '20S. SAD-AND-DEPRESSED '90S.

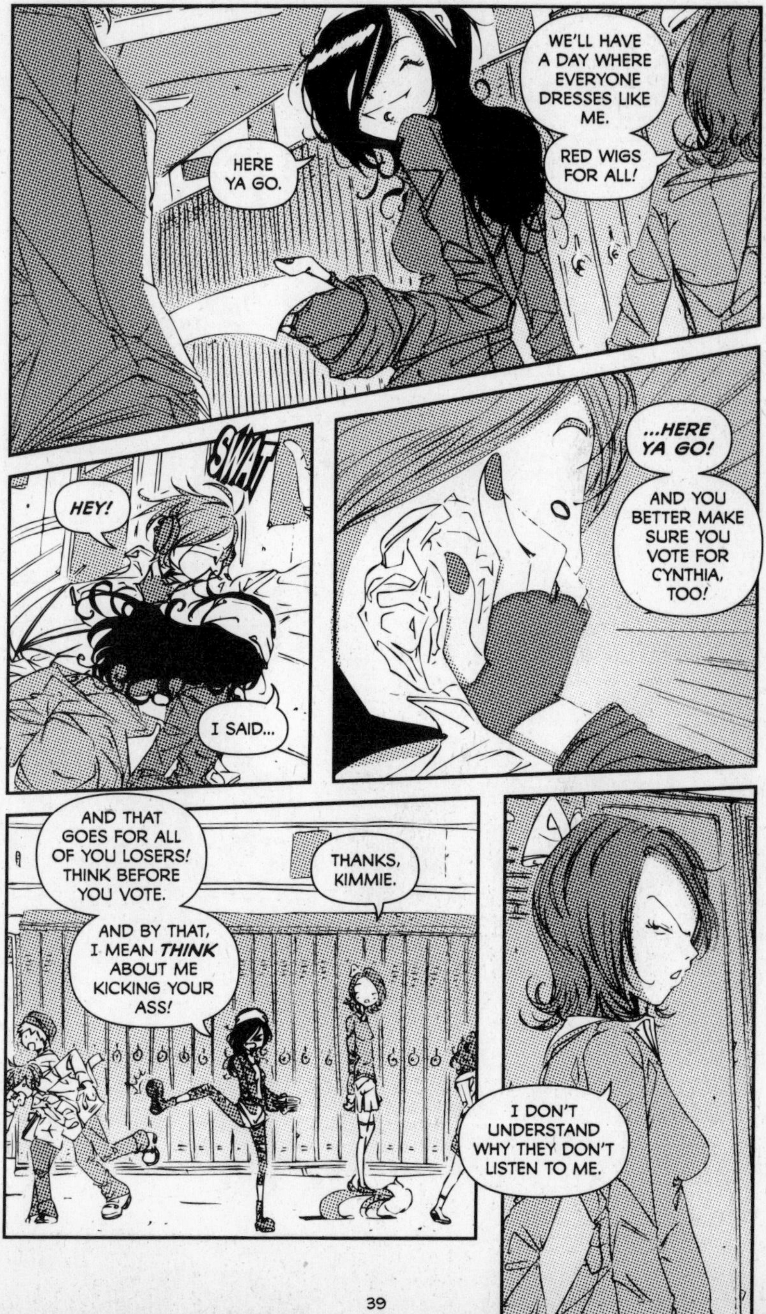
WE'LL HAVE A DAY WHERE EVERYONE DRESSES LIKE ME.
RED WIGS FOR ALL!
HERE YA GO.
SWAT
HEY!
I SAID...
...HERE YA GO!
AND YOU BETTER MAKE SURE YOU VOTE FOR CYNTHIA, TOO!
AND THAT GOES FOR ALL OF YOU LOSERS! THINK BEFORE YOU VOTE.
AND BY THAT, I MEAN *THINK* ABOUT ME KICKING YOUR ASS!
THANKS, KIMMIE.
I DON'T UNDERSTAND WHY THEY DON'T LISTEN TO ME.

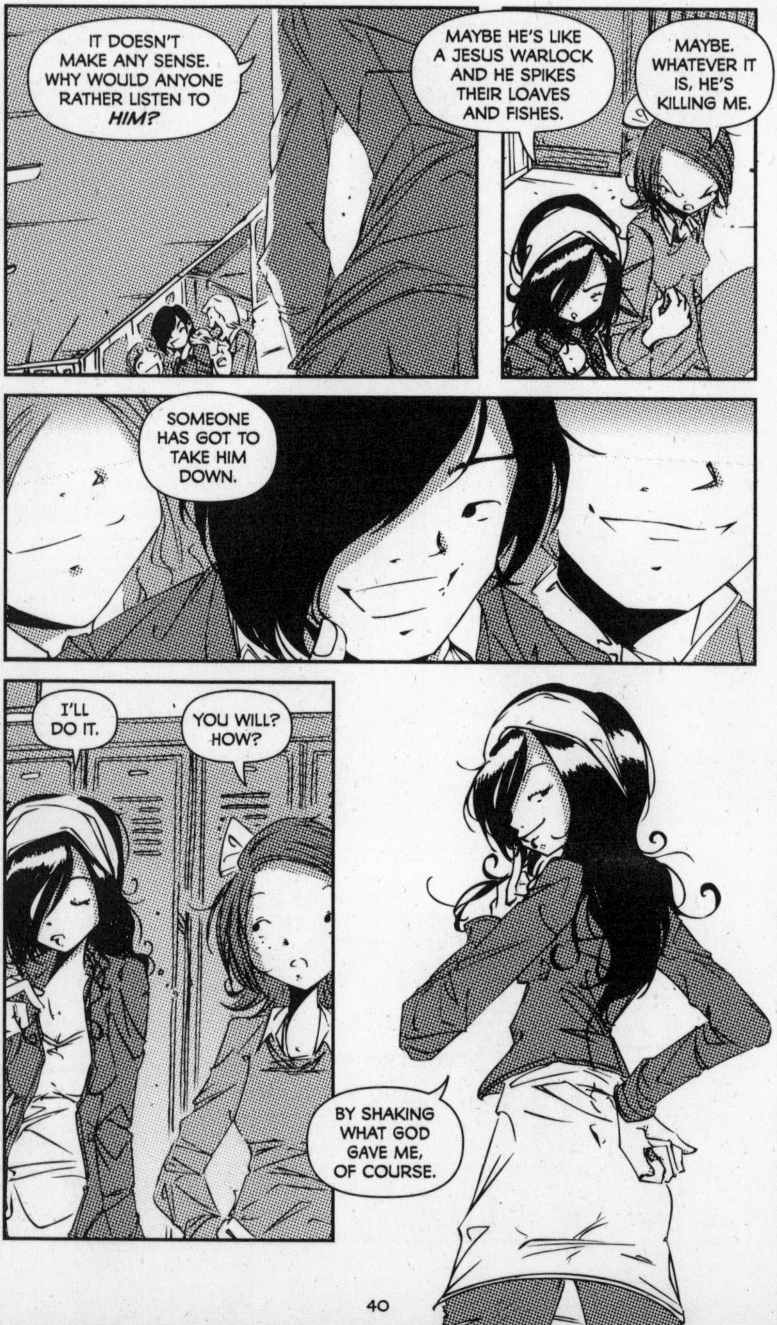
IT DOESN'T MAKE ANY SENSE. WHY WOULD ANYONE RATHER LISTEN TO *HIM?*
MAYBE HE'S LIKE A JESUS WARLOCK AND HE SPIKES THEIR LOAVES AND FISHES.
MAYBE. WHATEVER IT IS, HE'S KILLING ME.
SOMEONE HAS GOT TO TAKE HIM DOWN.
I'LL DO IT.
YOU WILL? HOW?
BY SHAKING WHAT GOD GAVE ME, OF COURSE.

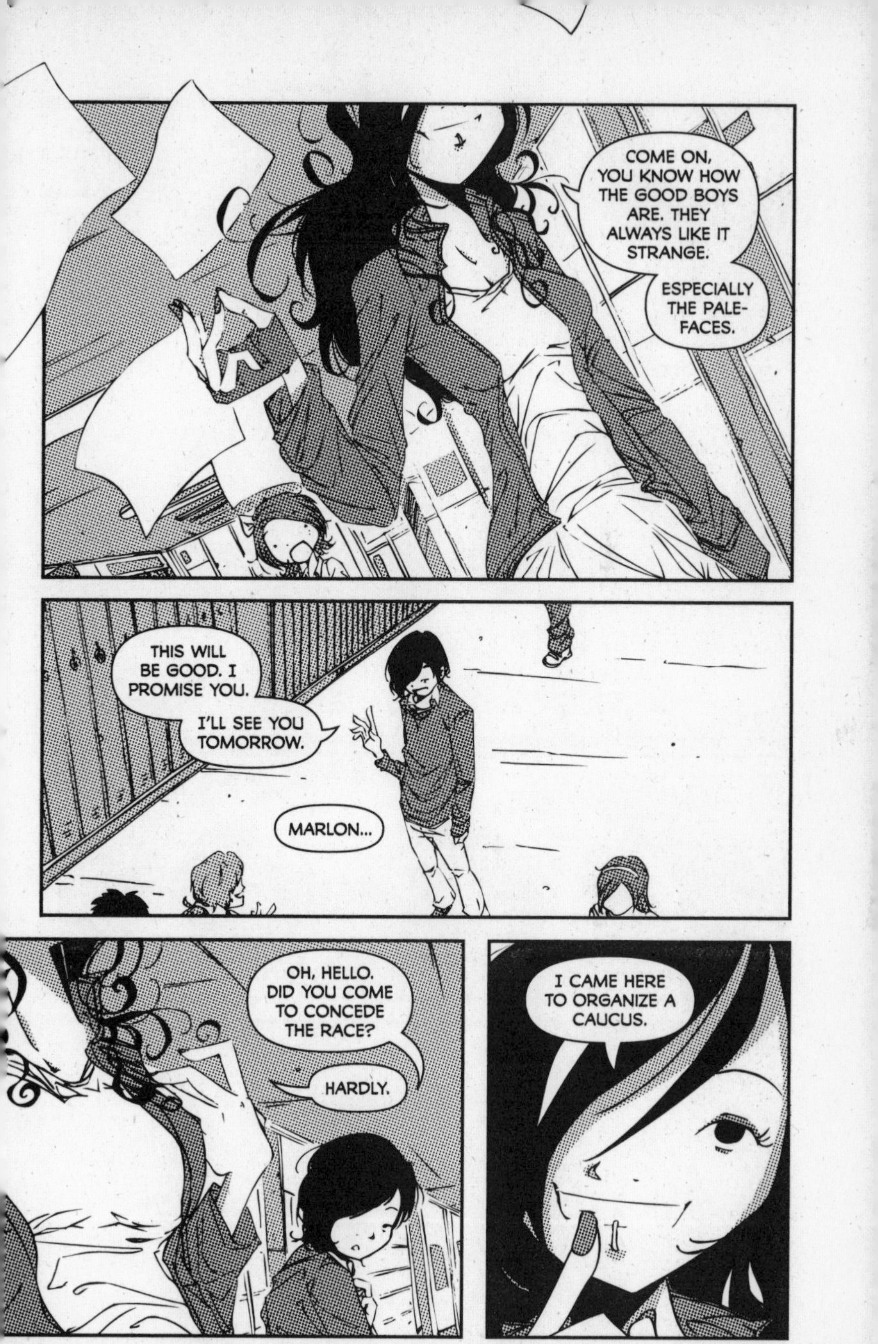
COME ON, YOU KNOW HOW THE GOOD BOYS ARE. THEY ALWAYS LIKE IT STRANGE.
ESPECIALLY THE PALE-FACES.
THIS WILL BE GOOD. I PROMISE YOU.
I'LL SEE YOU TOMORROW.
MARLON...
OH, HELLO. DID YOU COME TO CONCEDE THE RACE?
HARDLY.
I CAME HERE TO ORGANIZE A CAUCUS.

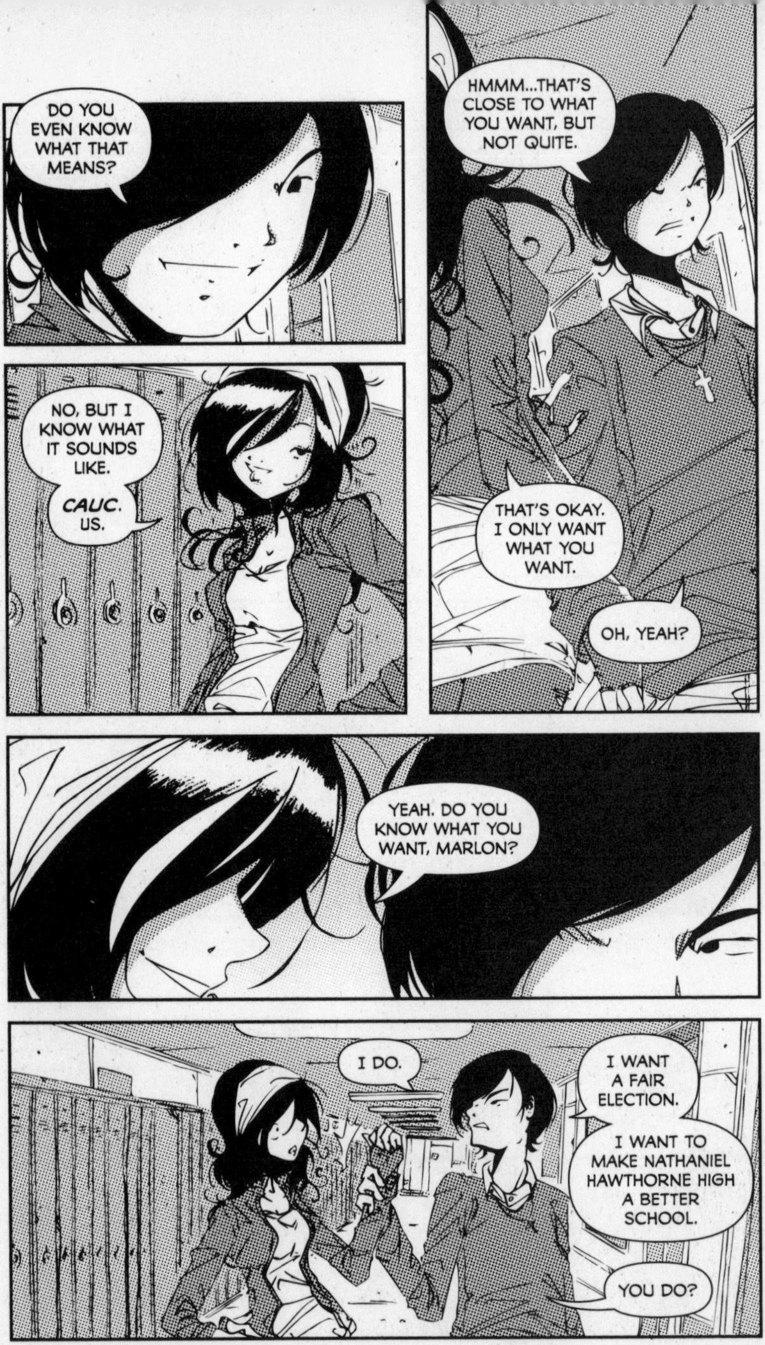
DO YOU EVEN KNOW WHAT THAT MEANS?
NO, BUT I KNOW WHAT IT SOUNDS LIKE.
CAUC. US.
HMMM...THAT'S CLOSE TO WHAT YOU WANT, BUT NOT QUITE.
THAT'S OKAY. I ONLY WANT WHAT YOU WANT.
OH, YEAH?
YEAH. DO YOU KNOW WHAT YOU WANT, MARLON?
I DO.
I WANT A FAIR ELECTION.
I WANT TO MAKE NATHANIEL HAWTHORNE HIGH A BETTER SCHOOL.
YOU DO?

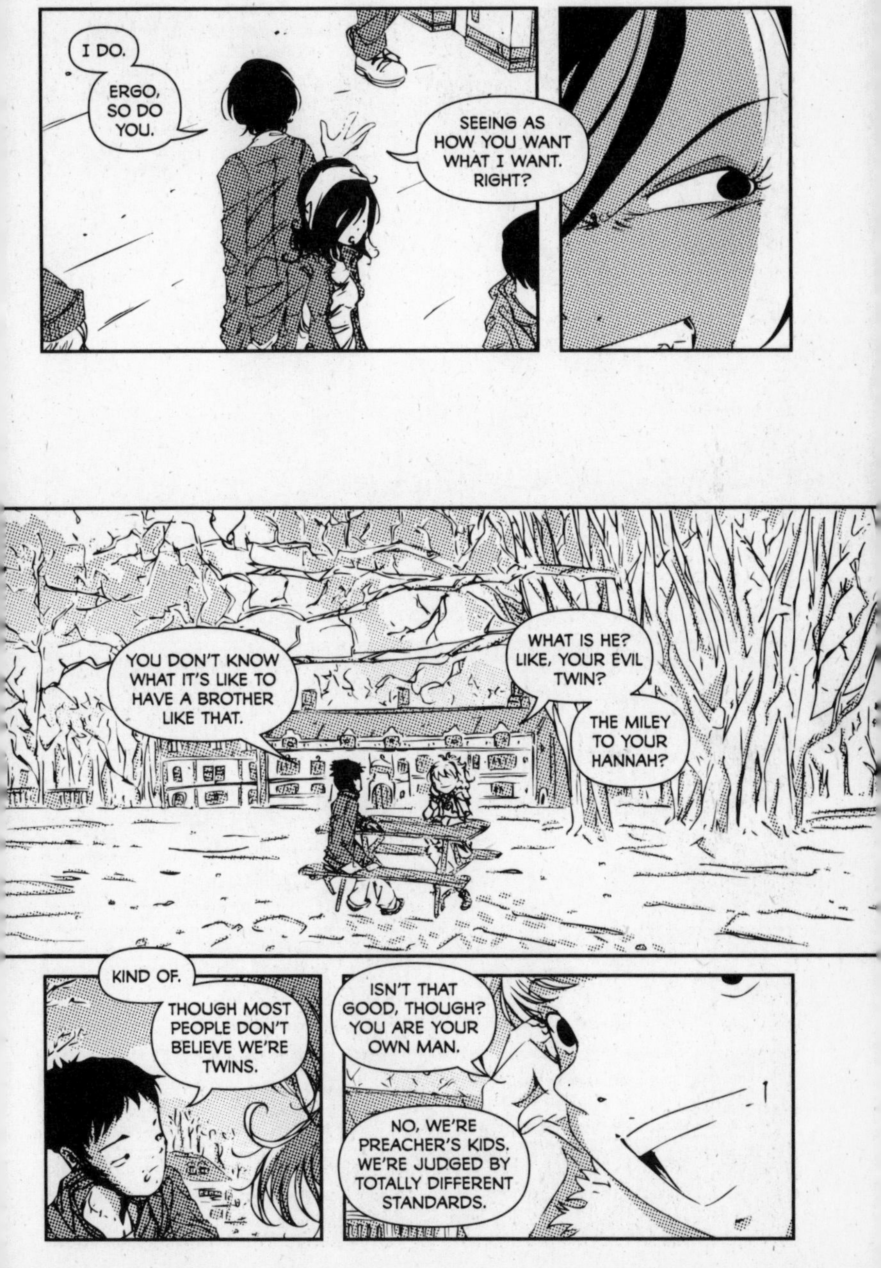
I DO.
ERGO, SO DO YOU.
SEEING AS HOW YOU WANT WHAT I WANT. RIGHT?
YOU DON'T KNOW WHAT IT'S LIKE TO HAVE A BROTHER LIKE THAT.
WHAT IS HE? LIKE, YOUR EVIL TWIN?
THE MILEY TO YOUR HANNAH?
KIND OF.
THOUGH MOST PEOPLE DON'T BELIEVE WE'RE TWINS.
ISN'T THAT GOOD, THOUGH? YOU ARE YOUR OWN MAN.
NO, WE'RE PREACHER'S KIDS. WE'RE JUDGED BY TOTALLY DIFFERENT STANDARDS.

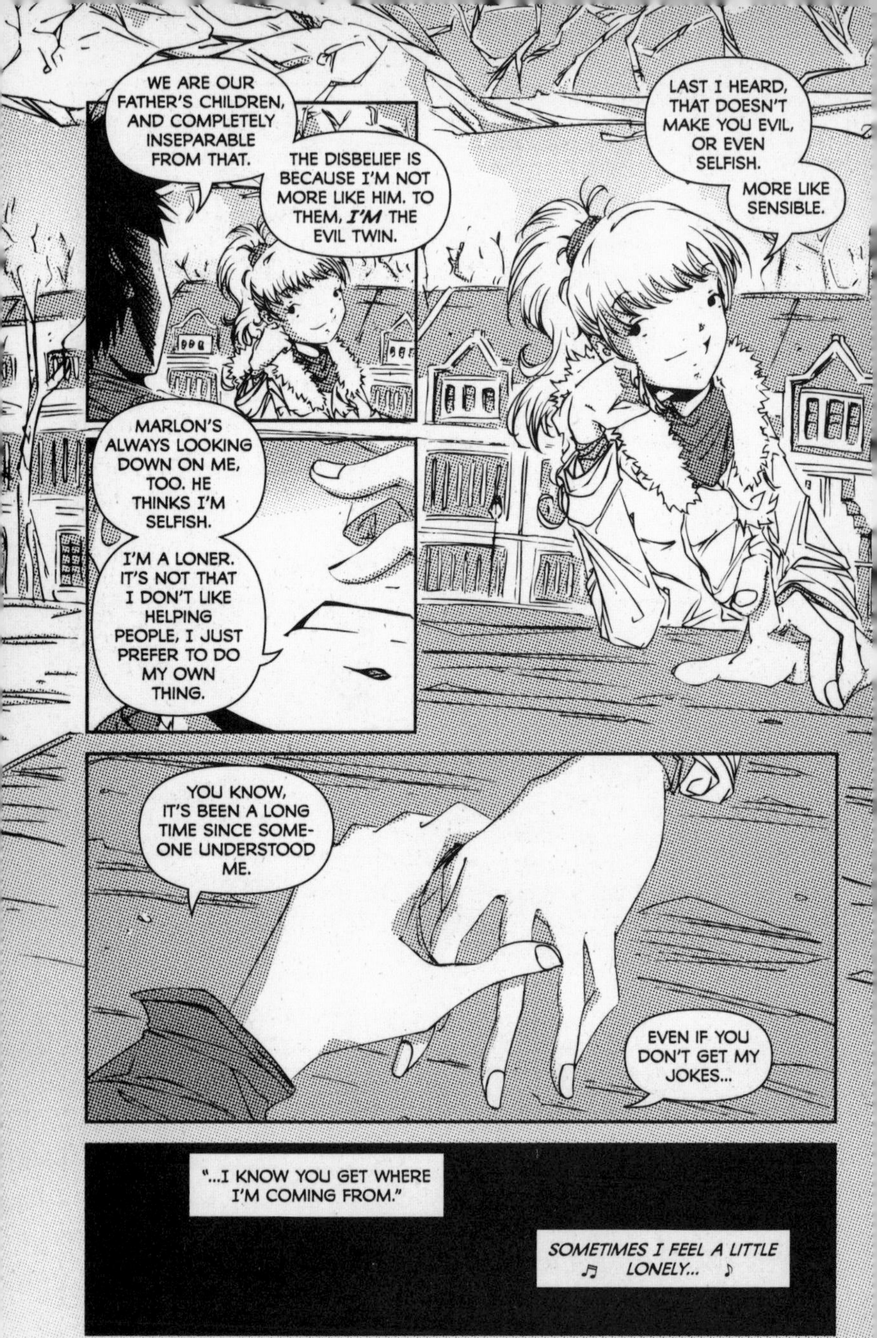
WE ARE OUR FATHER'S CHILDREN, AND COMPLETELY INSEPARABLE FROM THAT.
THE DISBELIEF IS BECAUSE I'M NOT MORE LIKE HIM. TO THEM, *I'M* THE EVIL TWIN.
LAST I HEARD, THAT DOESN'T MAKE YOU EVIL, OR EVEN SELFISH.
MORE LIKE SENSIBLE.
MARLON'S ALWAYS LOOKING DOWN ON ME, TOO. HE THINKS I'M SELFISH.
I'M A LONER. IT'S NOT THAT I DON'T LIKE HELPING PEOPLE, I JUST PREFER TO DO MY OWN THING.
YOU KNOW, IT'S BEEN A LONG TIME SINCE SOME-ONE UNDERSTOOD ME.
EVEN IF YOU DON'T GET MY JOKES...
"...I KNOW YOU GET WHERE I'M COMING FROM."
SOMETIMES I FEEL A LITTLE ♫ LONELY... ♪

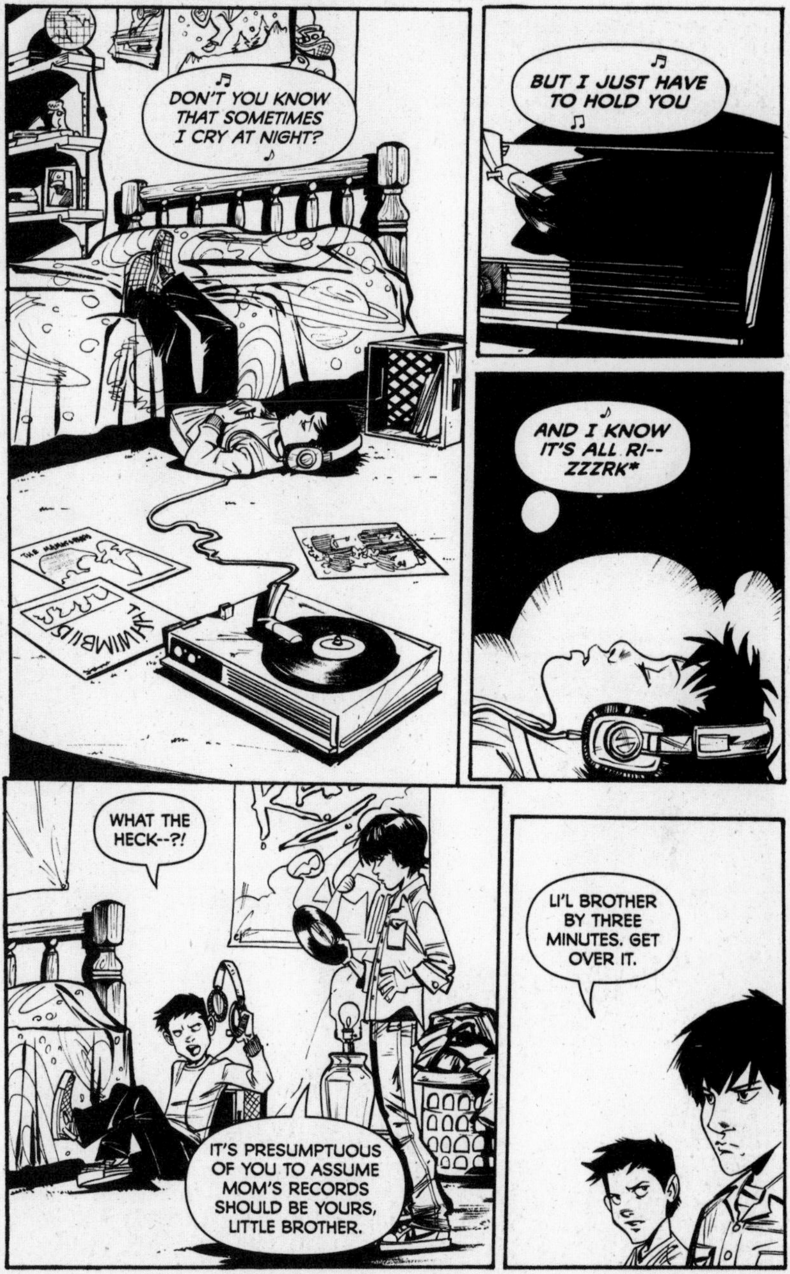
DON'T YOU KNOW THAT SOMETIMES I CRY AT NIGHT?
BUT I JUST HAVE TO HOLD YOU
AND I KNOW IT'S ALL RI-- ZZZRK*
WHAT THE HECK--?!
IT'S PRESUMPTUOUS OF YOU TO ASSUME MOM'S RECORDS SHOULD BE YOURS, LITTLE BROTHER.
LI'L BROTHER BY THREE MINUTES. GET OVER IT.

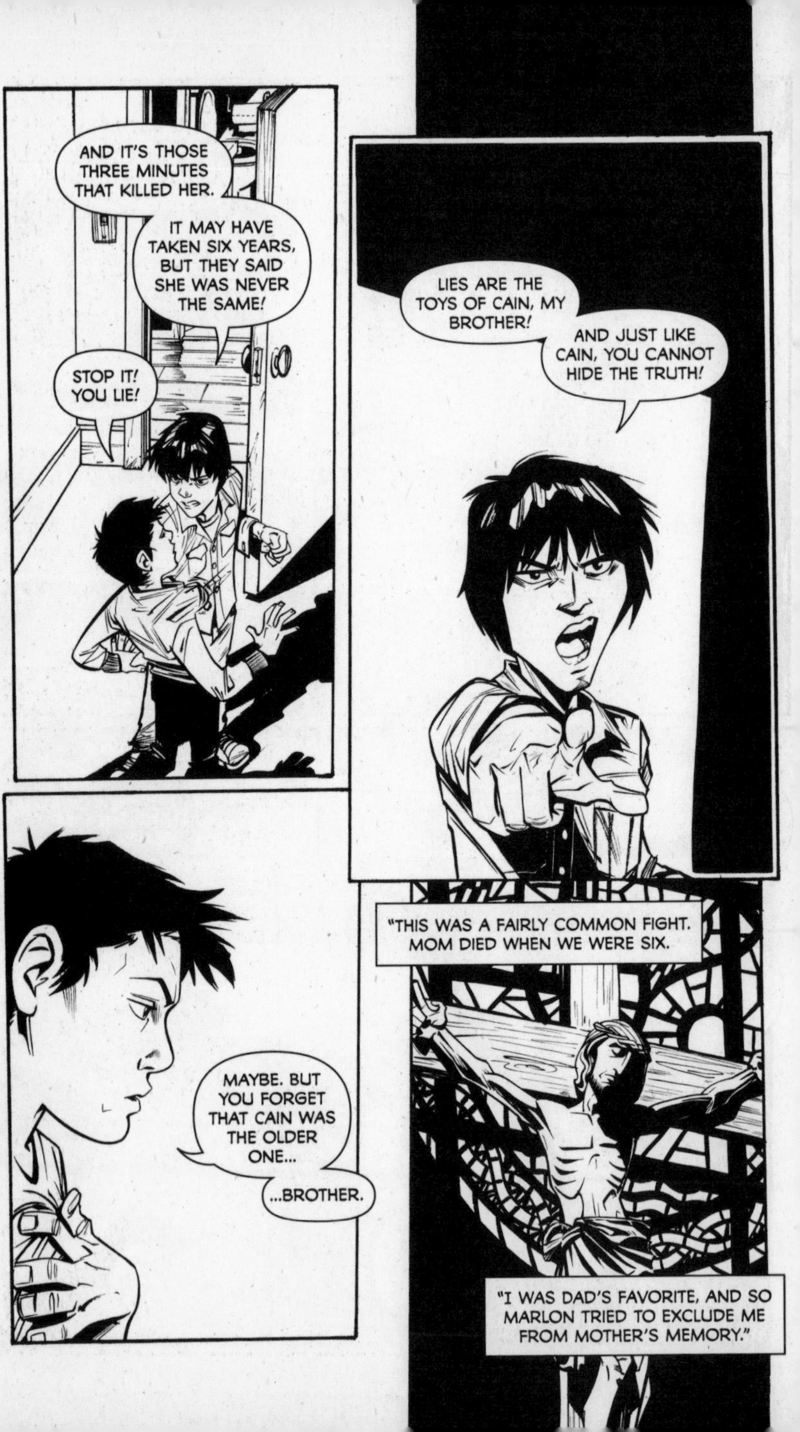
AND IT'S THOSE THREE MINUTES THAT KILLED HER.
IT MAY HAVE TAKEN SIX YEARS, BUT THEY SAID SHE WAS NEVER THE SAME!
STOP IT! YOU LIE!
LIES ARE THE TOYS OF CAIN, MY BROTHER!
AND JUST LIKE CAIN, YOU CANNOT HIDE THE TRUTH!
MAYBE. BUT YOU FORGET THAT CAIN WAS THE OLDER ONE...
...BROTHER.
"THIS WAS A FAIRLY COMMON FIGHT. MOM DIED WHEN WE WERE SIX.
"I WAS DAD'S FAVORITE, AND SO MARLON TRIED TO EXCLUDE ME FROM MOTHER'S MEMORY."

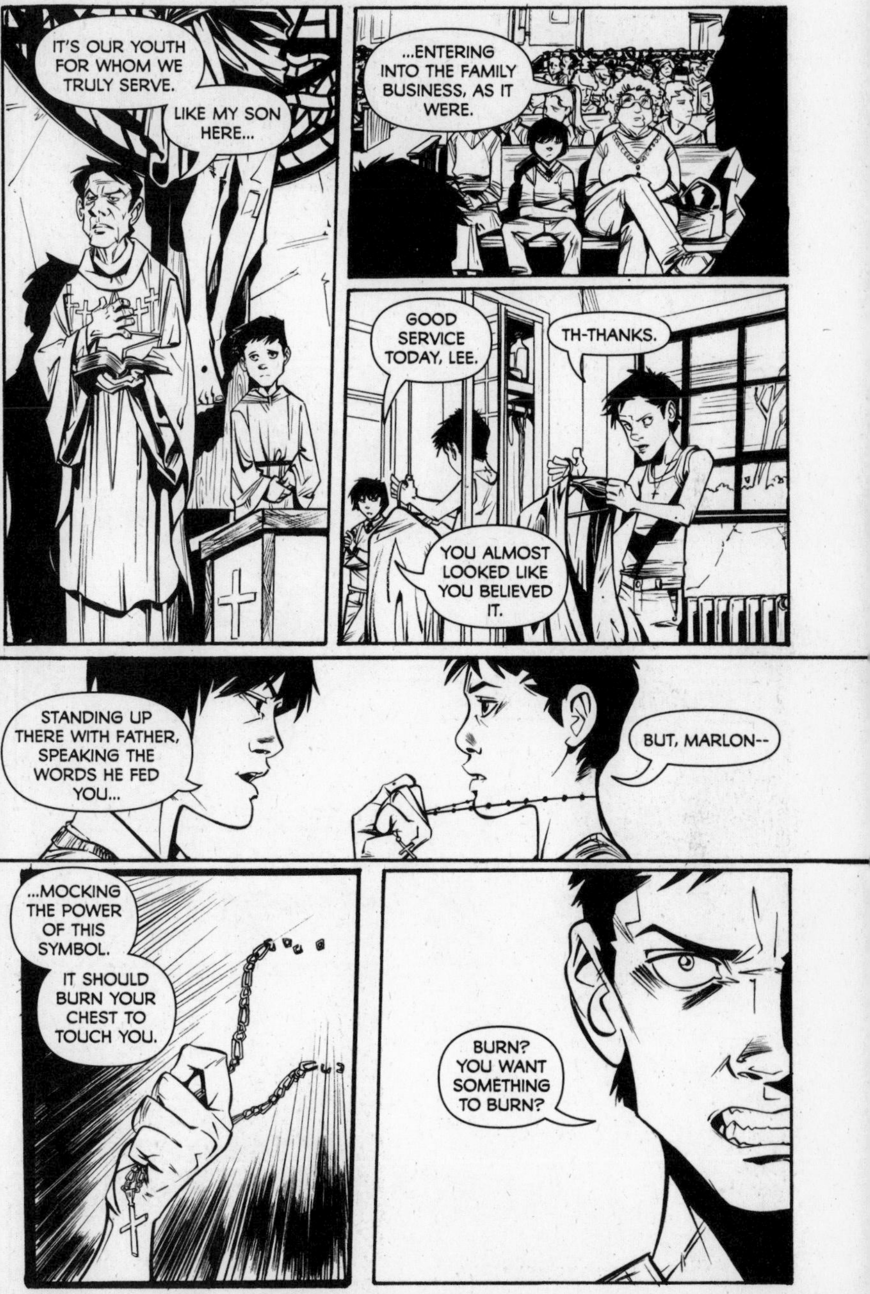
IT'S OUR YOUTH FOR WHOM WE TRULY SERVE.
LIKE MY SON HERE...
...ENTERING INTO THE FAMILY BUSINESS, AS IT WERE.
GOOD SERVICE TODAY, LEE.
TH-THANKS.
YOU ALMOST LOOKED LIKE YOU BELIEVED IT.
STANDING UP THERE WITH FATHER, SPEAKING THE WORDS HE FED YOU...
BUT, MARLON--
...MOCKING THE POWER OF THIS SYMBOL.
IT SHOULD BURN YOUR CHEST TO TOUCH YOU.
BURN? YOU WANT SOMETHING TO BURN?

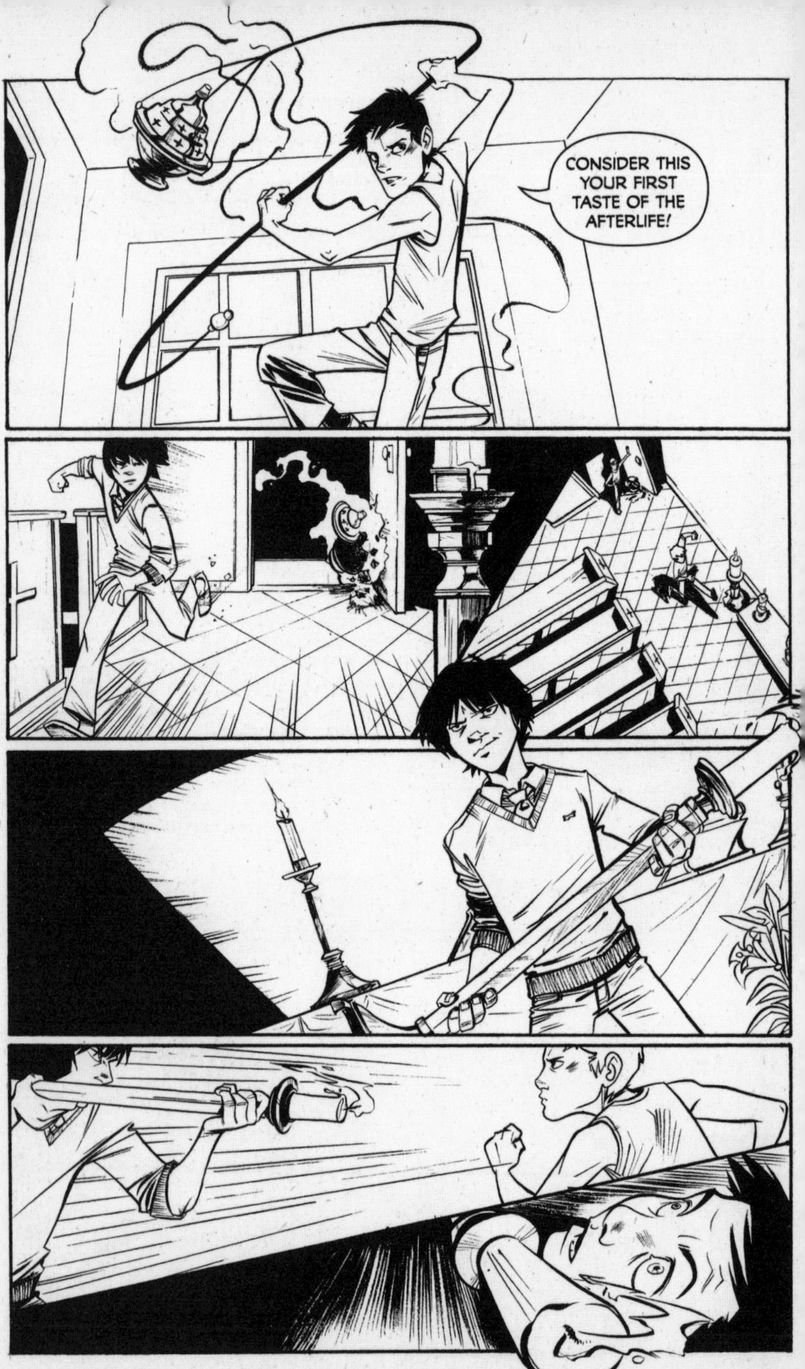
CONSIDER THIS YOUR FIRST TASTE OF THE AFTERLIFE!

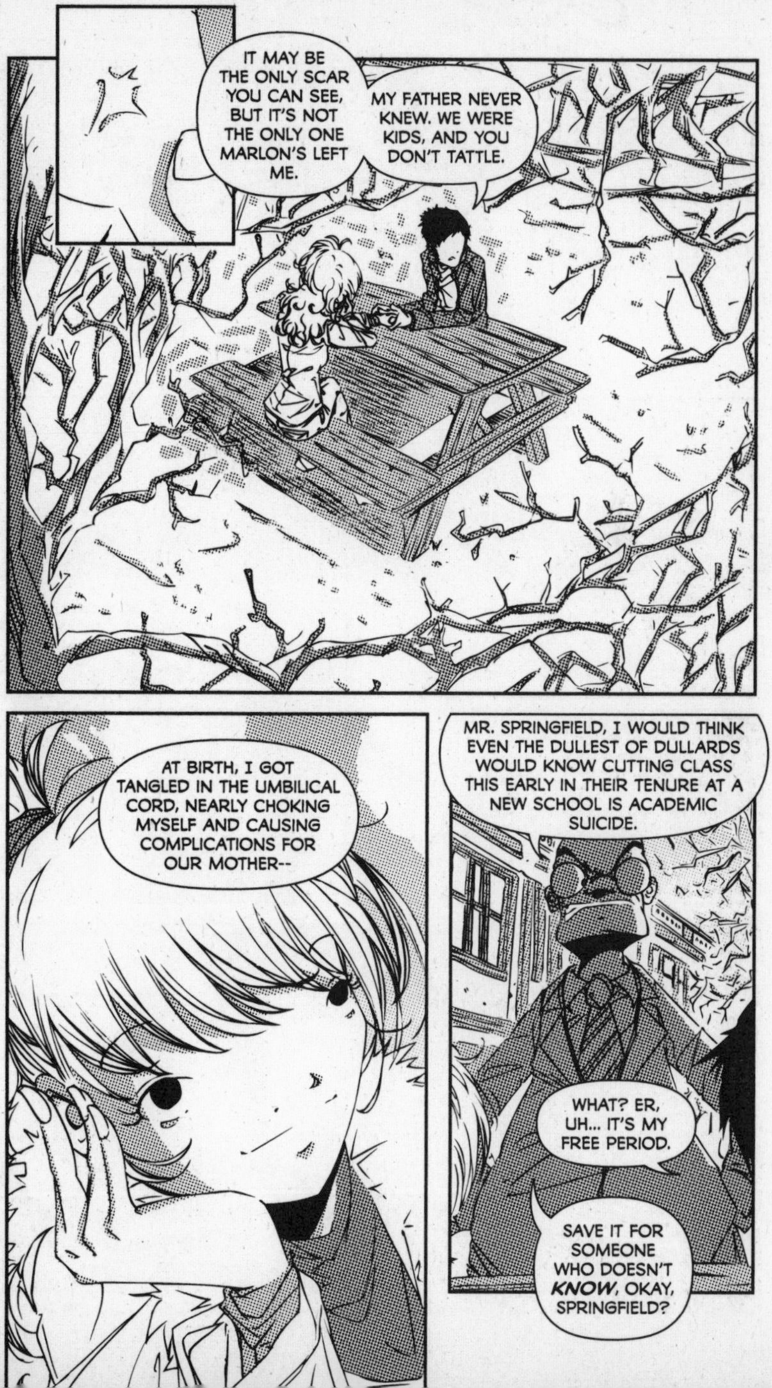
IT MAY BE THE ONLY SCAR YOU CAN SEE, BUT IT'S NOT THE ONLY ONE MARLON'S LEFT ME.
MY FATHER NEVER KNEW. WE WERE KIDS, AND YOU DON'T TATTLE.
AT BIRTH, I GOT TANGLED IN THE UMBILICAL CORD, NEARLY CHOKING MYSELF AND CAUSING COMPLICATIONS FOR OUR MOTHER--
MR. SPRINGFIELD, I WOULD THINK EVEN THE DULLEST OF DULLARDS WOULD KNOW CUTTING CLASS THIS EARLY IN THEIR TENURE AT A NEW SCHOOL IS ACADEMIC SUICIDE.
WHAT? ER, UH... IT'S MY FREE PERIOD.
SAVE IT FOR SOMEONE WHO DOESN'T ***KNOW***, OKAY, SPRINGFIELD?

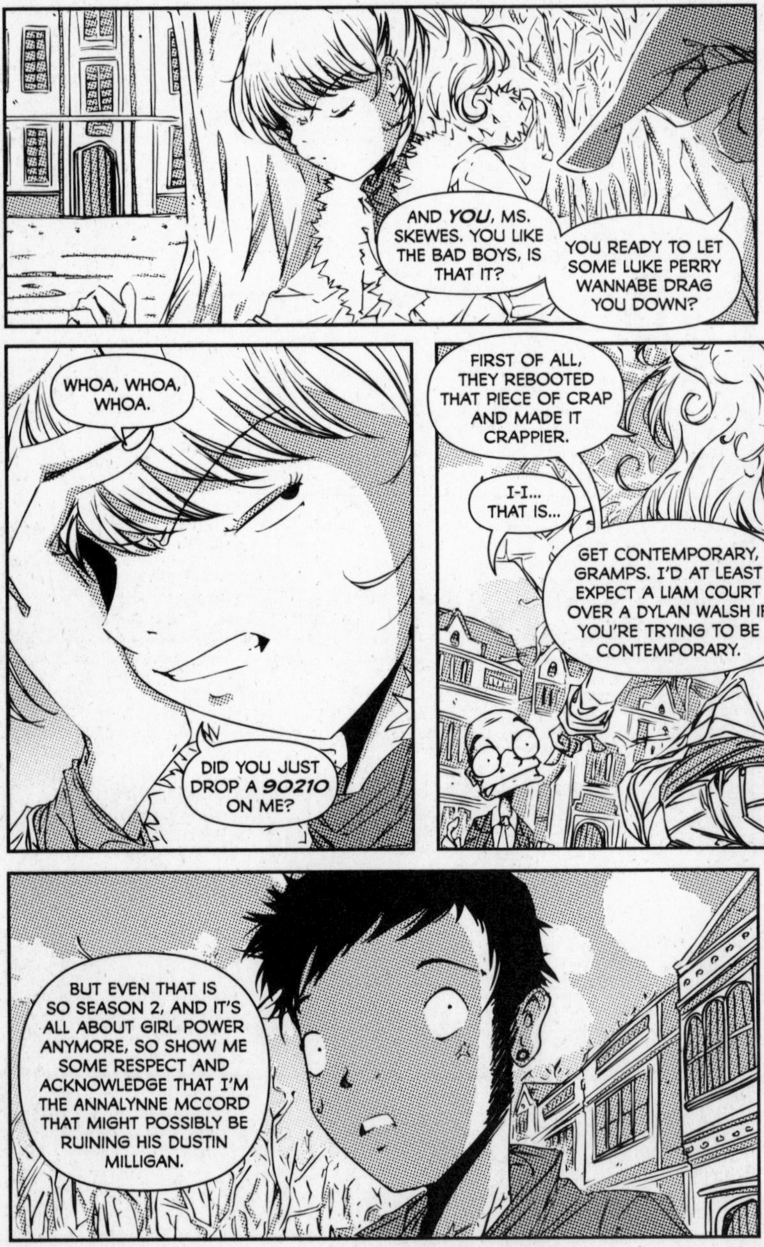
AND *YOU*, MS. SKEWES. YOU LIKE THE BAD BOYS, IS THAT IT?
YOU READY TO LET SOME LUKE PERRY WANNABE DRAG YOU DOWN?
WHOA, WHOA, WHOA.
DID YOU JUST DROP A *90210* ON ME?
FIRST OF ALL, THEY REBOOTED THAT PIECE OF CRAP AND MADE IT CRAPPIER.
I-I... THAT IS...
GET CONTEMPORARY, GRAMPS. I'D AT LEAST EXPECT A LIAM COURT OVER A DYLAN WALSH IF YOU'RE TRYING TO BE CONTEMPORARY.
BUT EVEN THAT IS SO SEASON 2, AND IT'S ALL ABOUT GIRL POWER ANYMORE, SO SHOW ME SOME RESPECT AND ACKNOWLEDGE THAT I'M THE ANNALYNNE MCCORD THAT MIGHT POSSIBLY BE RUINING HIS DUSTIN MILLIGAN.

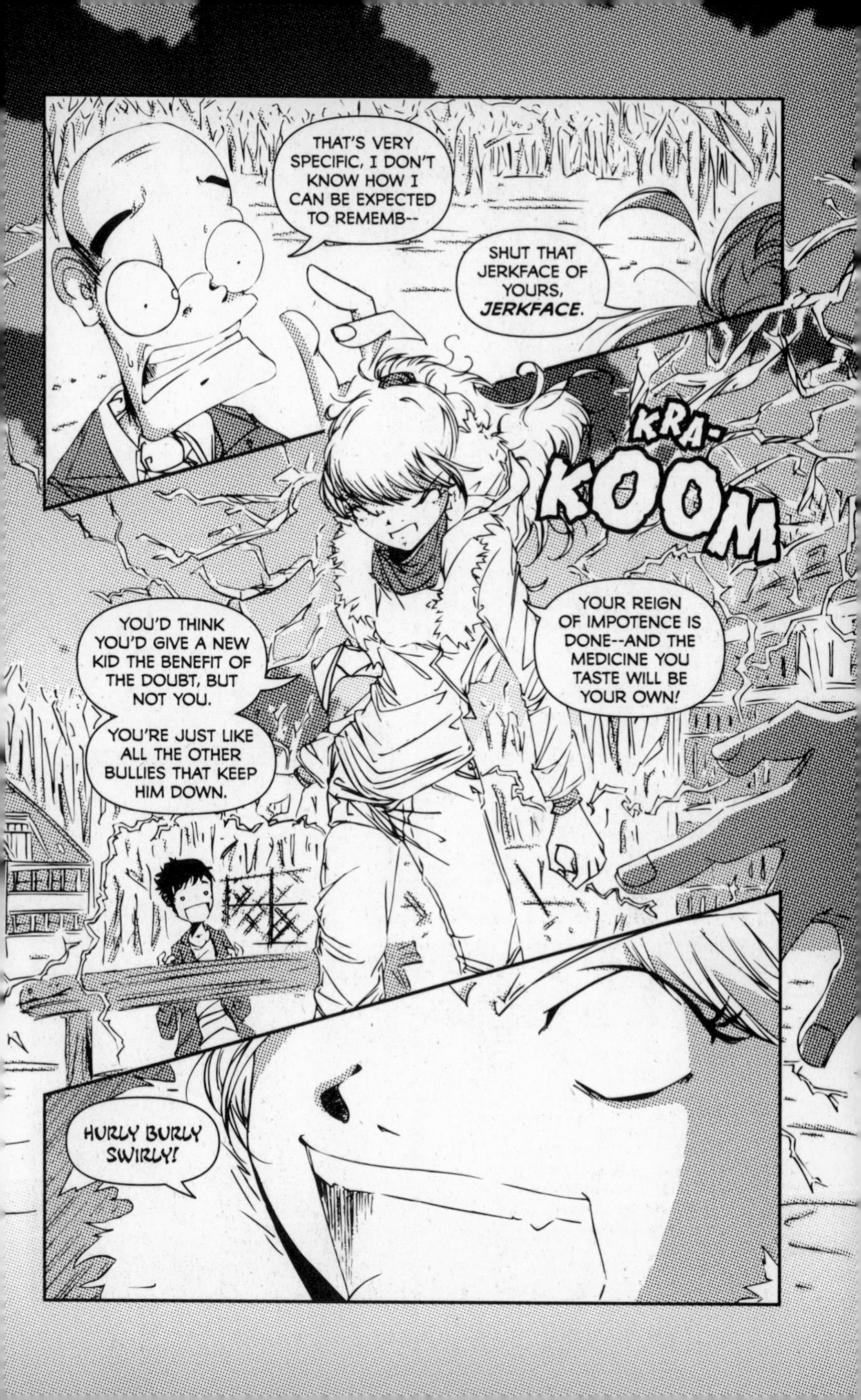
THAT'S VERY SPECIFIC, I DON'T KNOW HOW I CAN BE EXPECTED TO REMEMB--
SHUT THAT JERKFACE OF YOURS, *JERKFACE*.
KRA-KOOM
YOUR REIGN OF IMPOTENCE IS DONE--AND THE MEDICINE YOU TASTE WILL BE YOUR OWN!
YOU'D THINK YOU'D GIVE A NEW KID THE BENEFIT OF THE DOUBT, BUT NOT YOU.
YOU'RE JUST LIKE ALL THE OTHER BULLIES THAT KEEP HIM DOWN.
HURLY BURLY SWIRLY!

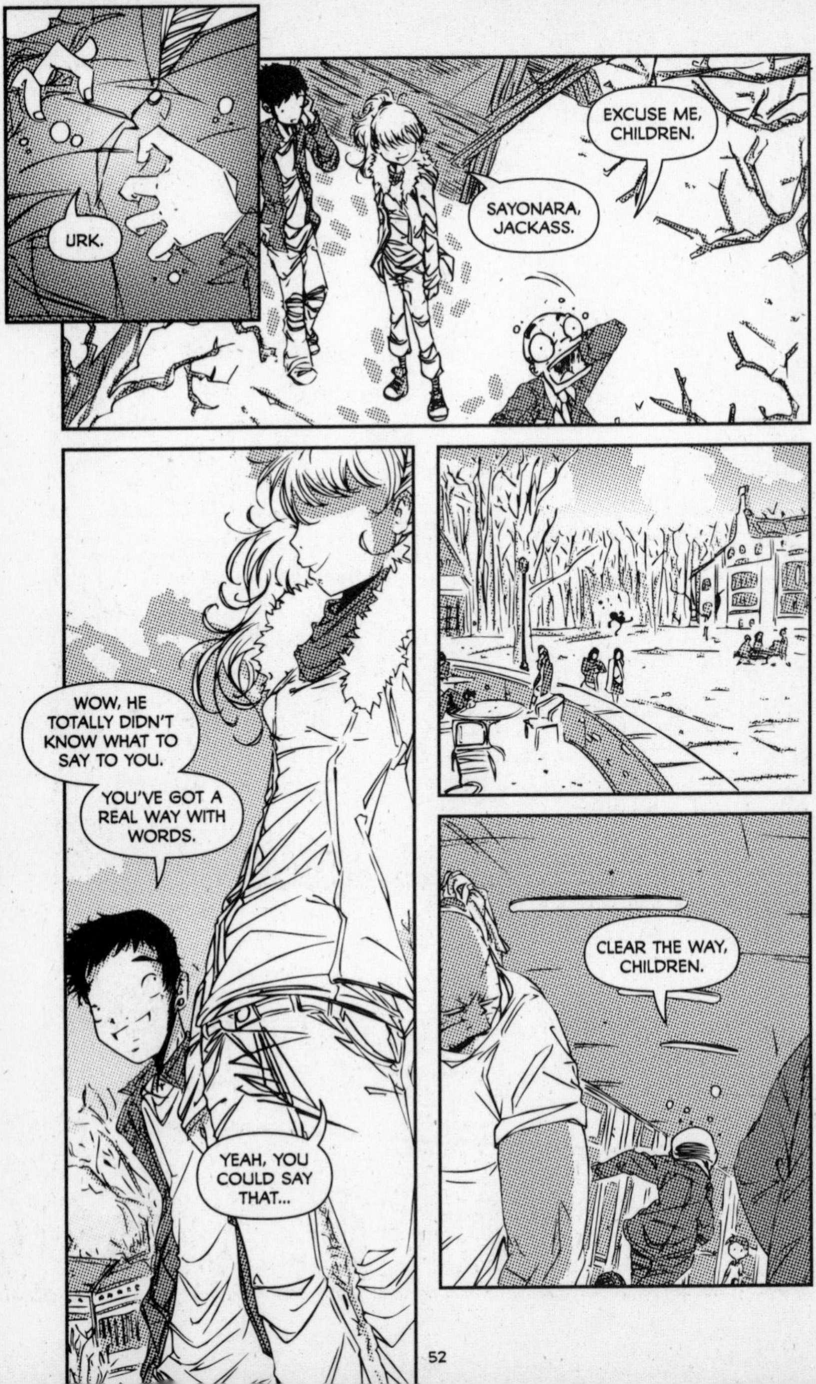
URK.
EXCUSE ME, CHILDREN.
SAYONARA, JACKASS.
WOW, HE TOTALLY DIDN'T KNOW WHAT TO SAY TO YOU.
YOU'VE GOT A REAL WAY WITH WORDS.
YEAH, YOU COULD SAY THAT...
CLEAR THE WAY, CHILDREN.

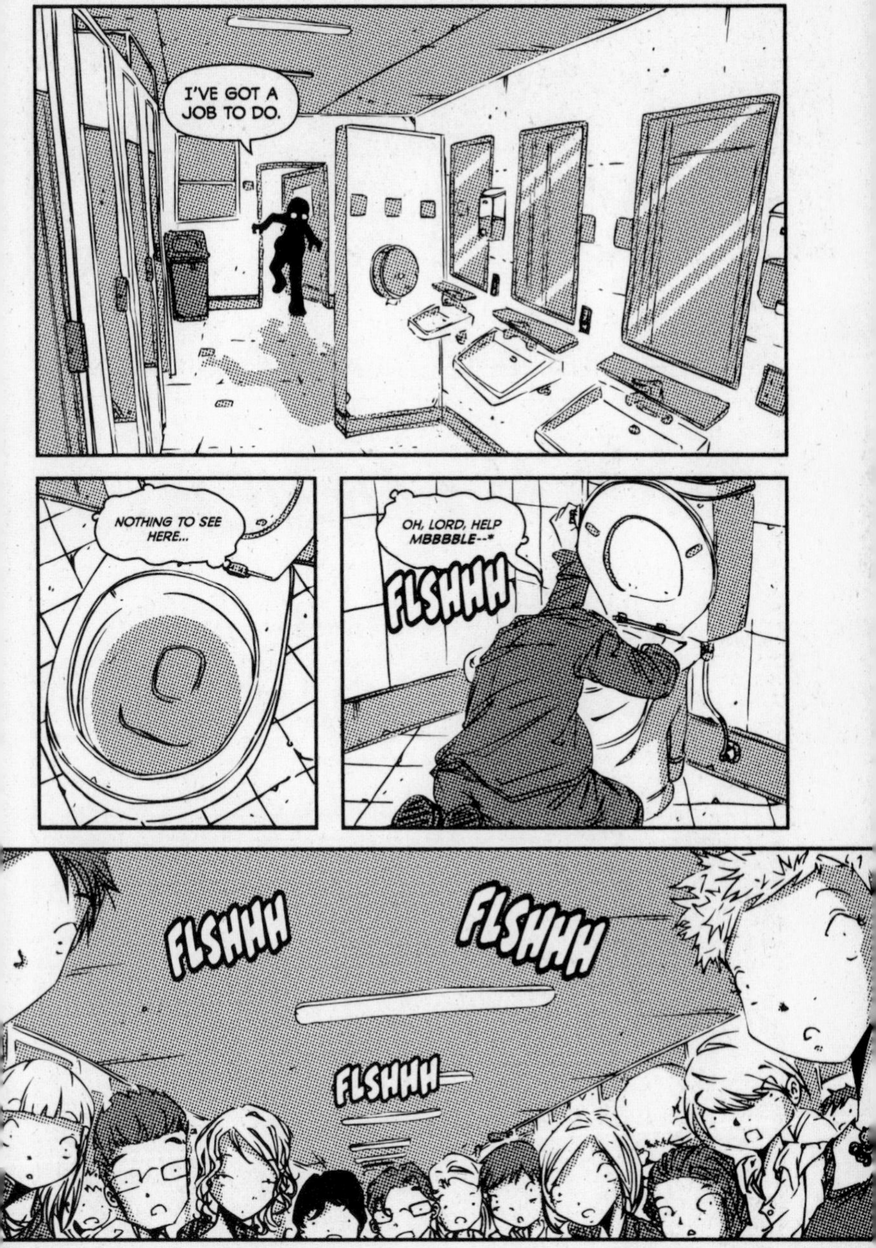
I'VE GOT A JOB TO DO.
NOTHING TO SEE HERE...
OH, LORD, HELP MBBBBLE--*
FLSHHH
FLSHHH
FLSHHH
FLSHHH

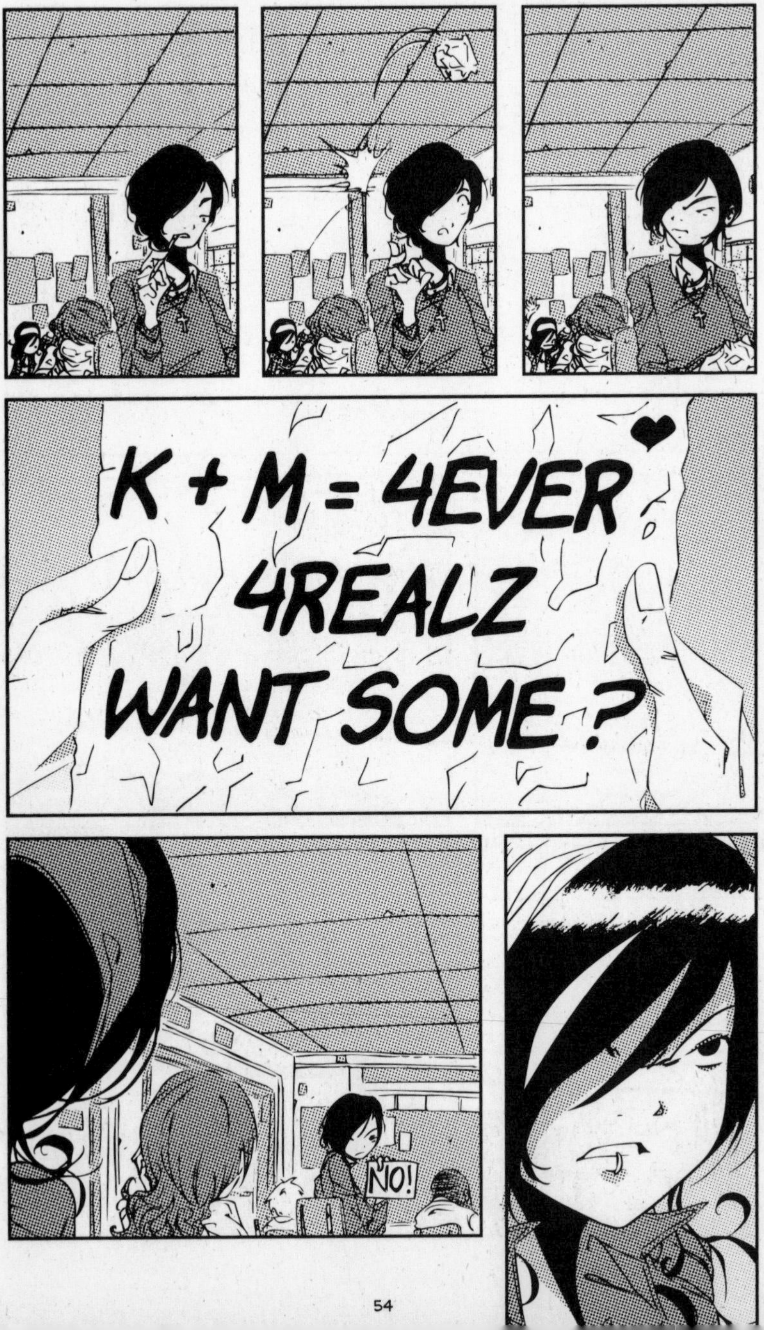
K + M = 4EVER
4REALZ
WANT SOME ?
NO!

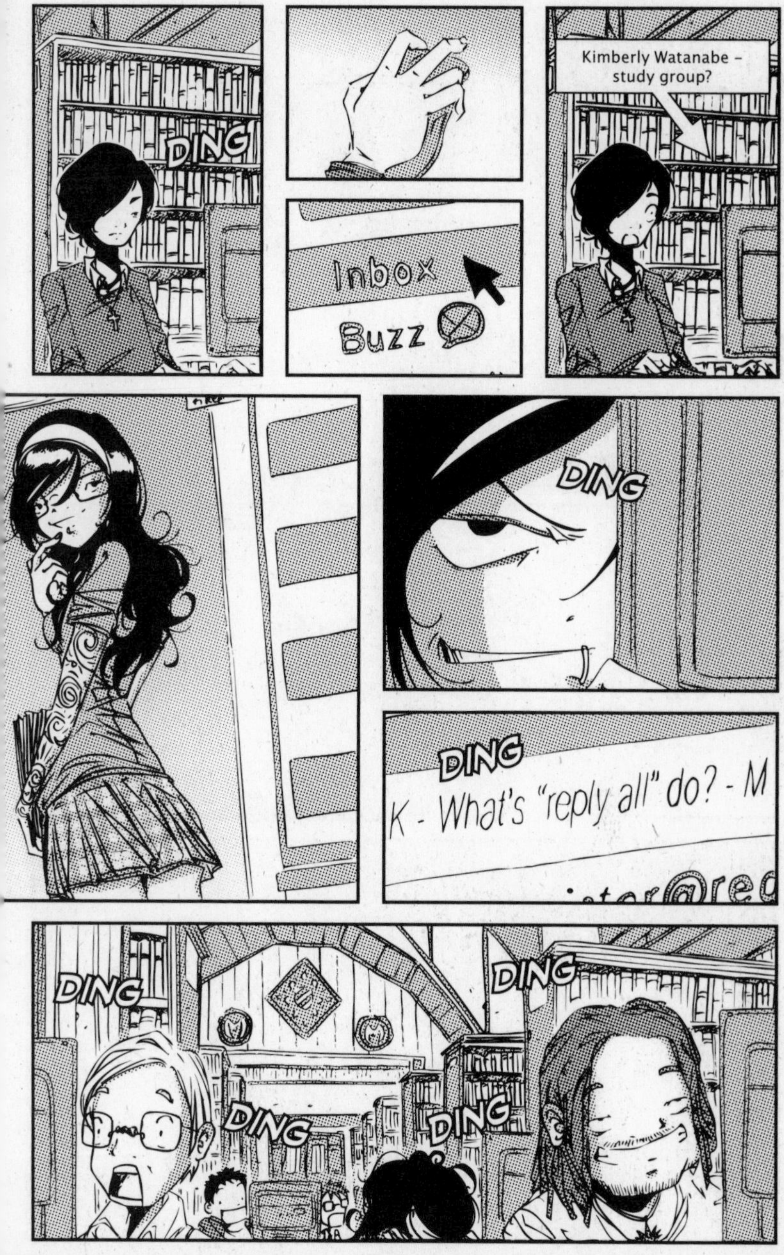
DING
Inbox
Buzz
Kimberly Watanabe – study group?
DING
DING
K - What's "reply all" do? - M
DING
DING
DING
DING

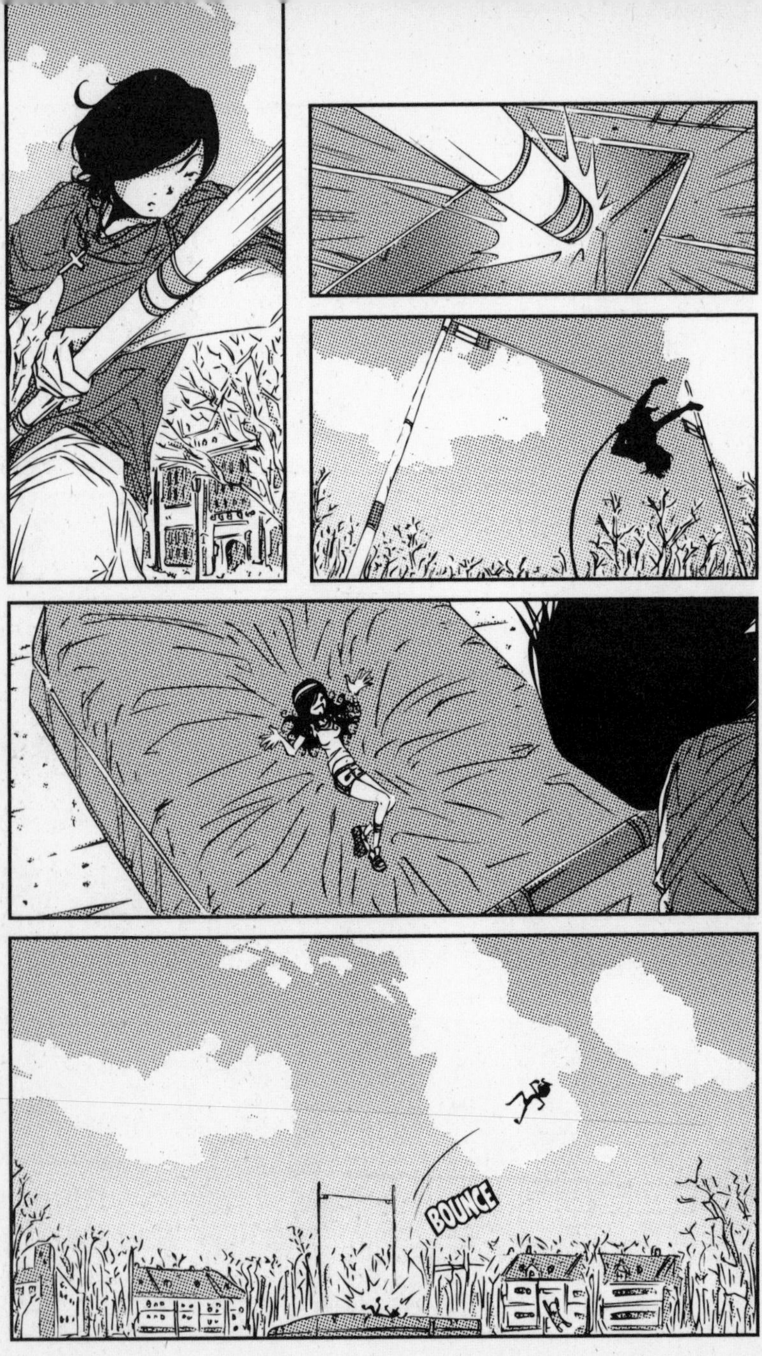
BOUNCE

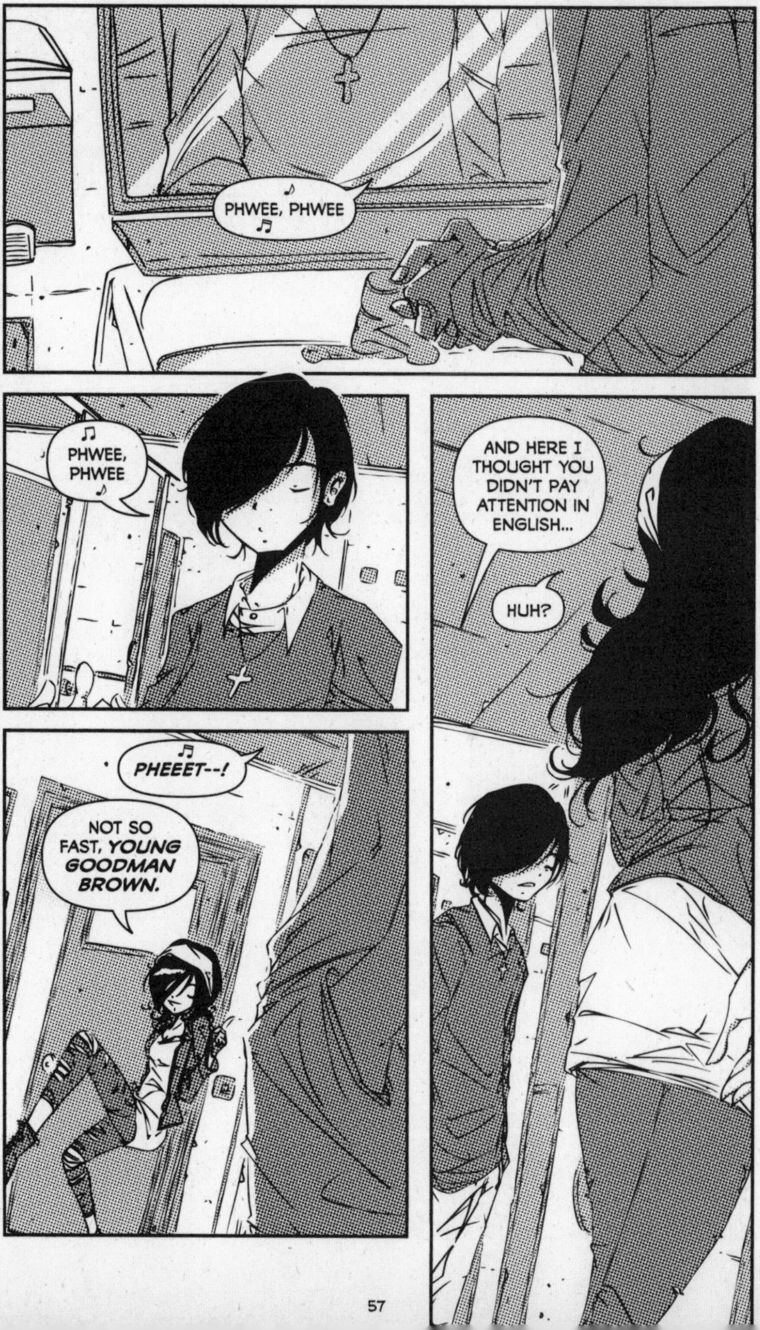
PHWEE, PHWEE
PHWEE, PHWEE
AND HERE I THOUGHT YOU DIDN'T PAY ATTENTION IN ENGLISH...
HUH?
PHEEET--!
NOT SO FAST, YOUNG GOODMAN BROWN.

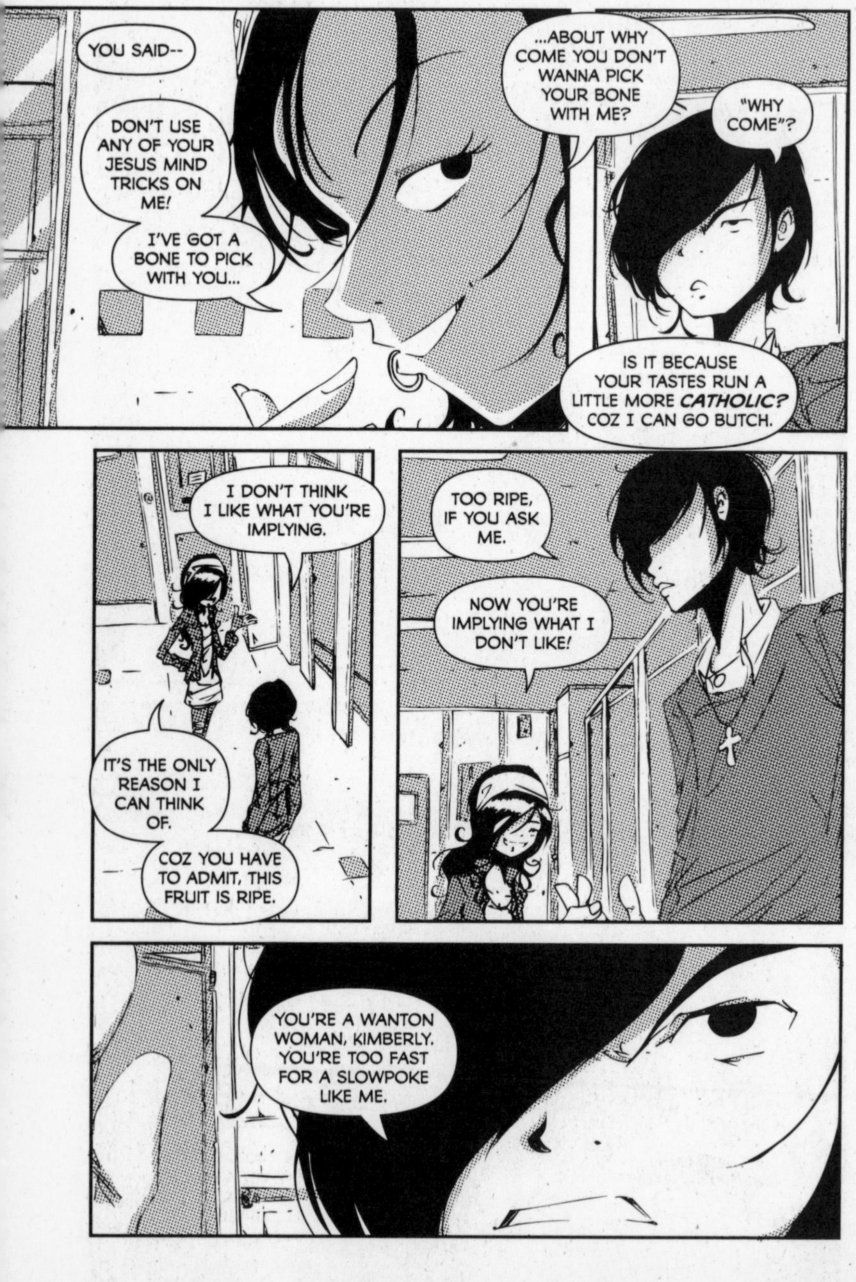
YOU SAID--
DON'T USE ANY OF YOUR JESUS MIND TRICKS ON ME!
I'VE GOT A BONE TO PICK WITH YOU...
...ABOUT WHY COME YOU DON'T WANNA PICK YOUR BONE WITH ME?
"WHY COME"?
IS IT BECAUSE YOUR TASTES RUN A LITTLE MORE CATHOLIC? COZ I CAN GO BUTCH.
I DON'T THINK I LIKE WHAT YOU'RE IMPLYING.
IT'S THE ONLY REASON I CAN THINK OF.
COZ YOU HAVE TO ADMIT, THIS FRUIT IS RIPE.
TOO RIPE, IF YOU ASK ME.
NOW YOU'RE IMPLYING WHAT I DON'T LIKE!
YOU'RE A WANTON WOMAN, KIMBERLY. YOU'RE TOO FAST FOR A SLOWPOKE LIKE ME.

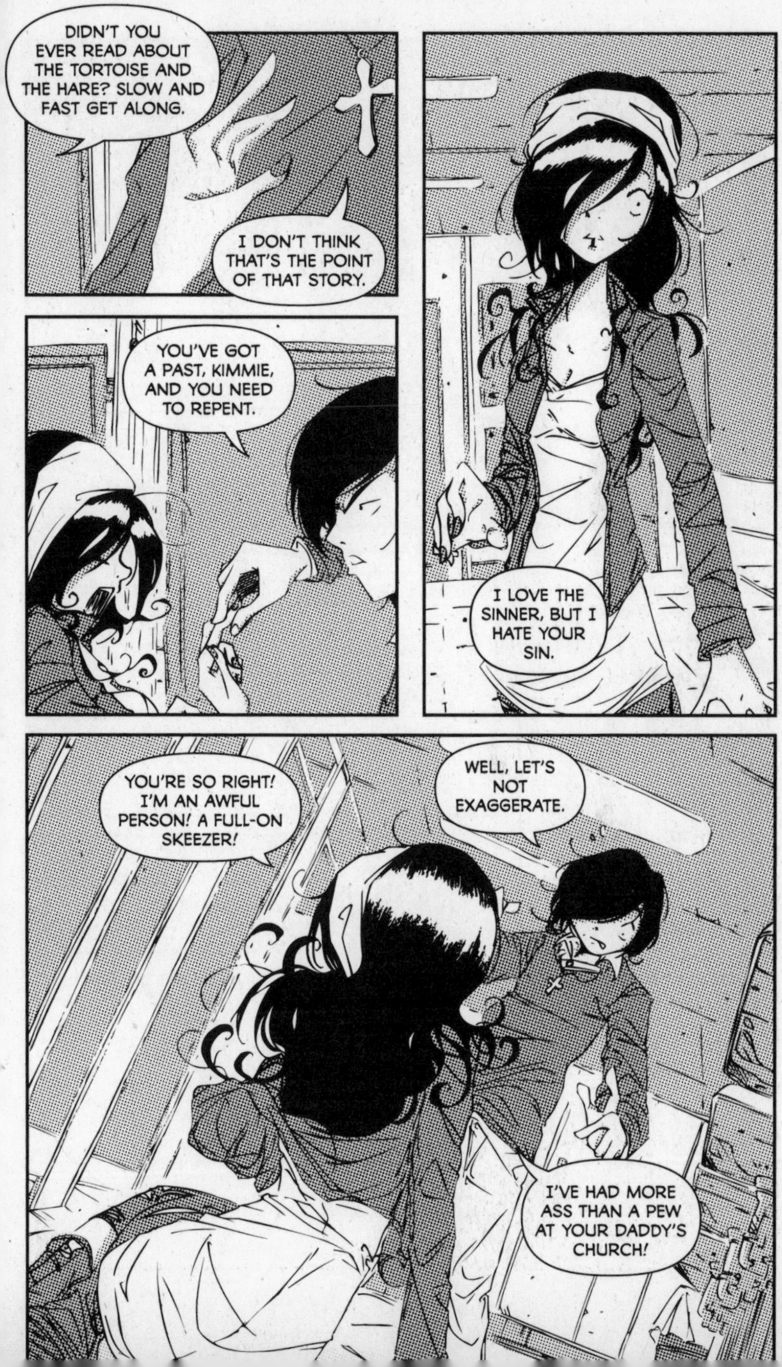
DIDN'T YOU EVER READ ABOUT THE TORTOISE AND THE HARE? SLOW AND FAST GET ALONG.
I DON'T THINK THAT'S THE POINT OF THAT STORY.
YOU'VE GOT A PAST, KIMMIE, AND YOU NEED TO REPENT.
I LOVE THE SINNER, BUT I HATE YOUR SIN.
YOU'RE SO RIGHT! I'M AN AWFUL PERSON! A FULL-ON SKEEZER!
WELL, LET'S NOT EXAGGERATE.
I'VE HAD MORE ASS THAN A PEW AT YOUR DADDY'S CHURCH!

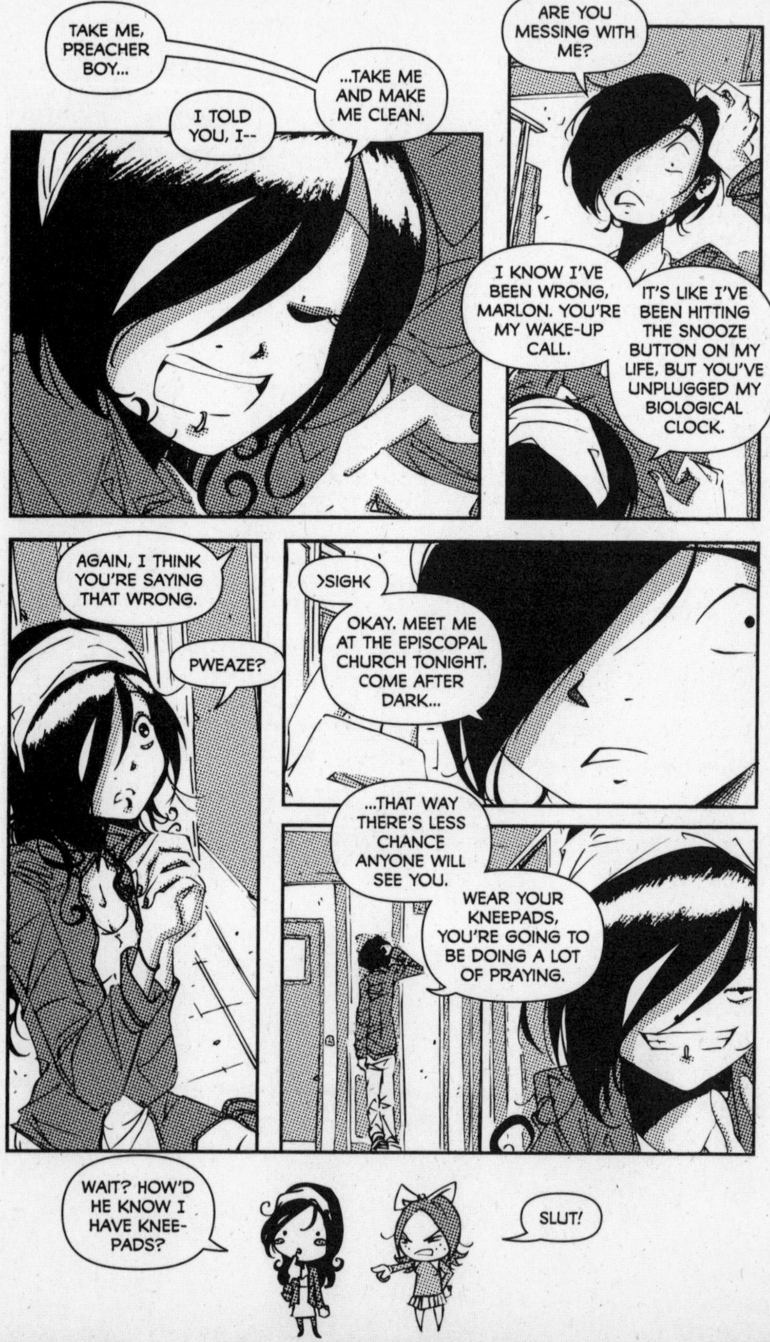
TAKE ME, PREACHER BOY...
...TAKE ME AND MAKE ME CLEAN.
I TOLD YOU, I--
ARE YOU MESSING WITH ME?
I KNOW I'VE BEEN WRONG, MARLON. YOU'RE MY WAKE-UP CALL.
IT'S LIKE I'VE BEEN HITTING THE SNOOZE BUTTON ON MY LIFE, BUT YOU'VE UNPLUGGED MY BIOLOGICAL CLOCK.
AGAIN, I THINK YOU'RE SAYING THAT WRONG.
PWEAZE?
>SIGH<
OKAY. MEET ME AT THE EPISCOPAL CHURCH TONIGHT. COME AFTER DARK...
...THAT WAY THERE'S LESS CHANCE ANYONE WILL SEE YOU.
WEAR YOUR KNEEPADS, YOU'RE GOING TO BE DOING A LOT OF PRAYING.
WAIT? HOW'D HE KNOW I HAVE KNEE-PADS?
SLUT!

Chapter 3
"Whole Lotta History"

3

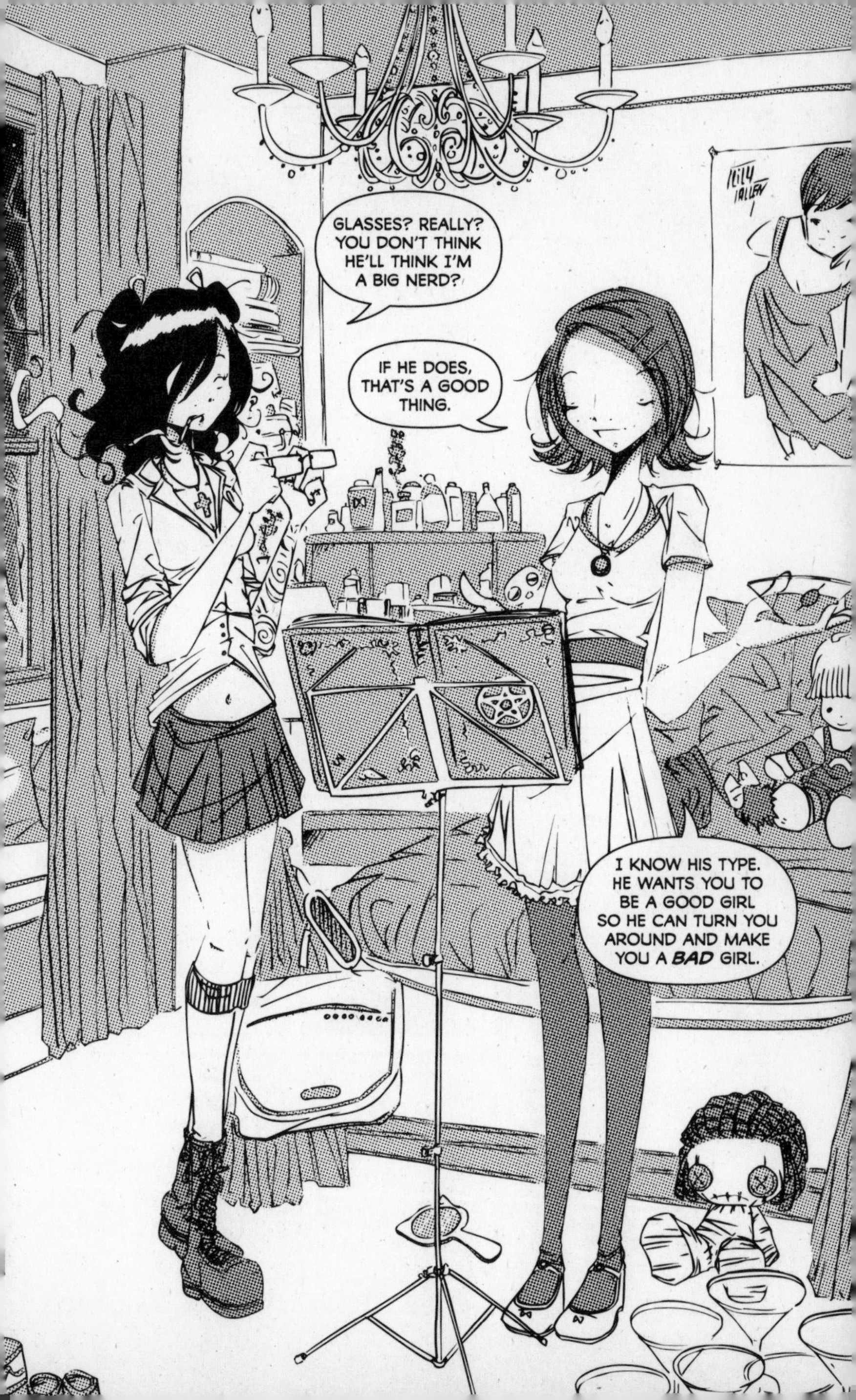
GLASSES? REALLY? YOU DON'T THINK HE'LL THINK I'M A BIG NERD?
IF HE DOES, THAT'S A GOOD THING.
I KNOW HIS TYPE. HE WANTS YOU TO BE A GOOD GIRL SO HE CAN TURN YOU AROUND AND MAKE YOU A ***BAD*** GIRL.
LILY ALLEN

YOU KNOW, WE MAY HAVE A BIGGER SCANDAL ON OUR HANDS THAN JUST MARLON GETTING FREAKY.

WHAT IF HE PULLS ON ME WHAT HE PULLED ON CHRISTINA SNYDER?

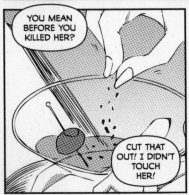

YOU MEAN BEFORE YOU KILLED HER?

CUT THAT OUT! I DIDN'T TOUCH HER!

SOLVING CRIMES WOULD BE GOOD FOR SOME BONUS POINTS, I GUESS.

BUT LET'S NOT GET ALL *VERONICA MARS*...

frog legs

...BECAUSE THAT SHOW WAS CANCELLED FOR A REASON.

PTUI!

MY LUCK, IT WOULD BE ALL LAME AND *GHOST WHISPERER*, ANYWAY.

WHATEVER. YOU *WISH* YOU HAD J. LOVE'S RACK.

JEEPERS CREEPERS...

PEEP THOSE PEEPERS!

FWSHH

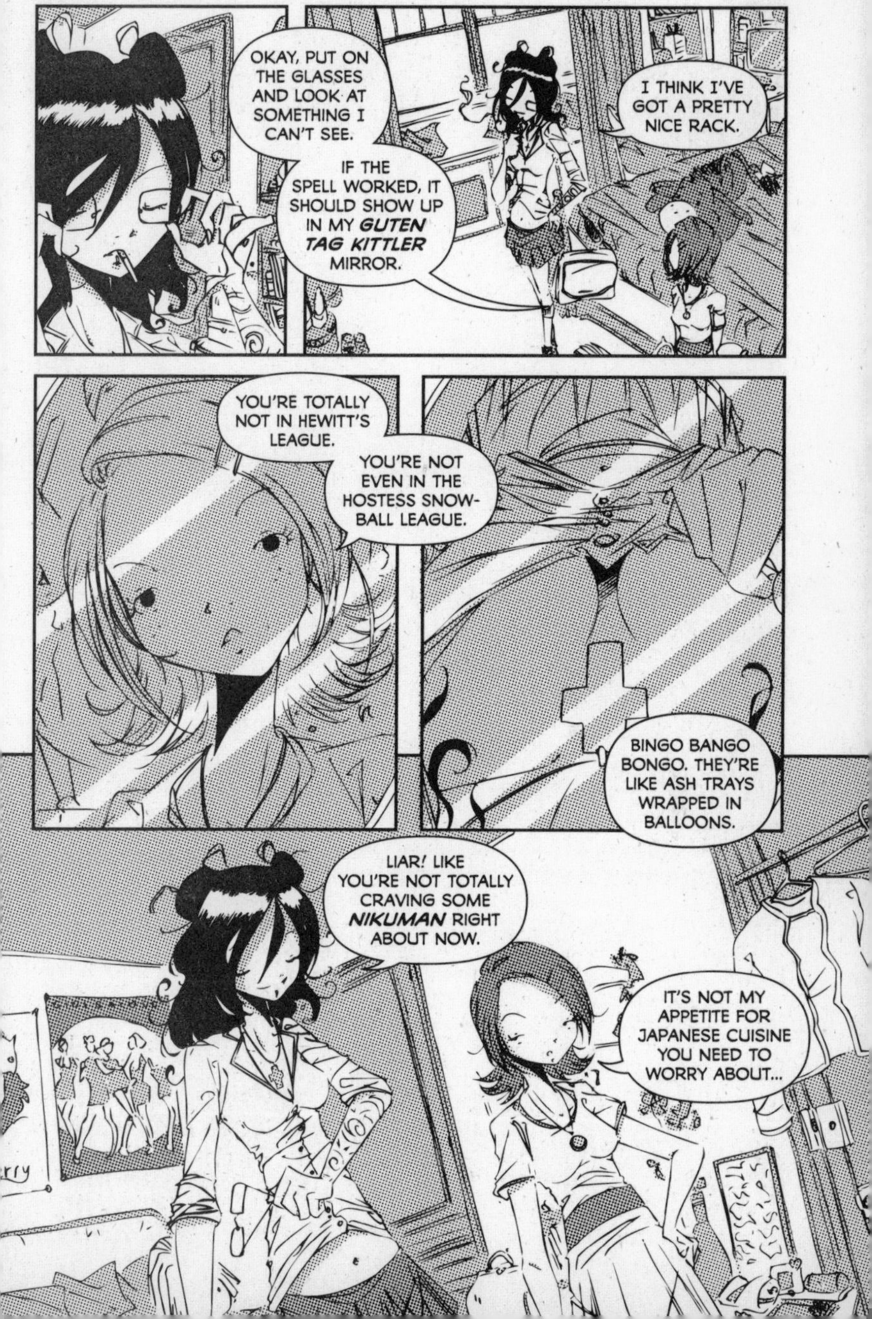
OKAY, PUT ON THE GLASSES AND LOOK AT SOMETHING I CAN'T SEE.
IF THE SPELL WORKED, IT SHOULD SHOW UP IN MY *GUTEN TAG KITTLER* MIRROR.
I THINK I'VE GOT A PRETTY NICE RACK.
YOU'RE TOTALLY NOT IN HEWITT'S LEAGUE.
YOU'RE NOT EVEN IN THE HOSTESS SNOW-BALL LEAGUE.
BINGO BANGO BONGO. THEY'RE LIKE ASH TRAYS WRAPPED IN BALLOONS.
LIAR! LIKE YOU'RE NOT TOTALLY CRAVING SOME *NIKUMAN* RIGHT ABOUT NOW.
IT'S NOT MY APPETITE FOR JAPANESE CUISINE YOU NEED TO WORRY ABOUT...

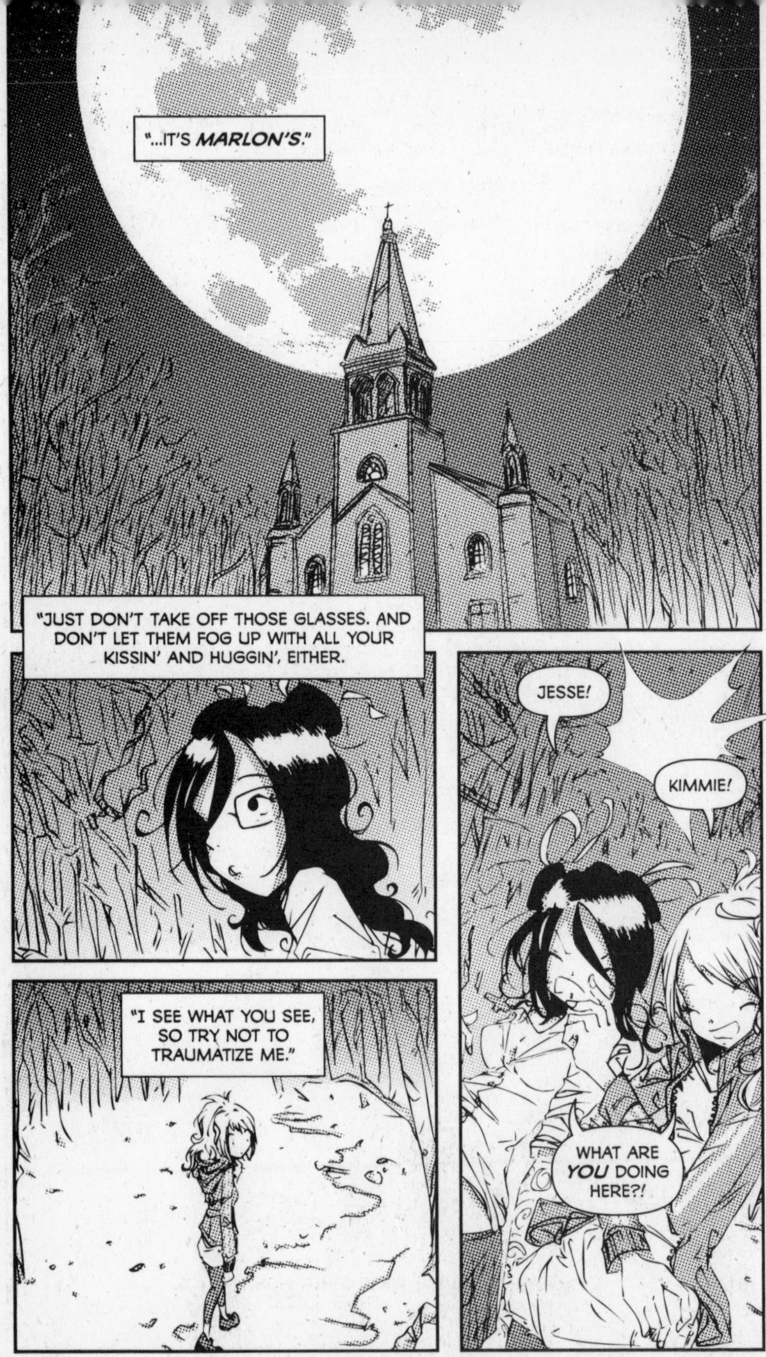
"...IT'S MARLON'S."
"JUST DON'T TAKE OFF THOSE GLASSES. AND DON'T LET THEM FOG UP WITH ALL YOUR KISSIN' AND HUGGIN', EITHER.
"I SEE WHAT YOU SEE, SO TRY NOT TO TRAUMATIZE ME."
JESSE!
KIMMIE!
WHAT ARE YOU DOING HERE?!

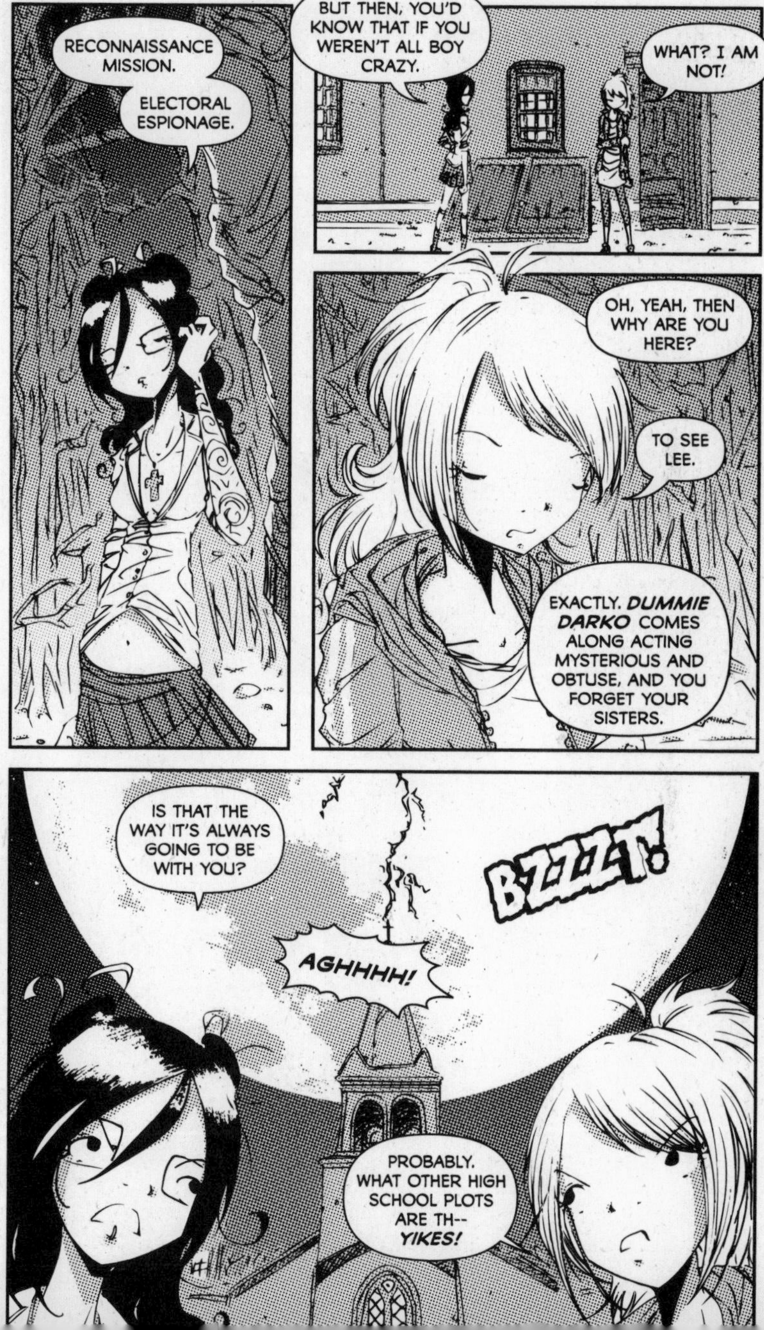
RECONNAISSANCE MISSION.
ELECTORAL ESPIONAGE.
BUT THEN, YOU'D KNOW THAT IF YOU WEREN'T ALL BOY CRAZY.
WHAT? I AM NOT!
OH, YEAH, THEN WHY ARE YOU HERE?
TO SEE LEE.
EXACTLY. DUMMIE DARKO COMES ALONG ACTING MYSTERIOUS AND OBTUSE, AND YOU FORGET YOUR SISTERS.
IS THAT THE WAY IT'S ALWAYS GOING TO BE WITH YOU?
BZZZZT!
AGHHHH!
PROBABLY. WHAT OTHER HIGH SCHOOL PLOTS ARE TH-- YIKES!

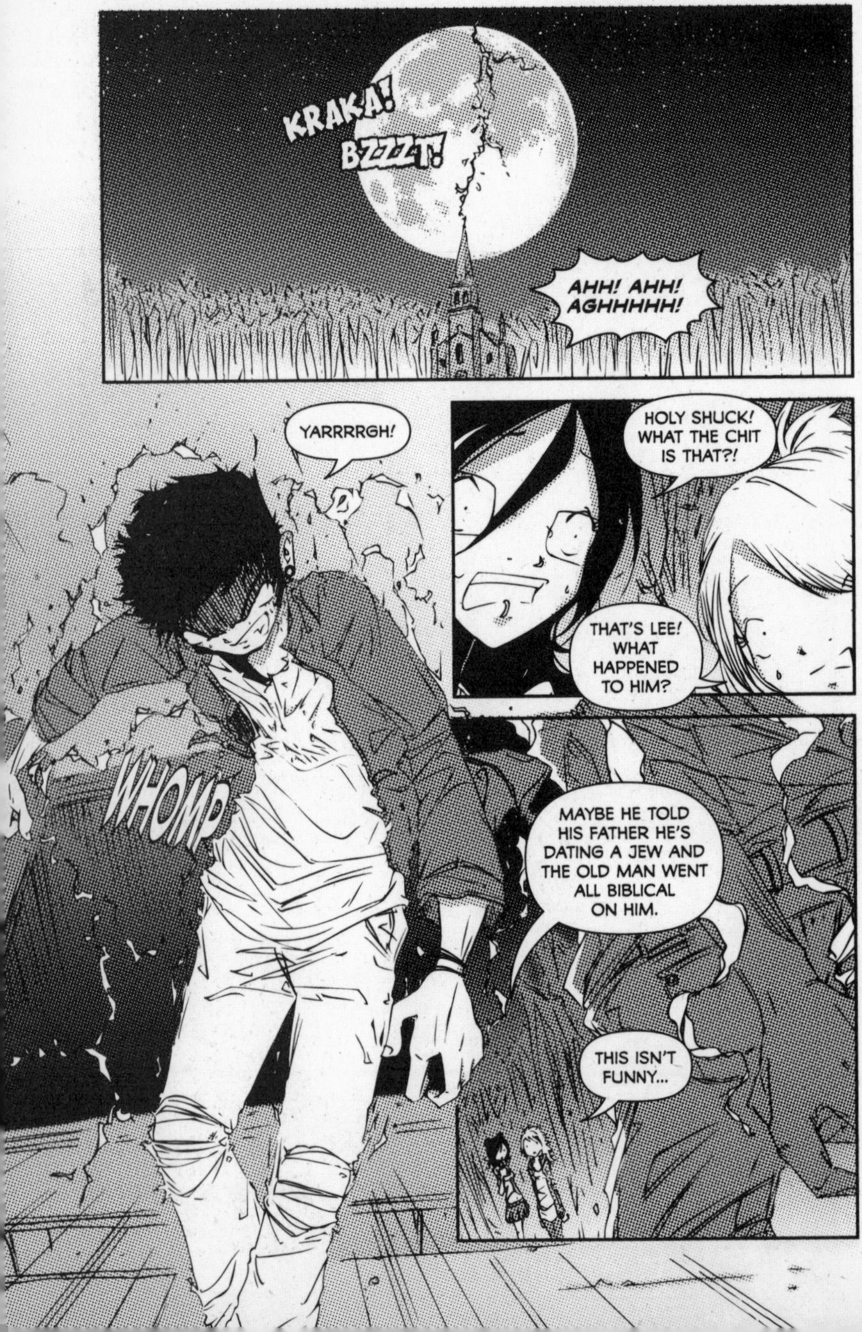
KRAKA!
BZZZT!
AHH! AHH! AGHHHHH!
YARRRRGH!
WHOMP
HOLY SHUCK! WHAT THE CHIT IS THAT?!
THAT'S LEE! WHAT HAPPENED TO HIM?
MAYBE HE TOLD HIS FATHER HE'S DATING A JEW AND THE OLD MAN WENT ALL BIBLICAL ON HIM.
THIS ISN'T FUNNY...

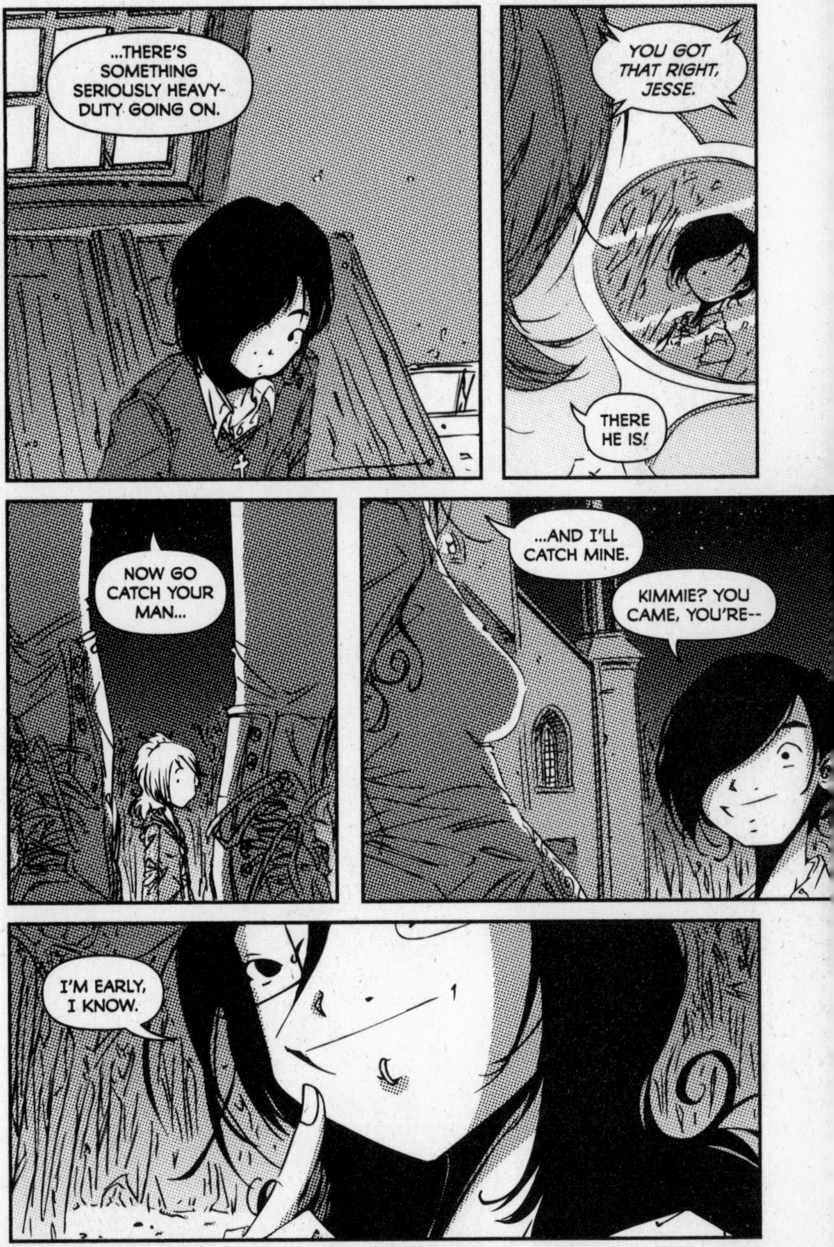
...THERE'S SOMETHING SERIOUSLY HEAVY-DUTY GOING ON.
YOU GOT THAT RIGHT, JESSE.
THERE HE IS!
NOW GO CATCH YOUR MAN...
...AND I'LL CATCH MINE.
KIMMIE? YOU CAME, YOU'RE--
I'M EARLY, I KNOW.

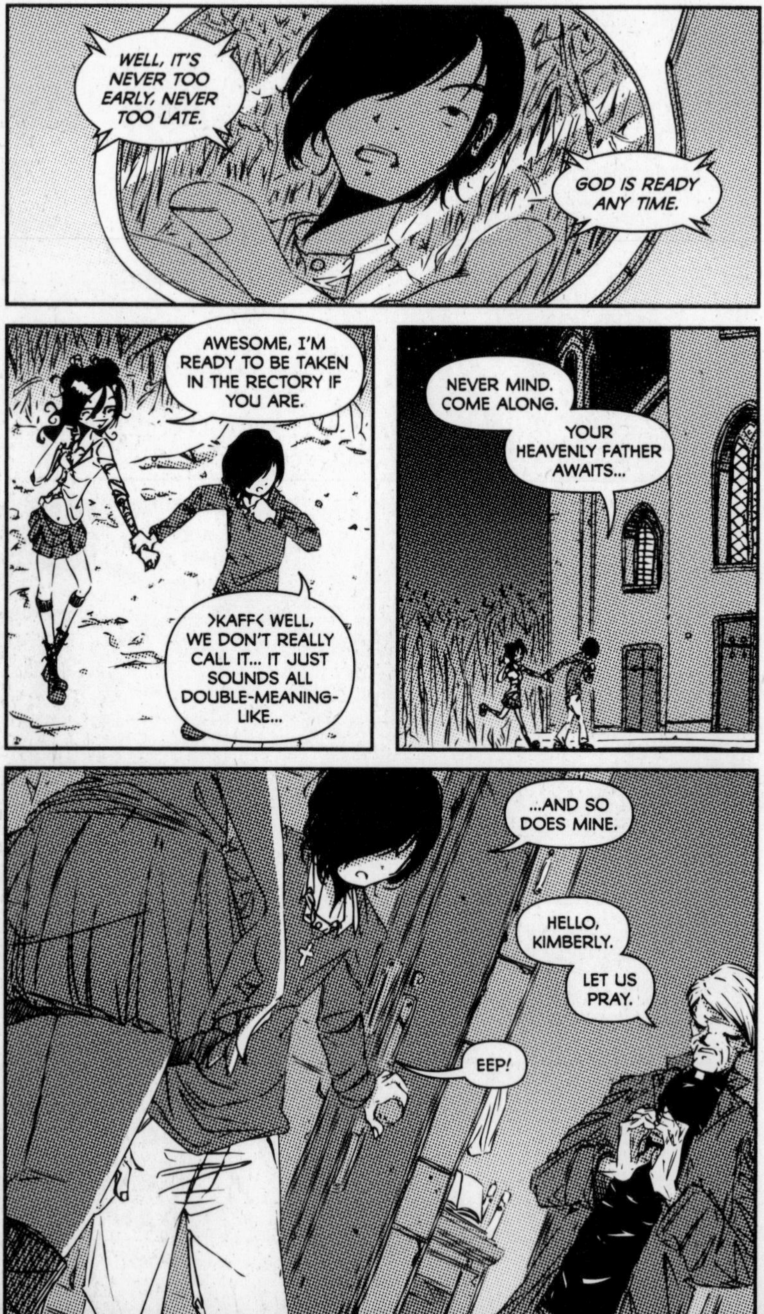
WELL, IT'S NEVER TOO EARLY, NEVER TOO LATE.
GOD IS READY ANY TIME.
AWESOME, I'M READY TO BE TAKEN IN THE RECTORY IF YOU ARE.
>KAFF< WELL, WE DON'T REALLY CALL IT... IT JUST SOUNDS ALL DOUBLE-MEANING-LIKE...
NEVER MIND. COME ALONG.
YOUR HEAVENLY FATHER AWAITS...
...AND SO DOES MINE.
HELLO, KIMBERLY.
LET US PRAY.
EEP!

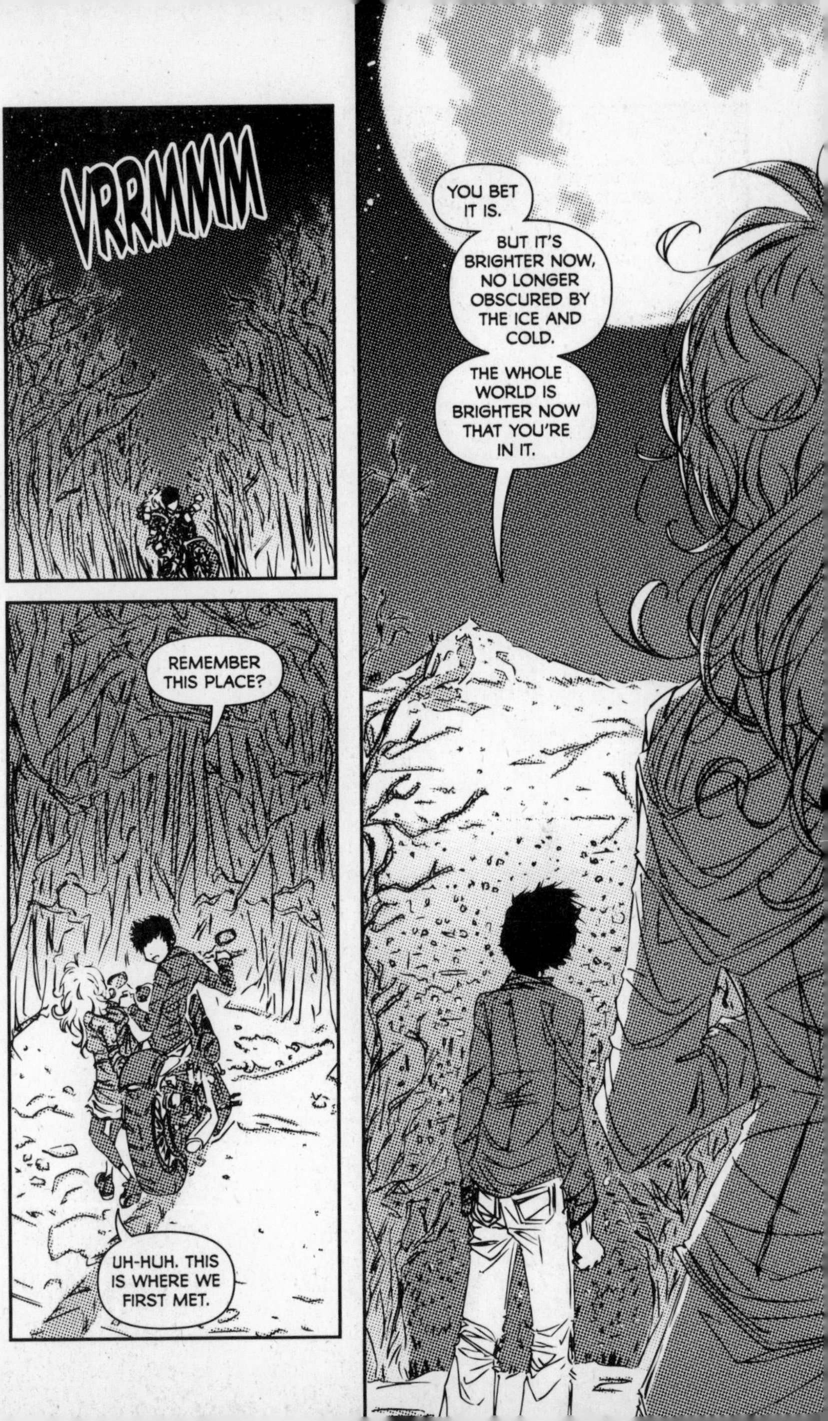
VRRMMM
REMEMBER THIS PLACE?
UH-HUH. THIS IS WHERE WE FIRST MET.
YOU BET IT IS.
BUT IT'S BRIGHTER NOW, NO LONGER OBSCURED BY THE ICE AND COLD.
THE WHOLE WORLD IS BRIGHTER NOW THAT YOU'RE IN IT.

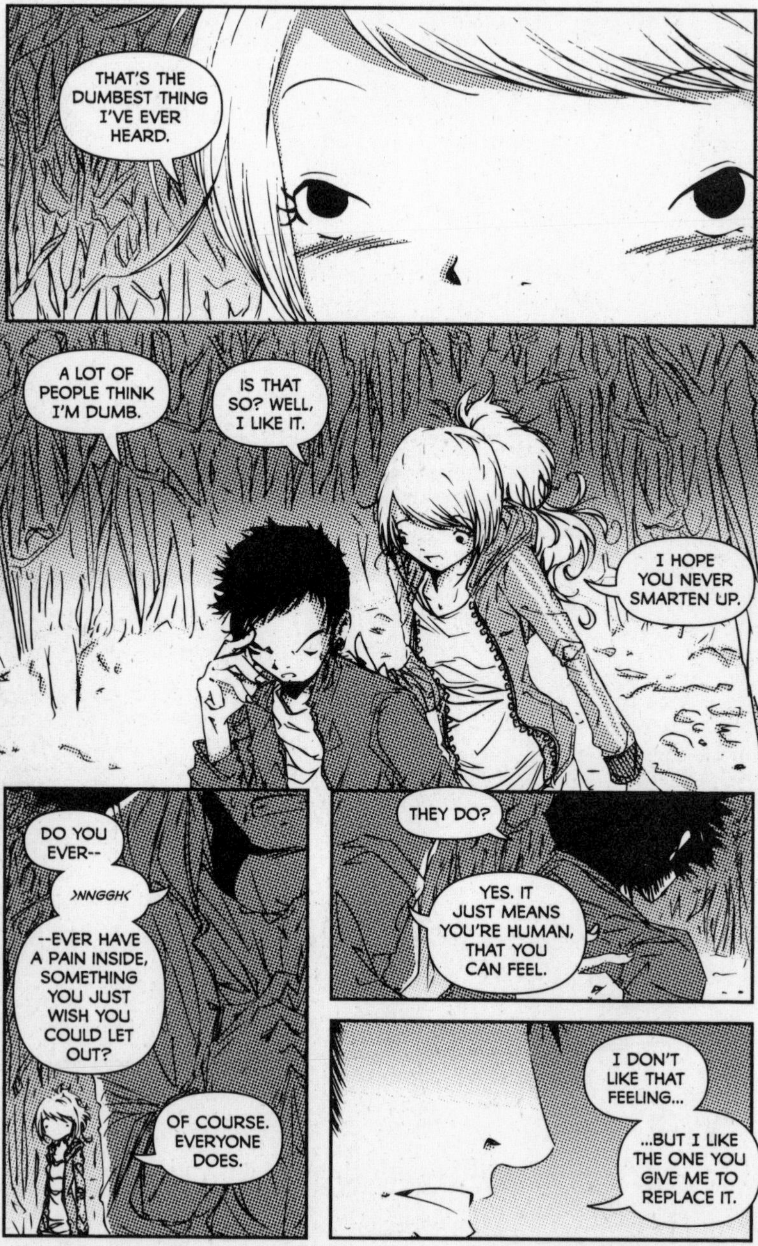
THAT'S THE DUMBEST THING I'VE EVER HEARD.
A LOT OF PEOPLE THINK I'M DUMB.
IS THAT SO? WELL, I LIKE IT.
I HOPE YOU NEVER SMARTEN UP.
DO YOU EVER--
>NNGGH<
--EVER HAVE A PAIN INSIDE, SOMETHING YOU JUST WISH YOU COULD LET OUT?
OF COURSE. EVERYONE DOES.
THEY DO?
YES. IT JUST MEANS YOU'RE HUMAN, THAT YOU CAN FEEL.
I DON'T LIKE THAT FEELING...
...BUT I LIKE THE ONE YOU GIVE ME TO REPLACE IT.

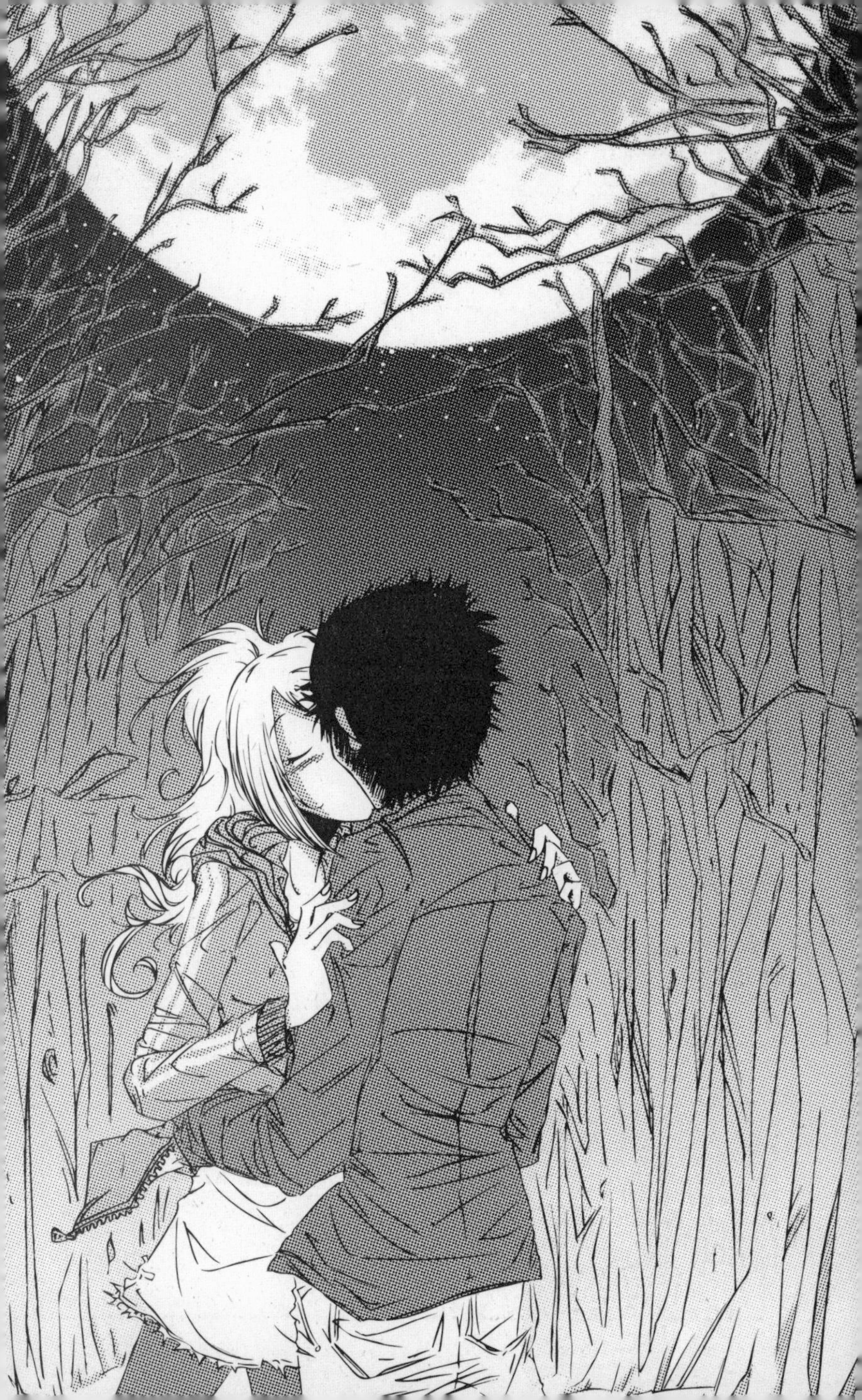

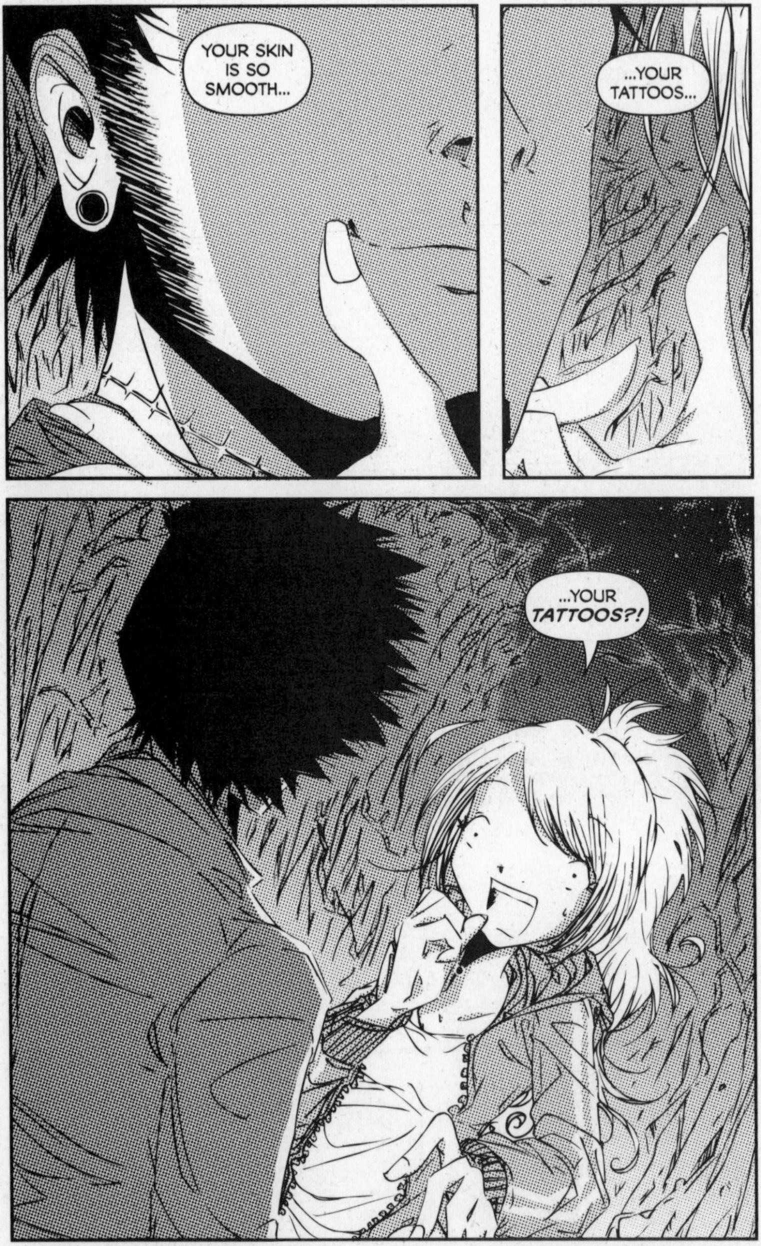
YOUR SKIN IS SO SMOOTH...
...YOUR TATTOOS...
...YOUR *TATTOOS?!*

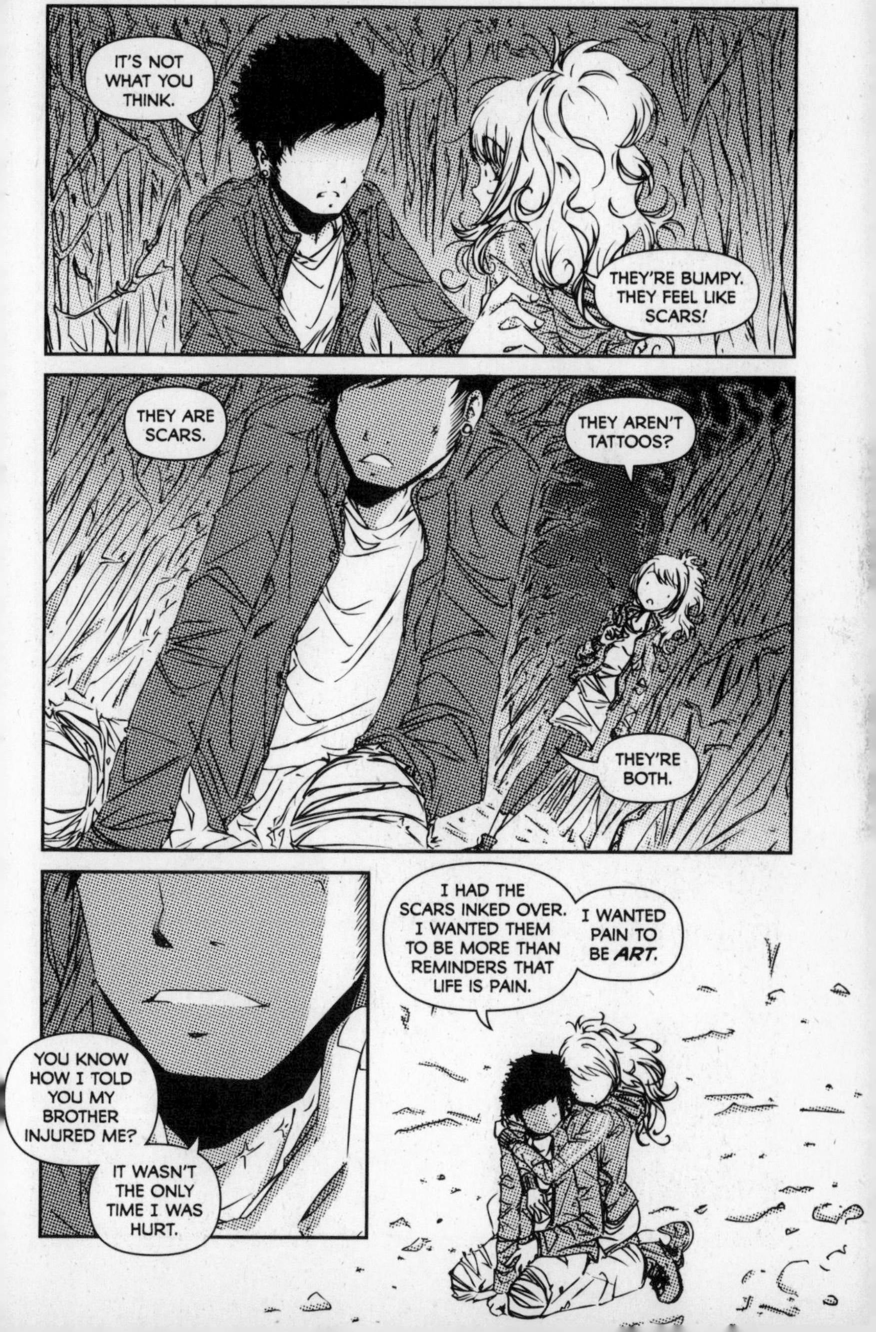
IT'S NOT WHAT YOU THINK.
THEY'RE BUMPY. THEY FEEL LIKE SCARS!
THEY ARE SCARS.
THEY AREN'T TATTOOS?
THEY'RE BOTH.
YOU KNOW HOW I TOLD YOU MY BROTHER INJURED ME?
IT WASN'T THE ONLY TIME I WAS HURT.
I HAD THE SCARS INKED OVER. I WANTED THEM TO BE MORE THAN REMINDERS THAT LIFE IS PAIN.
I WANTED PAIN TO BE ART.

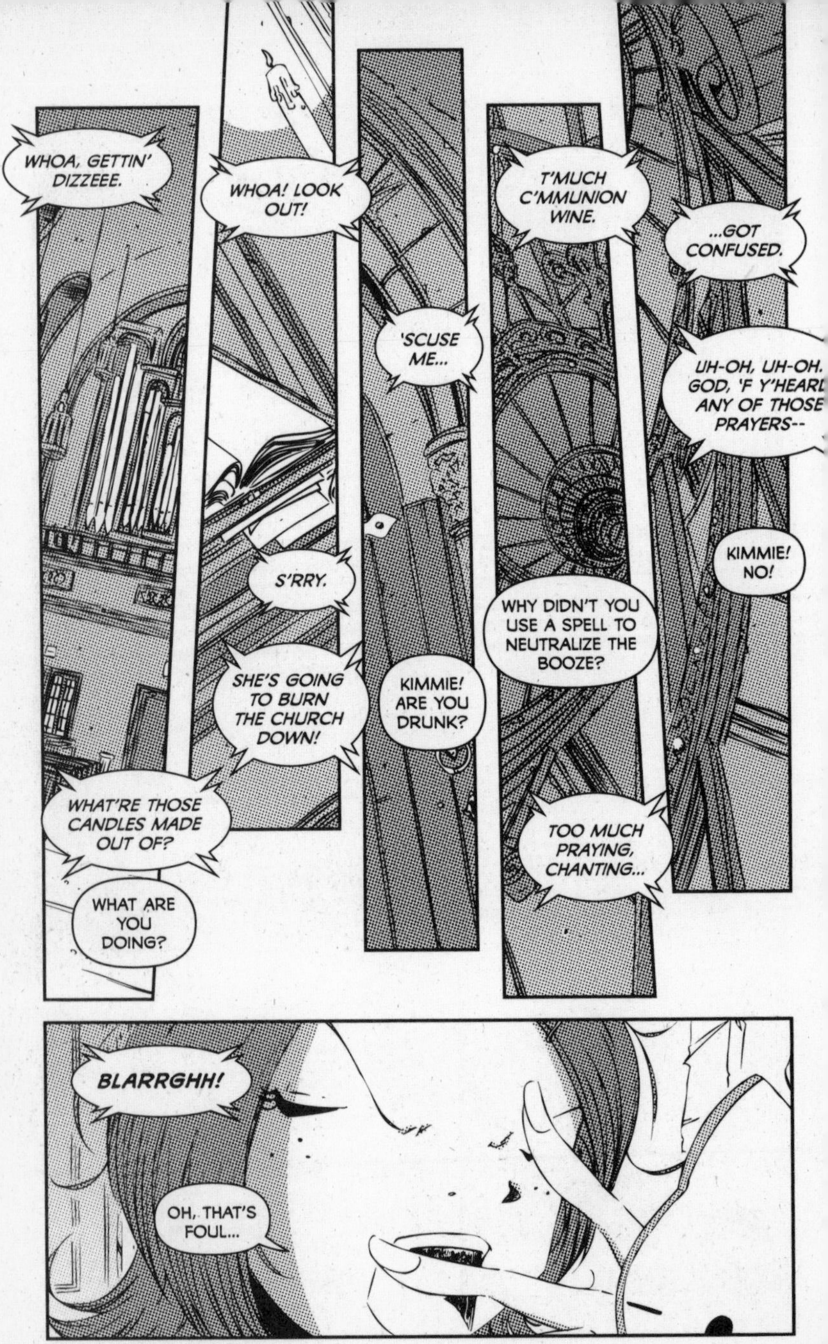

WHOA, GETTIN' DIZZEEE.
WHOA! LOOK OUT!
'SCUSE ME...
T'MUCH C'MMUNION WINE.
...GOT CONFUSED.
UH-OH, UH-OH. GOD, 'F Y'HEARD ANY OF THOSE PRAYERS--
S'RRY.
KIMMIE! NO!
WHY DIDN'T YOU USE A SPELL TO NEUTRALIZE THE BOOZE?
SHE'S GOING TO BURN THE CHURCH DOWN!
KIMMIE! ARE YOU DRUNK?
WHAT'RE THOSE CANDLES MADE OUT OF?
TOO MUCH PRAYING, CHANTING...
WHAT ARE YOU DOING?
BLARRGHH!
OH, THAT'S FOUL...

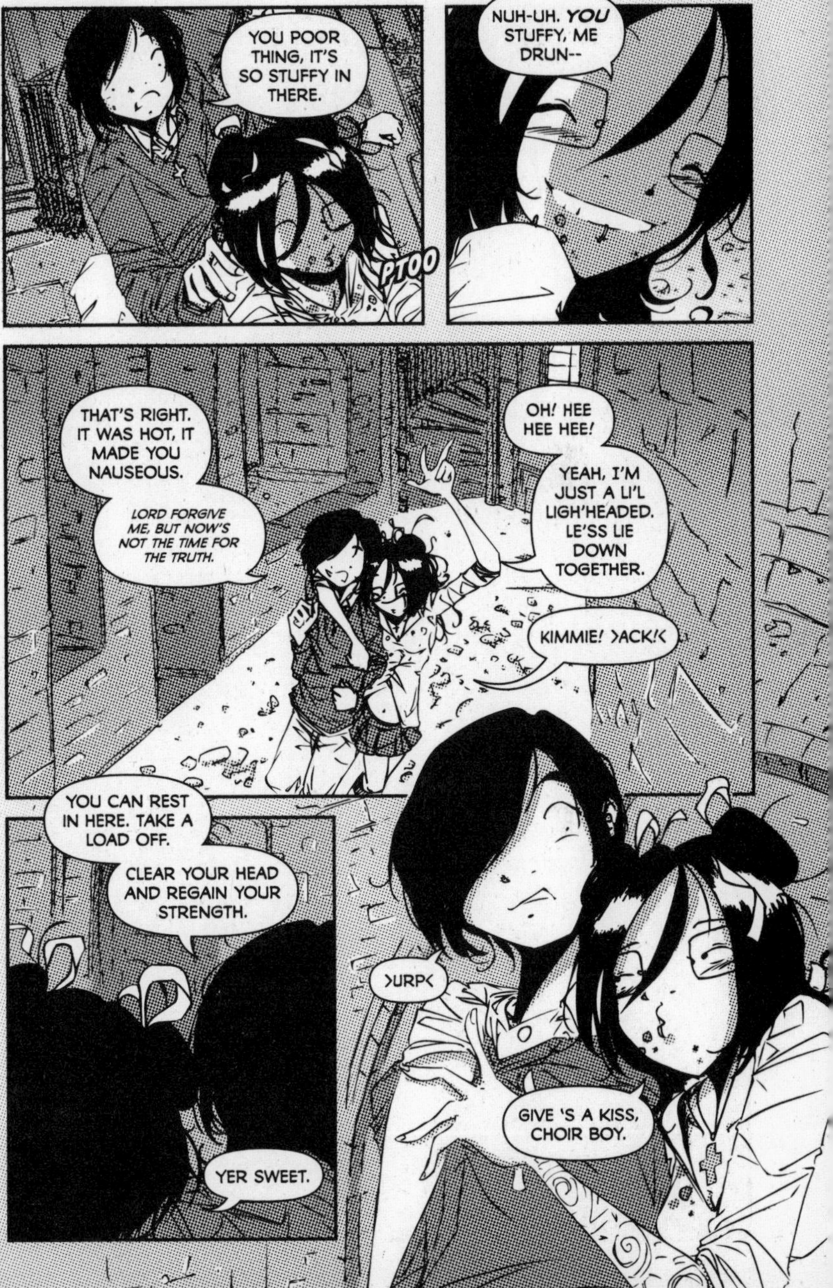
YOU POOR THING, IT'S SO STUFFY IN THERE.
PTOO
NUH-UH. *YOU* STUFFY, ME DRUN--
THAT'S RIGHT. IT WAS HOT, IT MADE YOU NAUSEOUS.
LORD FORGIVE ME, BUT NOW'S NOT THE TIME FOR THE TRUTH.
OH! HEE HEE HEE!
YEAH, I'M JUST A LI'L LIGH'HEADED. LE'SS LIE DOWN TOGETHER.
KIMMIE! >ACK!<
YOU CAN REST IN HERE. TAKE A LOAD OFF.
CLEAR YOUR HEAD AND REGAIN YOUR STRENGTH.
>URP<
GIVE 'S A KISS, CHOIR BOY.
YER SWEET.

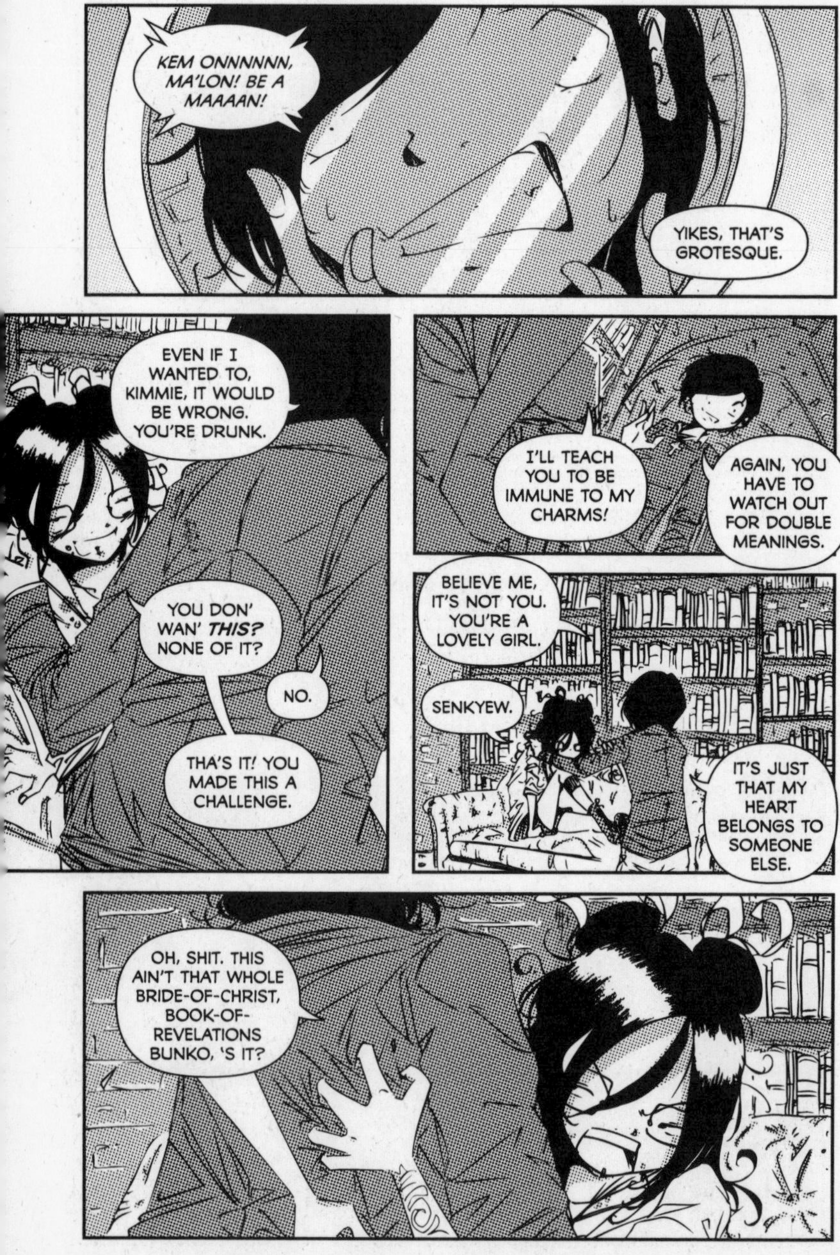
KEM ONNNNNN, MA'LON! BE A MAAAAN!
YIKES, THAT'S GROTESQUE.
EVEN IF I WANTED TO, KIMMIE, IT WOULD BE WRONG. YOU'RE DRUNK.
YOU DON' WAN' *THIS?* NONE OF IT?
NO.
THA'S IT! YOU MADE THIS A CHALLENGE.
I'LL TEACH YOU TO BE IMMUNE TO MY CHARMS!
AGAIN, YOU HAVE TO WATCH OUT FOR DOUBLE MEANINGS.
BELIEVE ME, IT'S NOT YOU. YOU'RE A LOVELY GIRL.
SENKYEW.
IT'S JUST THAT MY HEART BELONGS TO SOMEONE ELSE.
OH, SHIT. THIS AIN'T THAT WHOLE BRIDE-OF-CHRIST, BOOK-OF-REVELATIONS BUNKO, 'S IT?

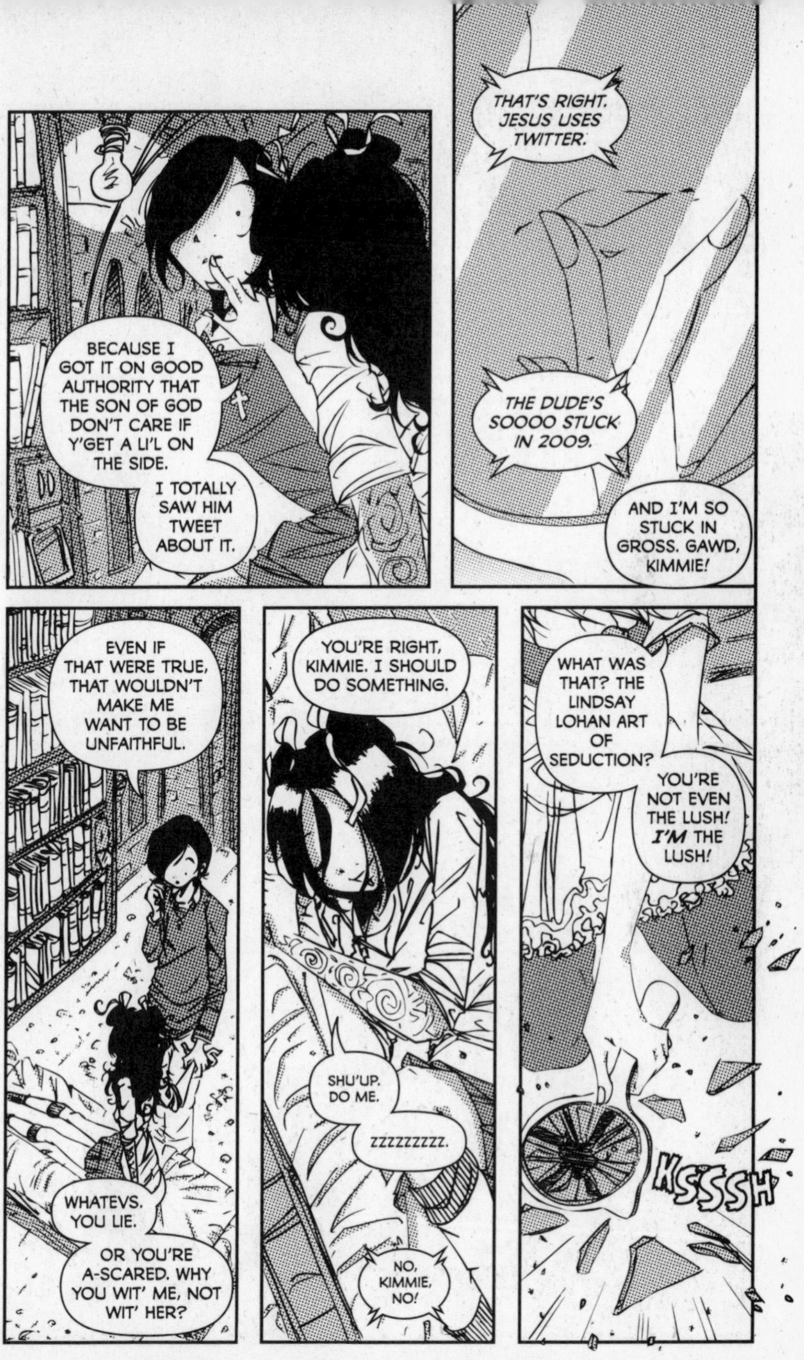

BECAUSE I GOT IT ON GOOD AUTHORITY THAT THE SON OF GOD DON'T CARE IF Y'GET A LI'L ON THE SIDE.
I TOTALLY SAW HIM TWEET ABOUT IT.
THAT'S RIGHT. JESUS USES TWITTER.
THE DUDE'S SOOOO STUCK IN 2009.
AND I'M SO STUCK IN GROSS. GAWD, KIMMIE!
EVEN IF THAT WERE TRUE, THAT WOULDN'T MAKE ME WANT TO BE UNFAITHFUL.
WHATEVS. YOU LIE.
OR YOU'RE A-SCARED. WHY YOU WIT' ME, NOT WIT' HER?
YOU'RE RIGHT, KIMMIE. I SHOULD DO SOMETHING.
SHU'UP. DO ME.
ZZZZZZZZZ.
NO, KIMMIE, NO!
WHAT WAS THAT? THE LINDSAY LOHAN ART OF SEDUCTION?
YOU'RE NOT EVEN THE LUSH! I'M THE LUSH!
KSSSH

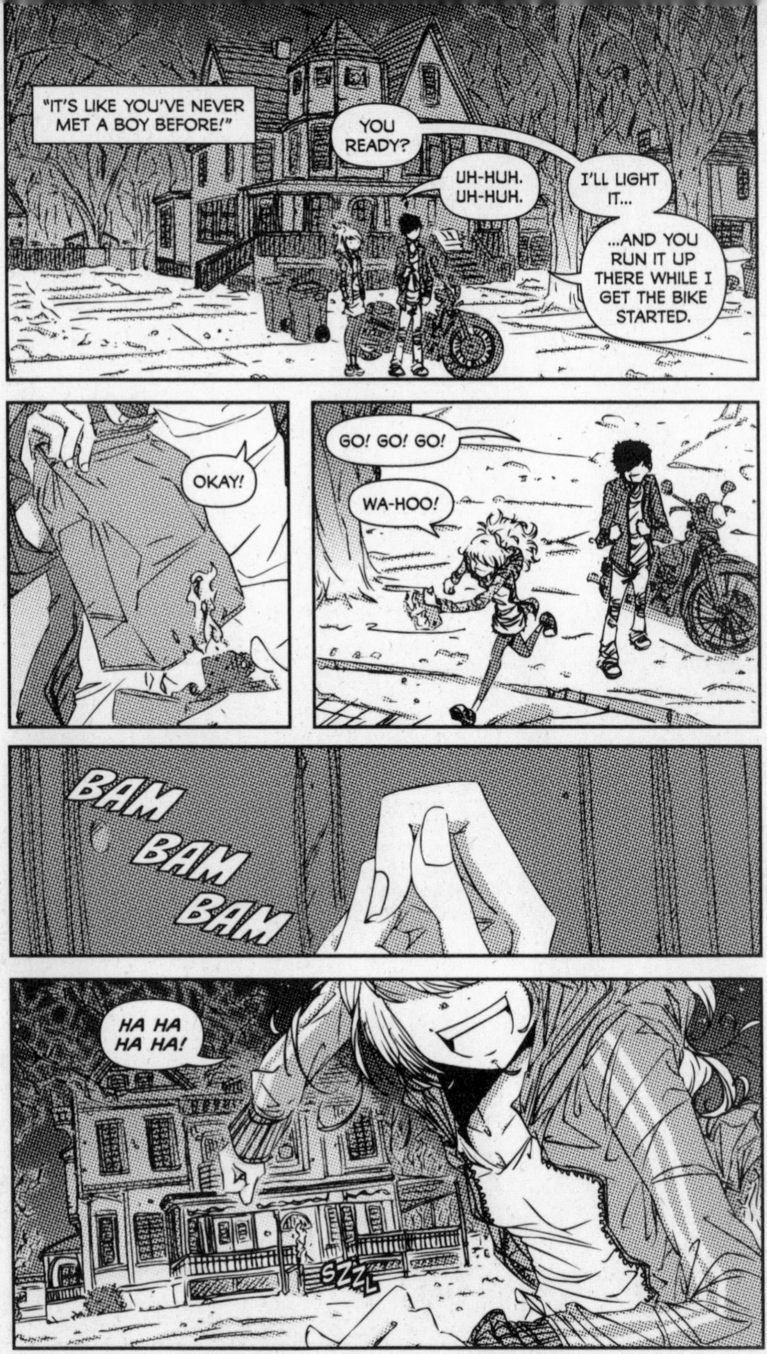
"IT'S LIKE YOU'VE NEVER MET A BOY BEFORE!"
YOU READY?
UH-HUH. UH-HUH.
I'LL LIGHT IT...
...AND YOU RUN IT UP THERE WHILE I GET THE BIKE STARTED.
OKAY!
GO! GO! GO!
WA-HOO!
BAM
BAM
BAM
HA HA HA HA!
SZZL

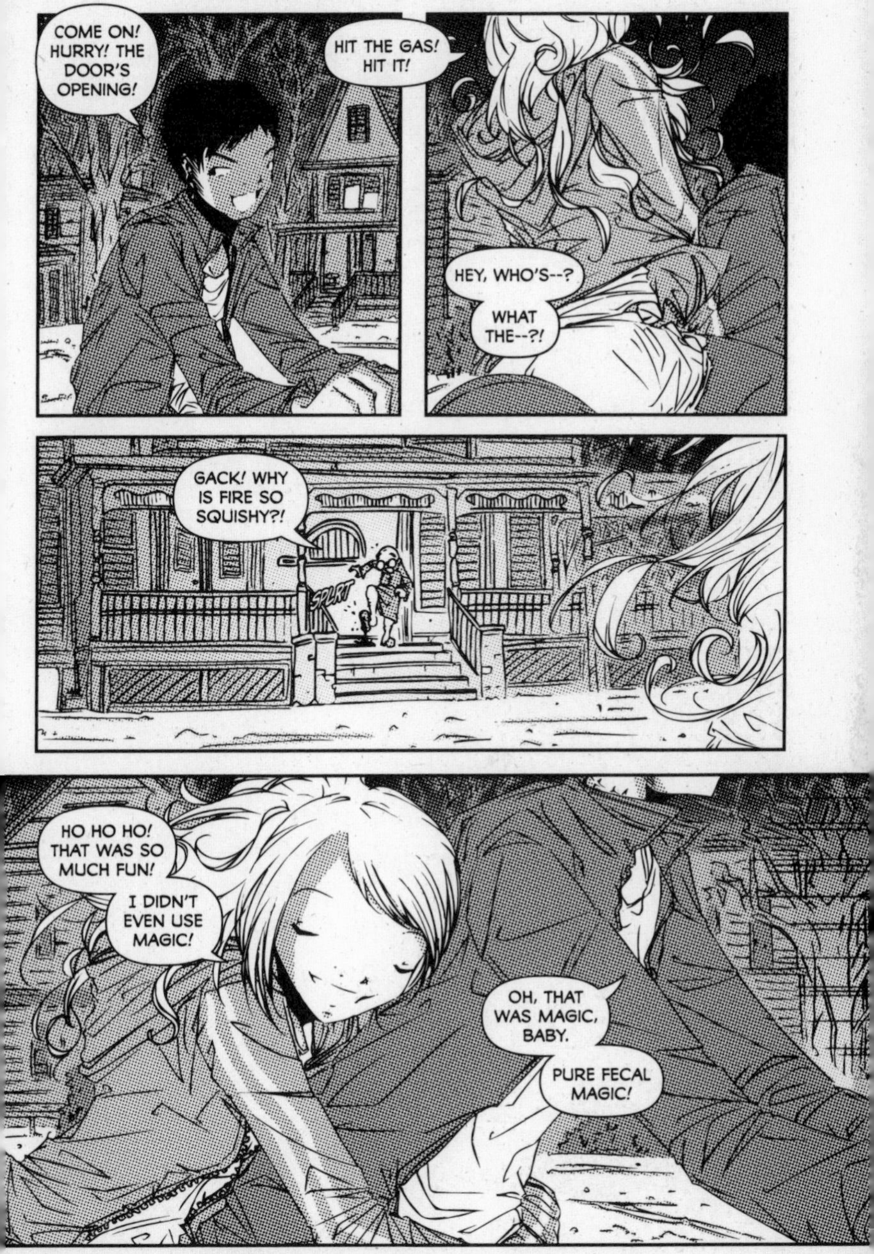
COME ON! HURRY! THE DOOR'S OPENING!
HIT THE GAS! HIT IT!
HEY, WHO'S--?
WHAT THE--?!
GACK! WHY IS FIRE SO SQUISHY?!
SPLRT
HO HO HO! THAT WAS SO MUCH FUN!
I DIDN'T EVEN USE MAGIC!
OH, THAT WAS MAGIC, BABY.
PURE FECAL MAGIC!

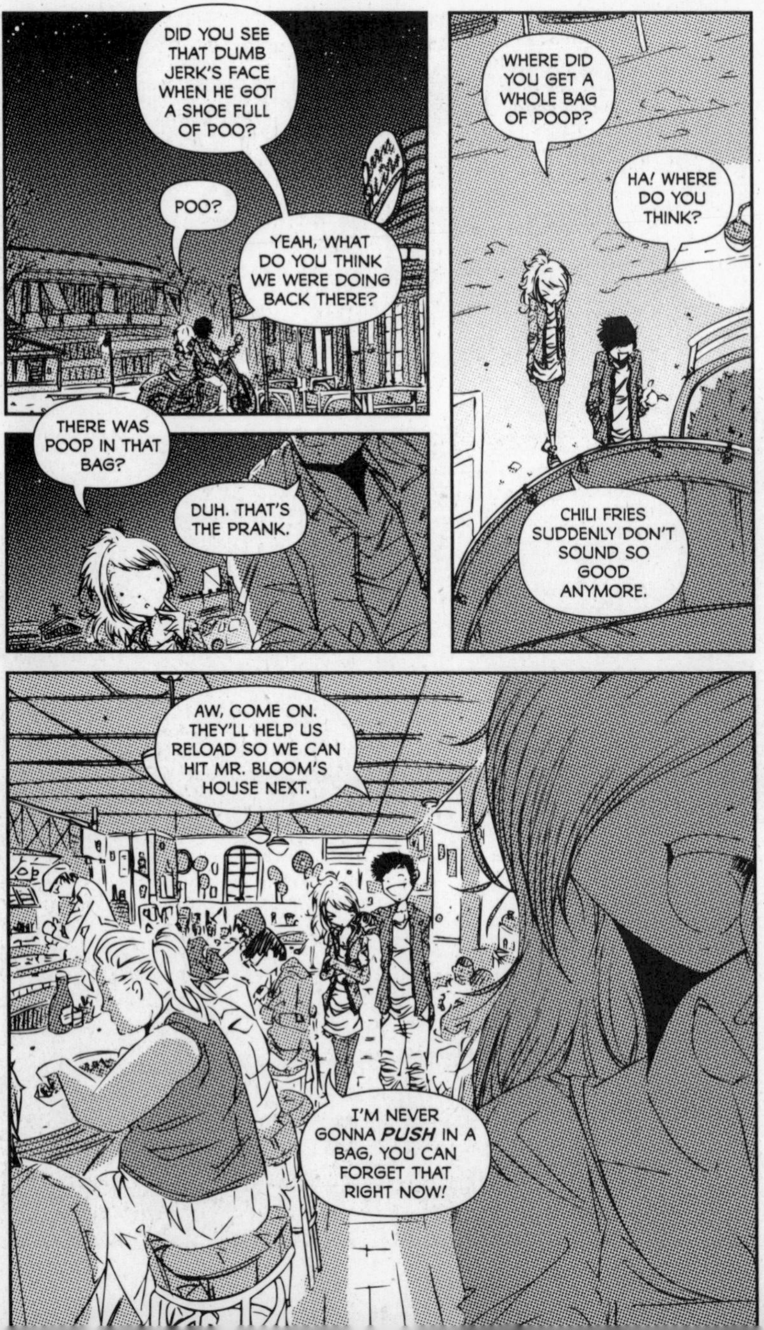
DID YOU SEE THAT DUMB JERK'S FACE WHEN HE GOT A SHOE FULL OF POO?
POO?
YEAH, WHAT DO YOU THINK WE WERE DOING BACK THERE?
THERE WAS POOP IN THAT BAG?
DUH. THAT'S THE PRANK.
WHERE DID YOU GET A WHOLE BAG OF POOP?
HA! WHERE DO YOU THINK?
CHILI FRIES SUDDENLY DON'T SOUND SO GOOD ANYMORE.
AW, COME ON. THEY'LL HELP US RELOAD SO WE CAN HIT MR. BLOOM'S HOUSE NEXT.
I'M NEVER GONNA *PUSH* IN A BAG, YOU CAN FORGET THAT RIGHT NOW!

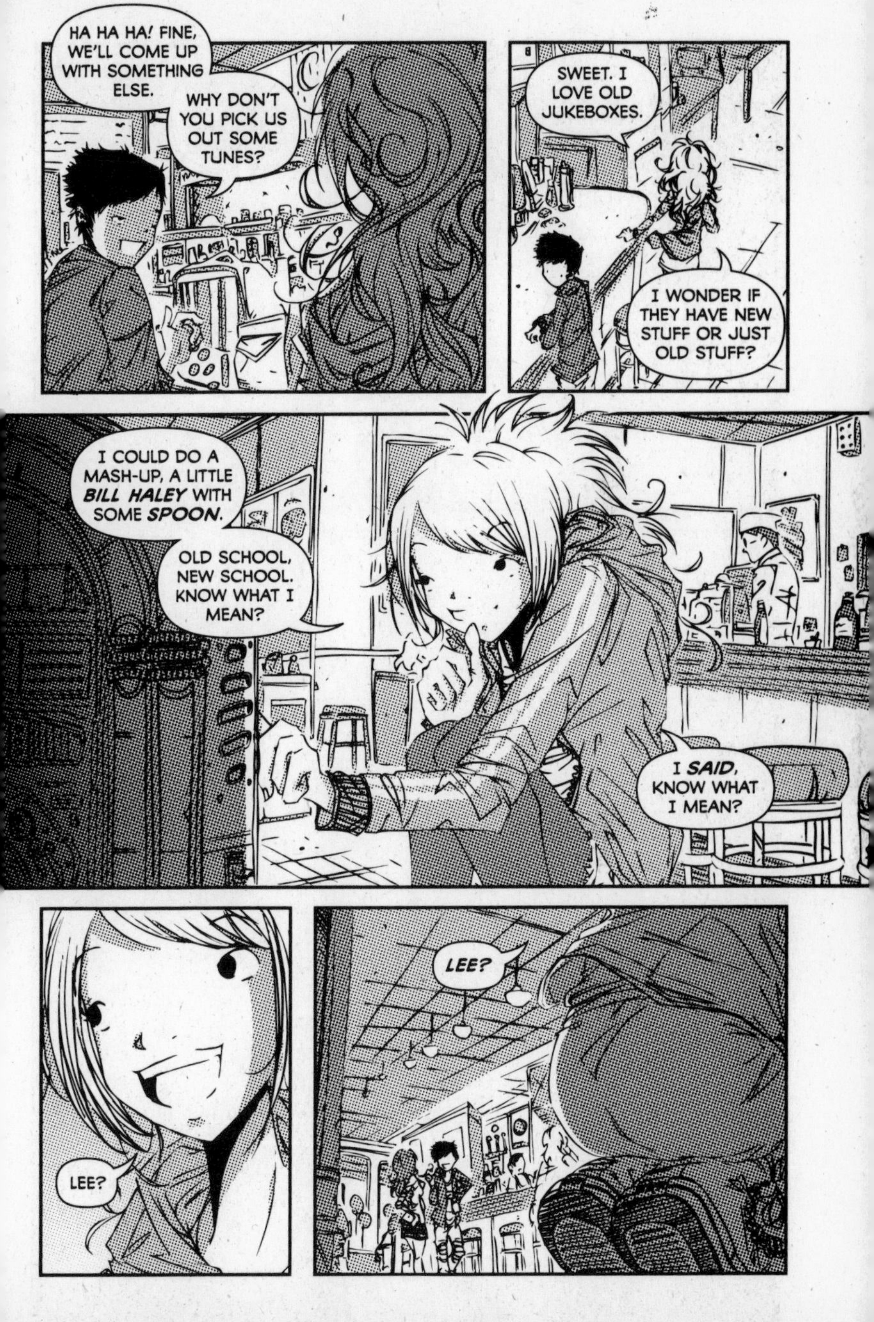
HA HA HA! FINE, WE'LL COME UP WITH SOMETHING ELSE.
WHY DON'T YOU PICK US OUT SOME TUNES?
SWEET. I LOVE OLD JUKEBOXES.
I WONDER IF THEY HAVE NEW STUFF OR JUST OLD STUFF?
I COULD DO A MASH-UP, A LITTLE BILL HALEY WITH SOME SPOON.
OLD SCHOOL, NEW SCHOOL. KNOW WHAT I MEAN?
I SAID, KNOW WHAT I MEAN?
LEE?
LEE?

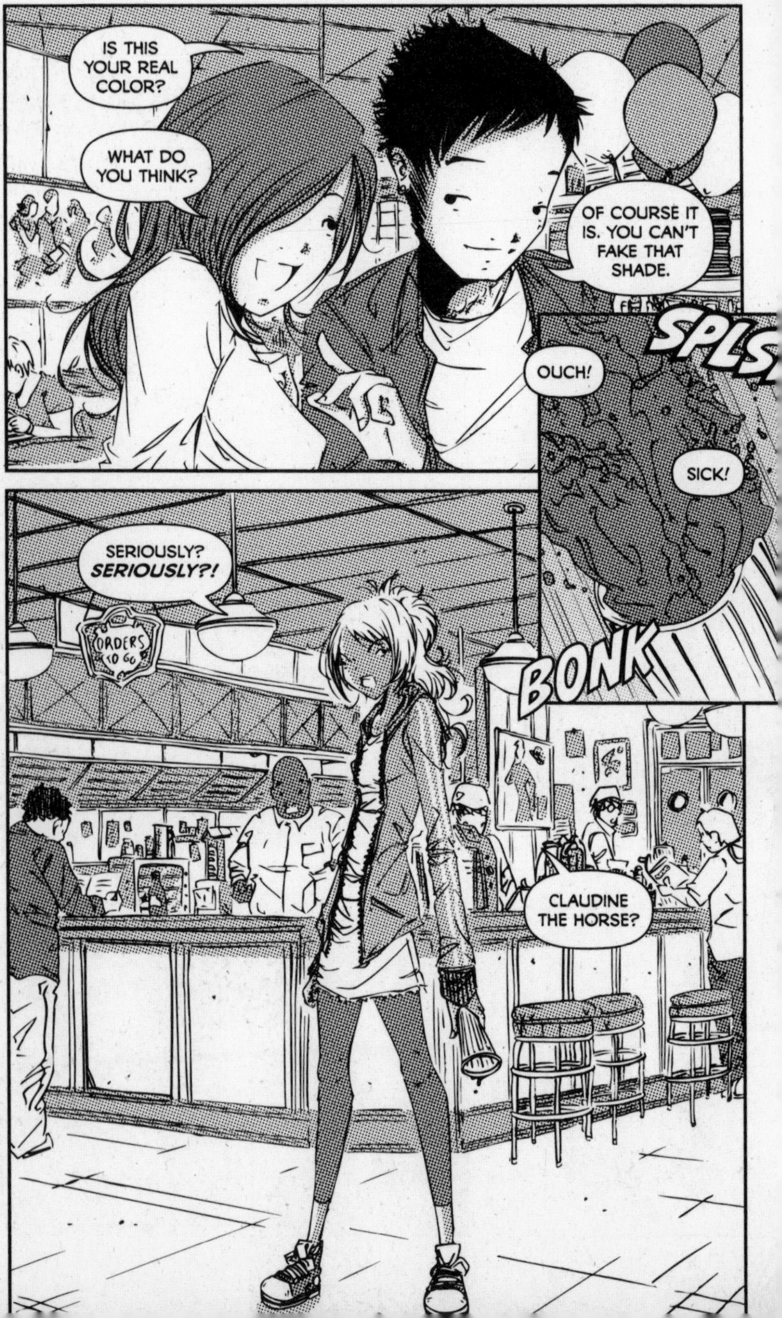
IS THIS YOUR REAL COLOR?
WHAT DO YOU THINK?
OF COURSE IT IS. YOU CAN'T FAKE THAT SHADE.
SPLS
OUCH!
SICK!
BONK
SERIOUSLY? *SERIOUSLY?!*
ORDERS TO GO
CLAUDINE THE HORSE?

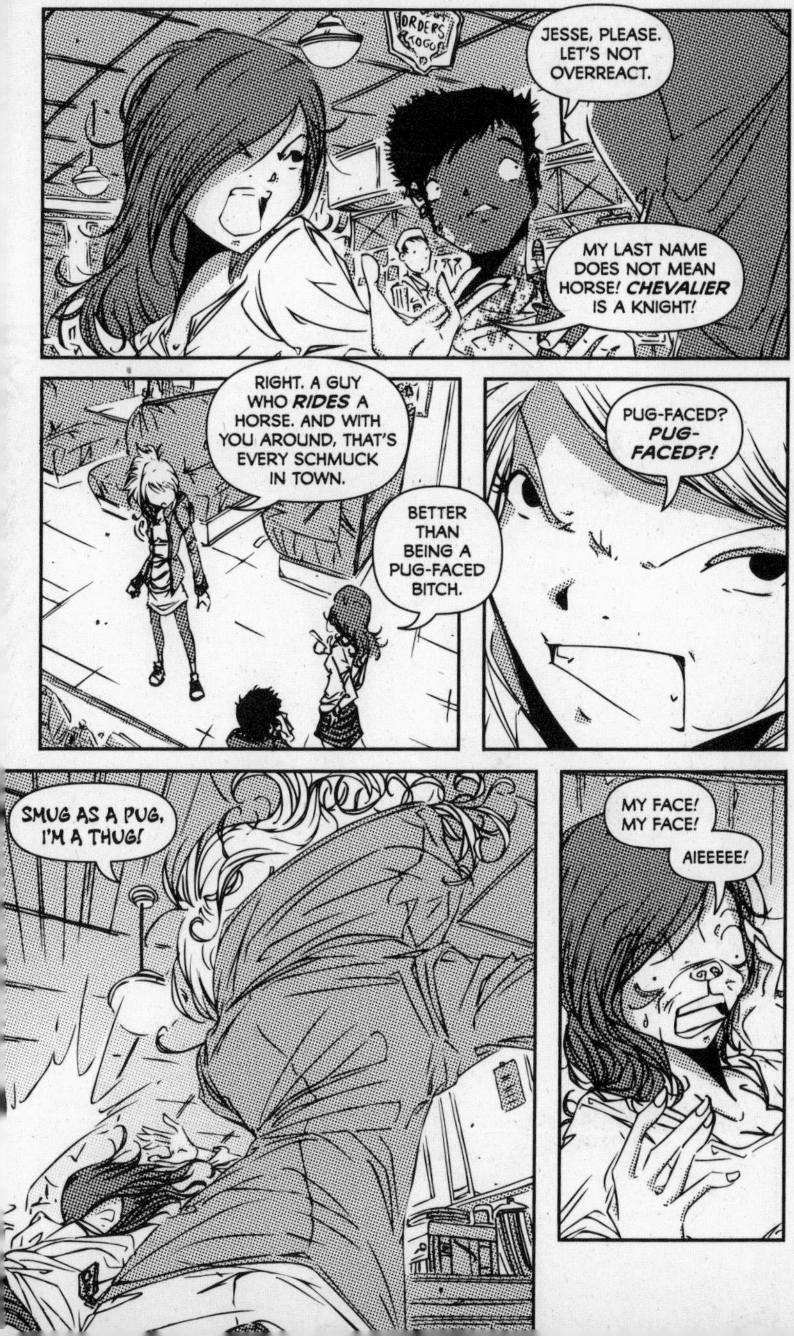
JESSE, PLEASE. LET'S NOT OVERREACT.
MY LAST NAME DOES NOT MEAN HORSE! CHEVALIER IS A KNIGHT!
RIGHT. A GUY WHO RIDES A HORSE. AND WITH YOU AROUND, THAT'S EVERY SCHMUCK IN TOWN.
BETTER THAN BEING A PUG-FACED BITCH.
PUG-FACED? PUG-FACED?!
SMUG AS A PUG, I'M A THUG!
MY FACE! MY FACE!
AIEEEEE!

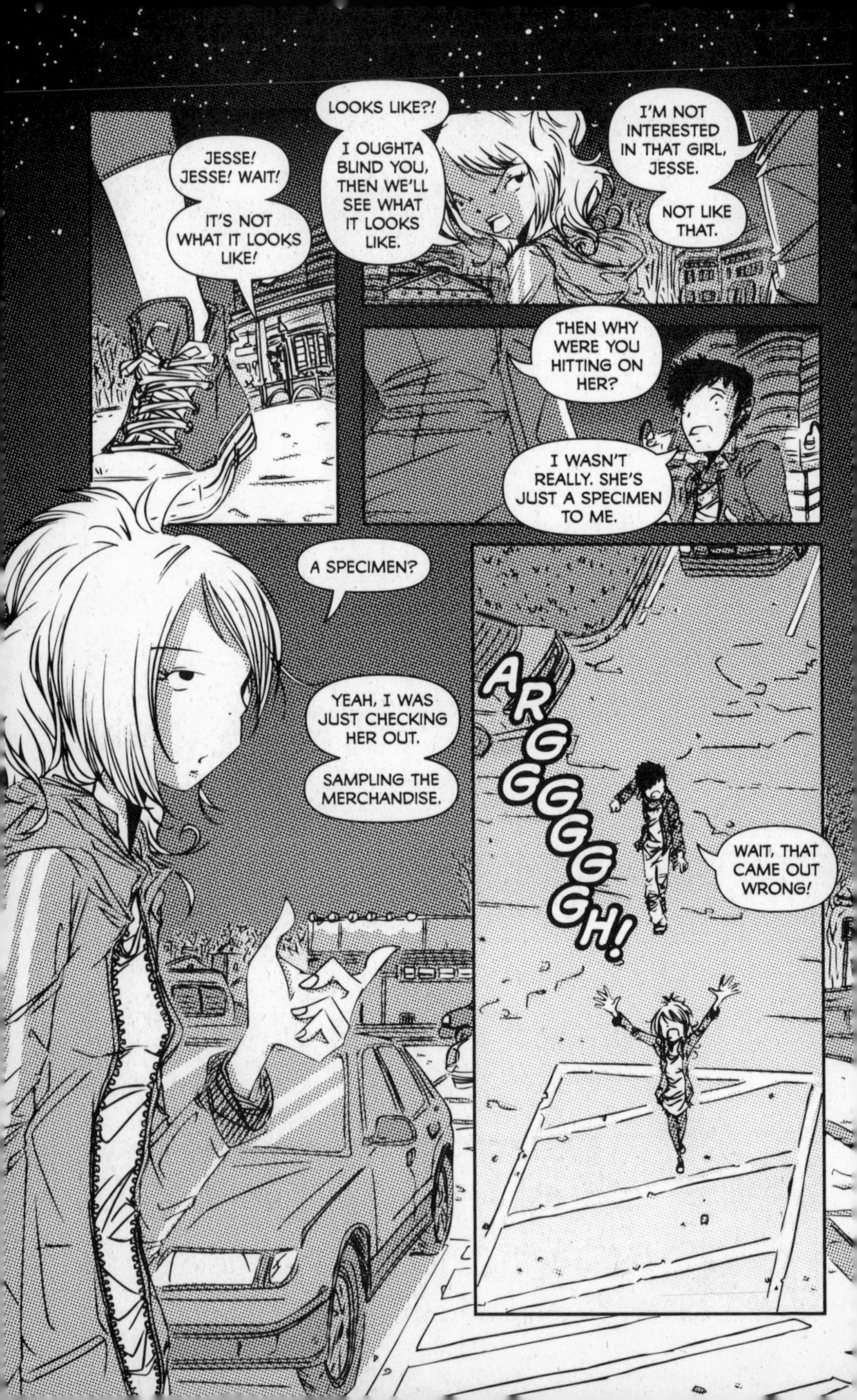
JESSE! JESSE! WAIT!
IT'S NOT WHAT IT LOOKS LIKE!
LOOKS LIKE?!
I OUGHTA BLIND YOU, THEN WE'LL SEE WHAT IT LOOKS LIKE.
I'M NOT INTERESTED IN THAT GIRL, JESSE.
NOT LIKE THAT.
THEN WHY WERE YOU HITTING ON HER?
I WASN'T REALLY. SHE'S JUST A SPECIMEN TO ME.
A SPECIMEN?
YEAH, I WAS JUST CHECKING HER OUT.
SAMPLING THE MERCHANDISE.
ARGGGGGH!
WAIT, THAT CAME OUT WRONG!

OOOPS, SORRY. MY LEG CAME OUT WRONG.
WHAT ARE YOU DOING?!
I CAN'T BELIEVE I CARRIED A BAG OF YOUR FLAMING SHIT!
FLAME FOR FLAME...
FENDERS BURN, AND CHROME BUBBLE!
ARRRR!

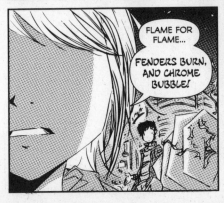

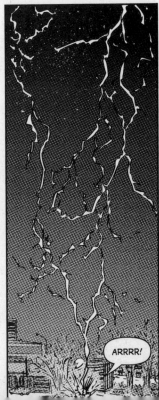

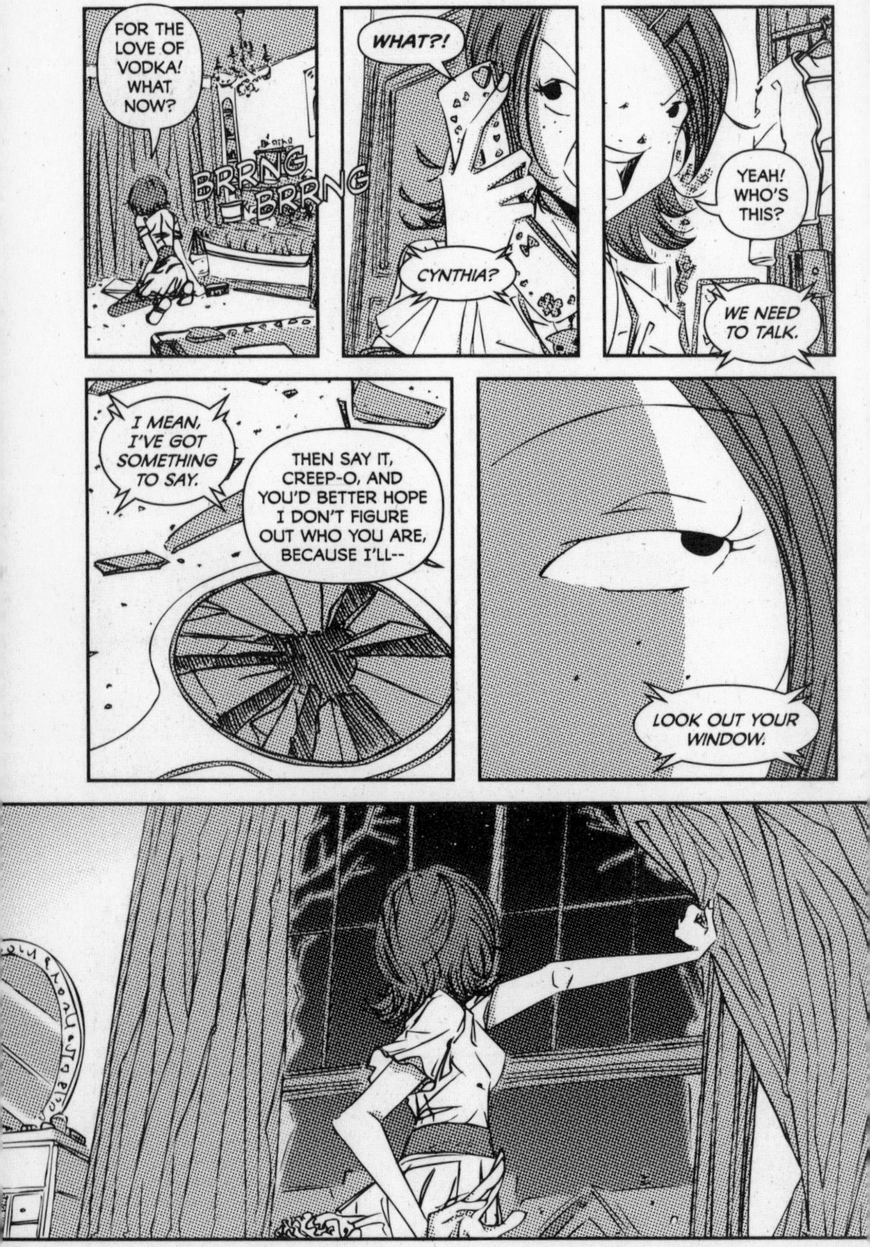
FOR THE LOVE OF VODKA! WHAT NOW?
BRRNG BRRNG
WHAT?!
CYNTHIA?
YEAH! WHO'S THIS?
WE NEED TO TALK.
I MEAN, I'VE GOT SOMETHING TO SAY.
THEN SAY IT, CREEP-O, AND YOU'D BETTER HOPE I DON'T FIGURE OUT WHO YOU ARE, BECAUSE I'LL--
LOOK OUT YOUR WINDOW.

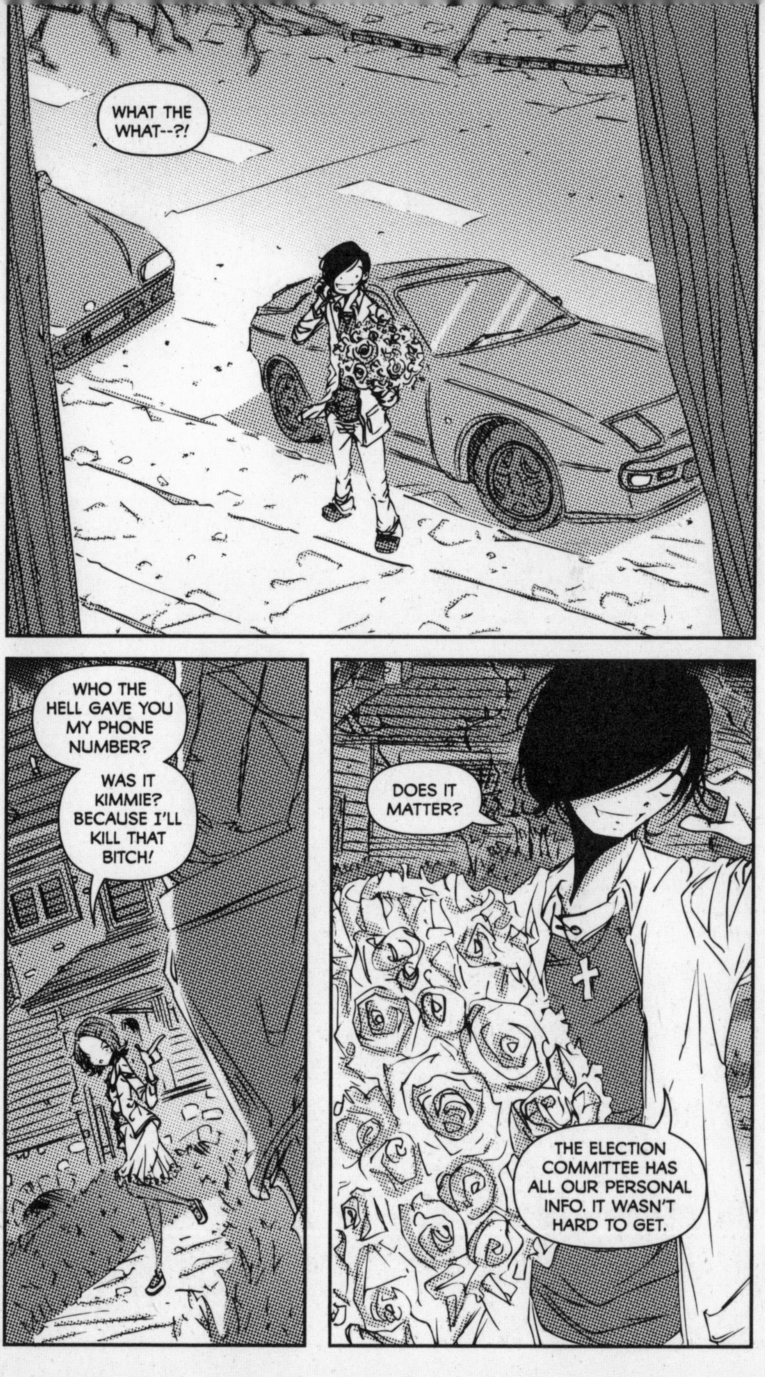
WHAT THE WHAT--?!
WHO THE HELL GAVE YOU MY PHONE NUMBER?
WAS IT KIMMIE? BECAUSE I'LL KILL THAT BITCH!
DOES IT MATTER?
THE ELECTION COMMITTEE HAS ALL OUR PERSONAL INFO. IT WASN'T HARD TO GET.

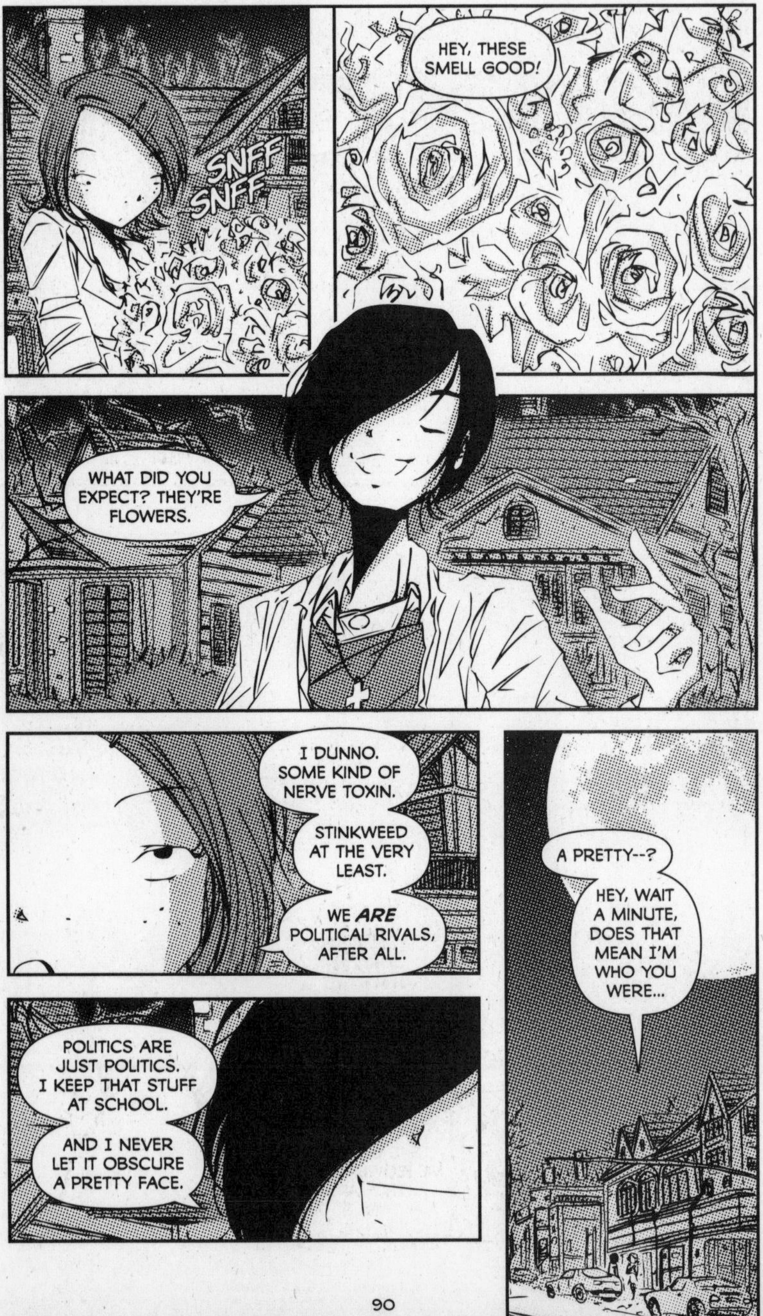
SNFF SNFF
HEY, THESE SMELL GOOD!
WHAT DID YOU EXPECT? THEY'RE FLOWERS.
I DUNNO. SOME KIND OF NERVE TOXIN.
STINKWEED AT THE VERY LEAST.
WE *ARE* POLITICAL RIVALS, AFTER ALL.
POLITICS ARE JUST POLITICS. I KEEP THAT STUFF AT SCHOOL.
AND I NEVER LET IT OBSCURE A PRETTY FACE.
A PRETTY--?
HEY, WAIT A MINUTE, DOES THAT MEAN I'M WHO YOU WERE...

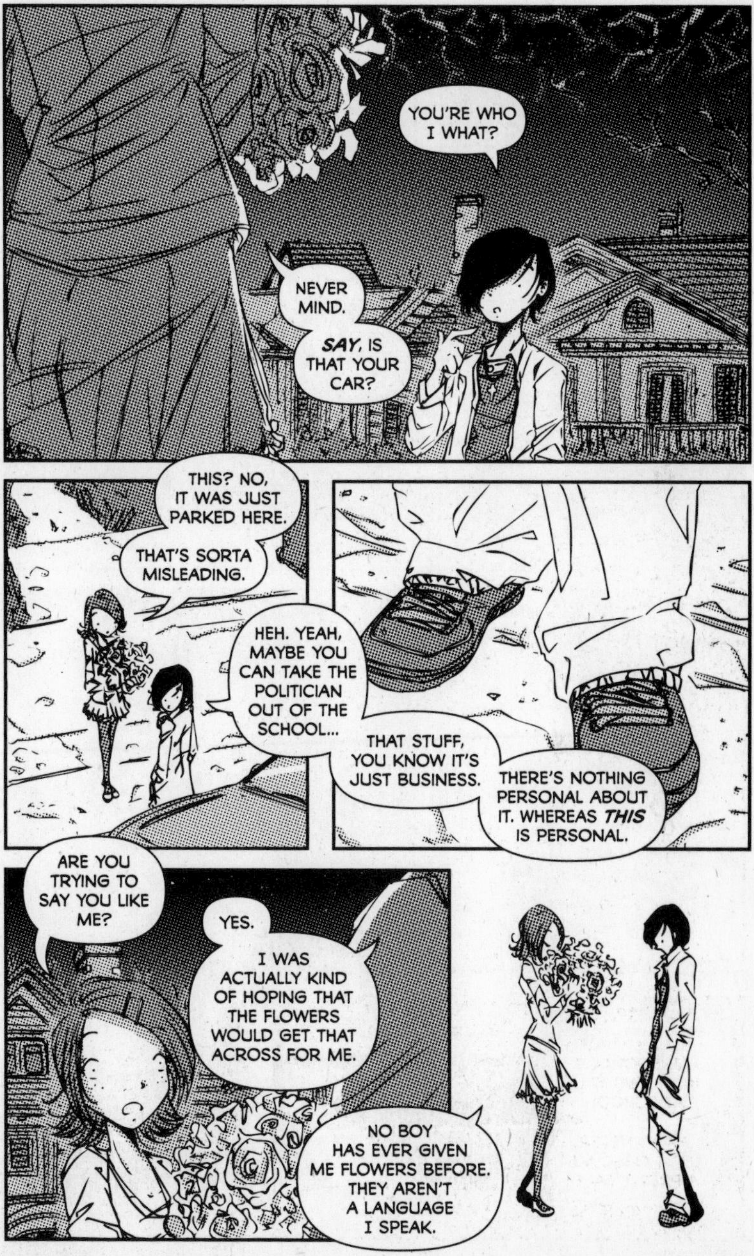

YOU'RE WHO I WHAT?
NEVER MIND.
SAY, IS THAT YOUR CAR?
THIS? NO, IT WAS JUST PARKED HERE.
THAT'S SORTA MISLEADING.
HEH. YEAH, MAYBE YOU CAN TAKE THE POLITICIAN OUT OF THE SCHOOL...
THAT STUFF, YOU KNOW IT'S JUST BUSINESS.
THERE'S NOTHING PERSONAL ABOUT IT. WHEREAS THIS IS PERSONAL.
ARE YOU TRYING TO SAY YOU LIKE ME?
YES.
I WAS ACTUALLY KIND OF HOPING THAT THE FLOWERS WOULD GET THAT ACROSS FOR ME.
NO BOY HAS EVER GIVEN ME FLOWERS BEFORE. THEY AREN'T A LANGUAGE I SPEAK.

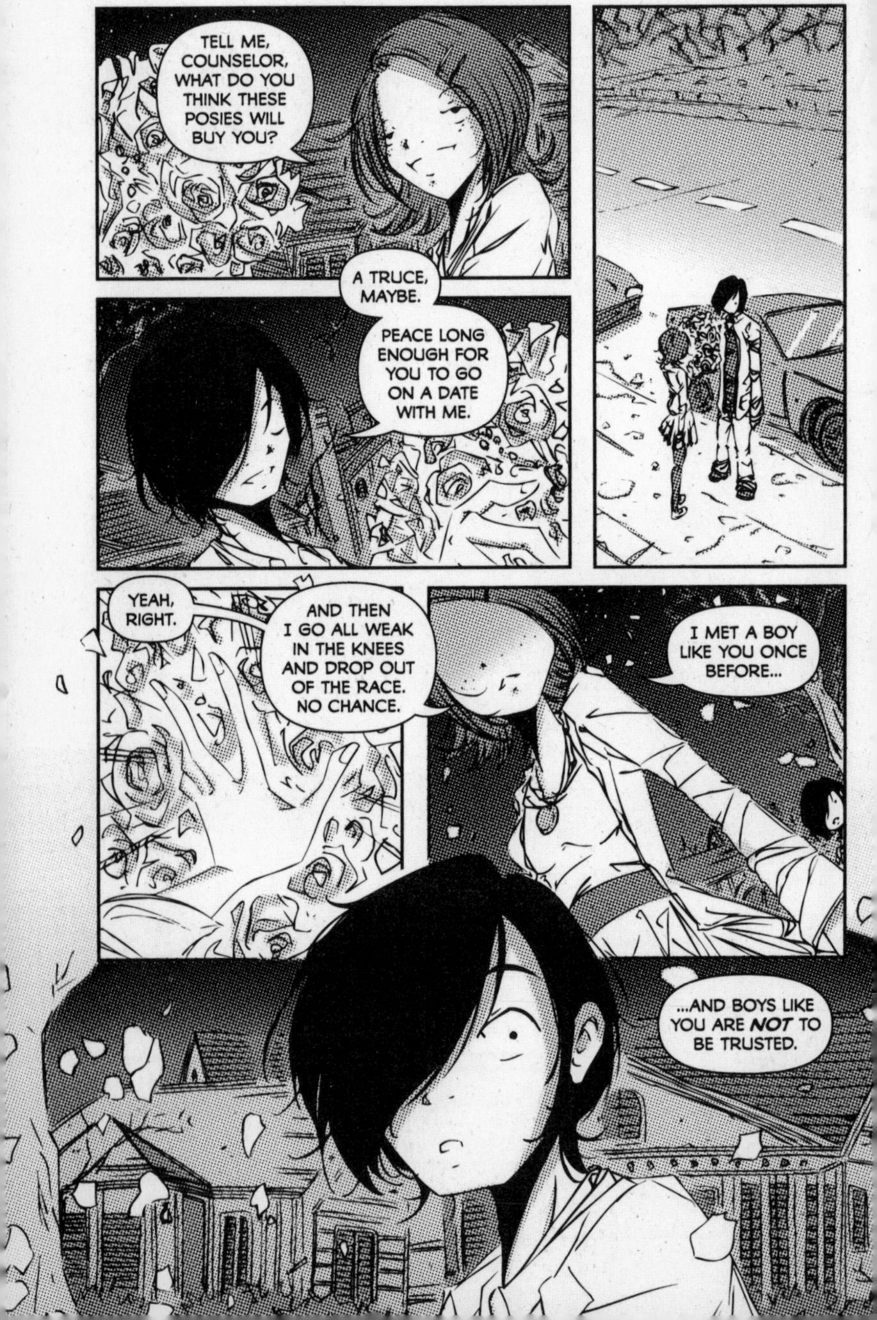
TELL ME, COUNSELOR, WHAT DO YOU THINK THESE POSIES WILL BUY YOU?
A TRUCE, MAYBE.
PEACE LONG ENOUGH FOR YOU TO GO ON A DATE WITH ME.
YEAH, RIGHT.
AND THEN I GO ALL WEAK IN THE KNEES AND DROP OUT OF THE RACE. NO CHANCE.
I MET A BOY LIKE YOU ONCE BEFORE...
...AND BOYS LIKE YOU ARE *NOT* TO BE TRUSTED.

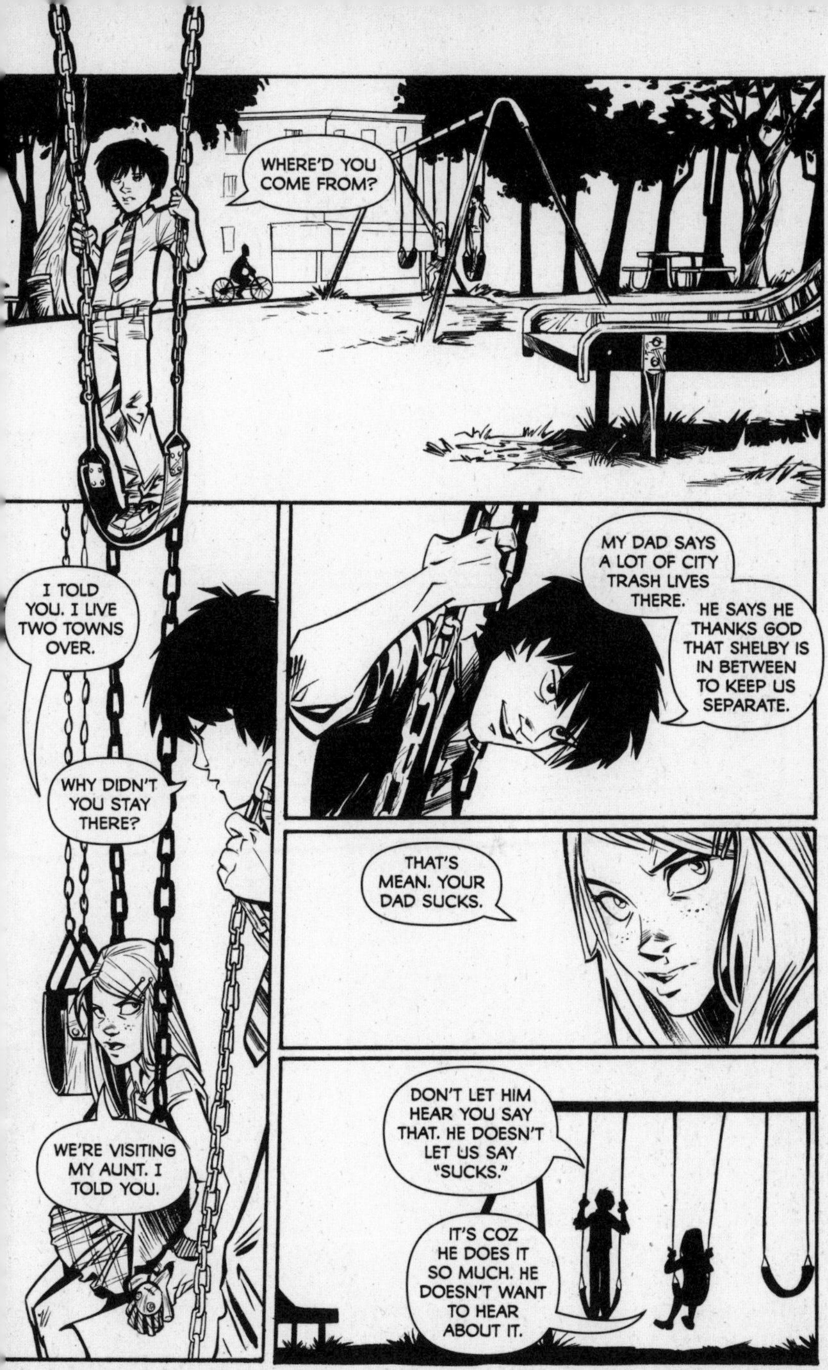
WHERE'D YOU COME FROM?
I TOLD YOU. I LIVE TWO TOWNS OVER.
WHY DIDN'T YOU STAY THERE?
WE'RE VISITING MY AUNT. I TOLD YOU.
MY DAD SAYS A LOT OF CITY TRASH LIVES THERE.
HE SAYS HE THANKS GOD THAT SHELBY IS IN BETWEEN TO KEEP US SEPARATE.
THAT'S MEAN. YOUR DAD SUCKS.
DON'T LET HIM HEAR YOU SAY THAT. HE DOESN'T LET US SAY "SUCKS."
IT'S COZ HE DOES IT SO MUCH. HE DOESN'T WANT TO HEAR ABOUT IT.

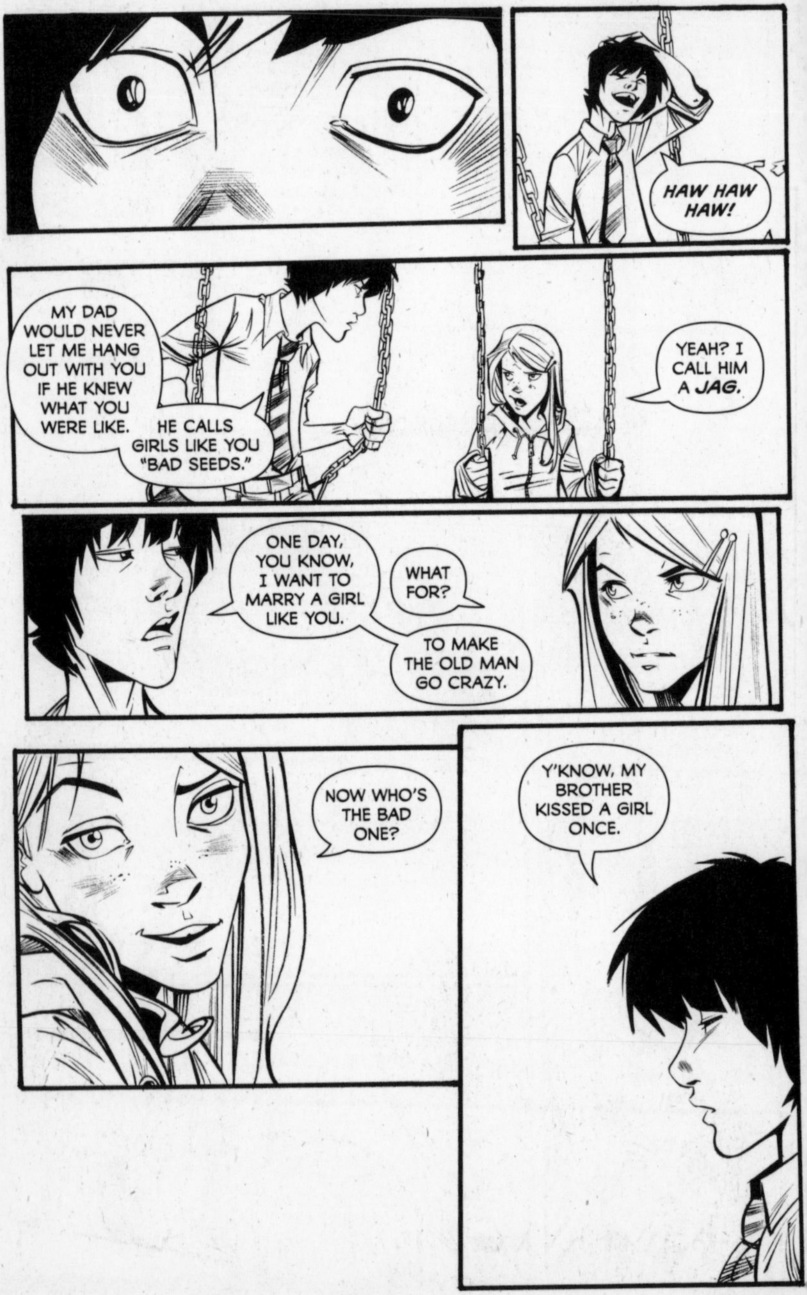
HAW HAW HAW!
MY DAD WOULD NEVER LET ME HANG OUT WITH YOU IF HE KNEW WHAT YOU WERE LIKE.
HE CALLS GIRLS LIKE YOU "BAD SEEDS."
YEAH? I CALL HIM A JAG.
ONE DAY, YOU KNOW, I WANT TO MARRY A GIRL LIKE YOU.
WHAT FOR?
TO MAKE THE OLD MAN GO CRAZY.
NOW WHO'S THE BAD ONE?
Y'KNOW, MY BROTHER KISSED A GIRL ONCE.

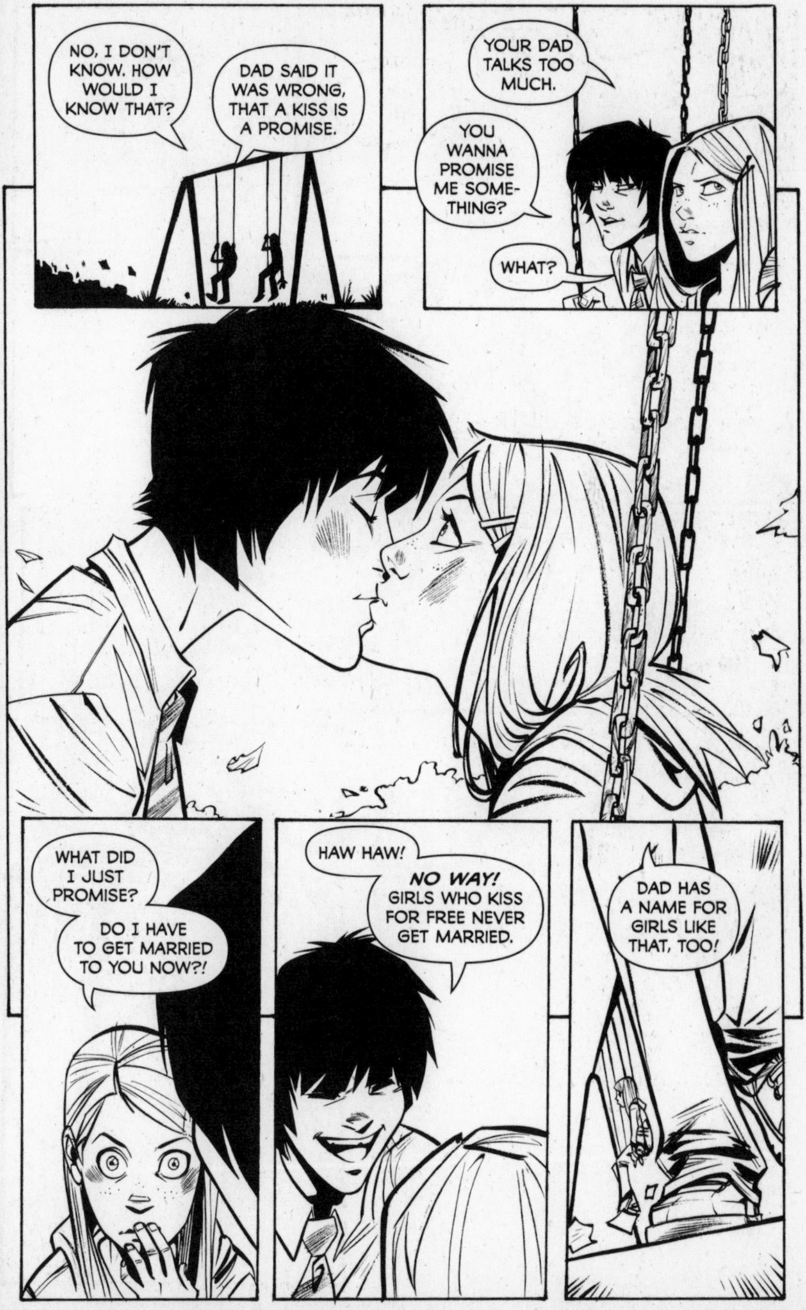
NO, I DON'T KNOW. HOW WOULD I KNOW THAT?
DAD SAID IT WAS WRONG, THAT A KISS IS A PROMISE.
YOUR DAD TALKS TOO MUCH.
YOU WANNA PROMISE ME SOMETHING?
WHAT?
WHAT DID I JUST PROMISE?
DO I HAVE TO GET MARRIED TO YOU NOW?!
HAW HAW!
NO WAY! GIRLS WHO KISS FOR FREE NEVER GET MARRIED.
DAD HAS A NAME FOR GIRLS LIKE THAT, TOO!

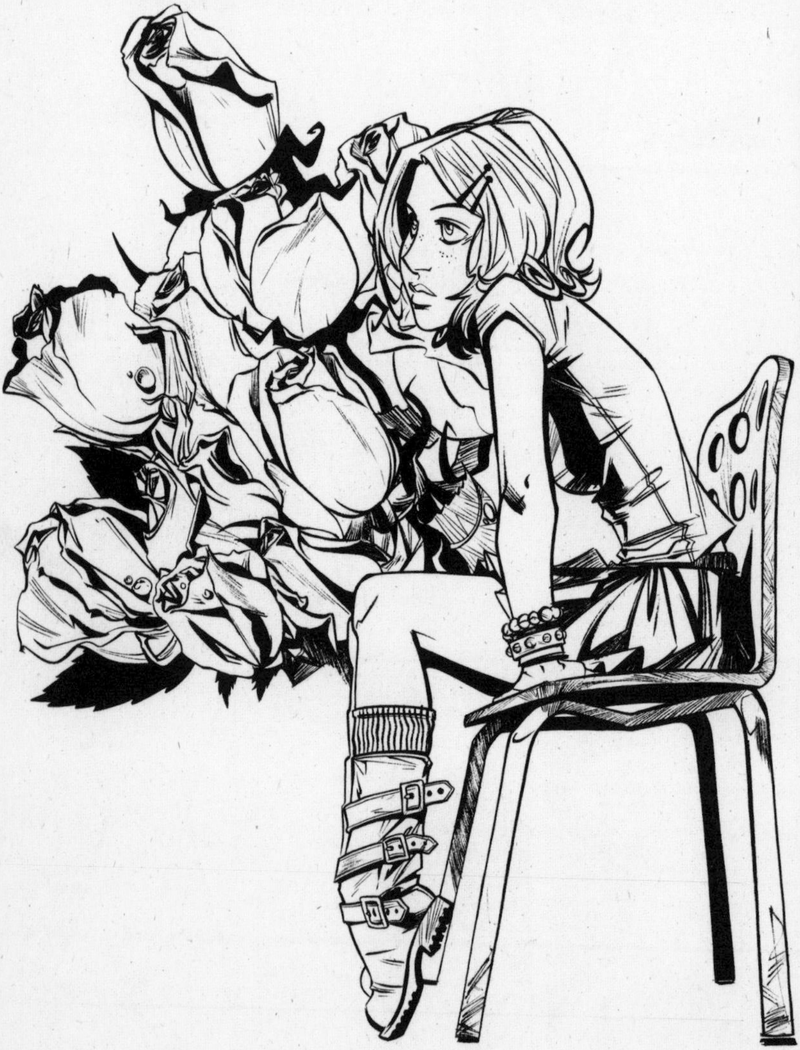

Chapter 4
"Meet Ze Monsta"

4

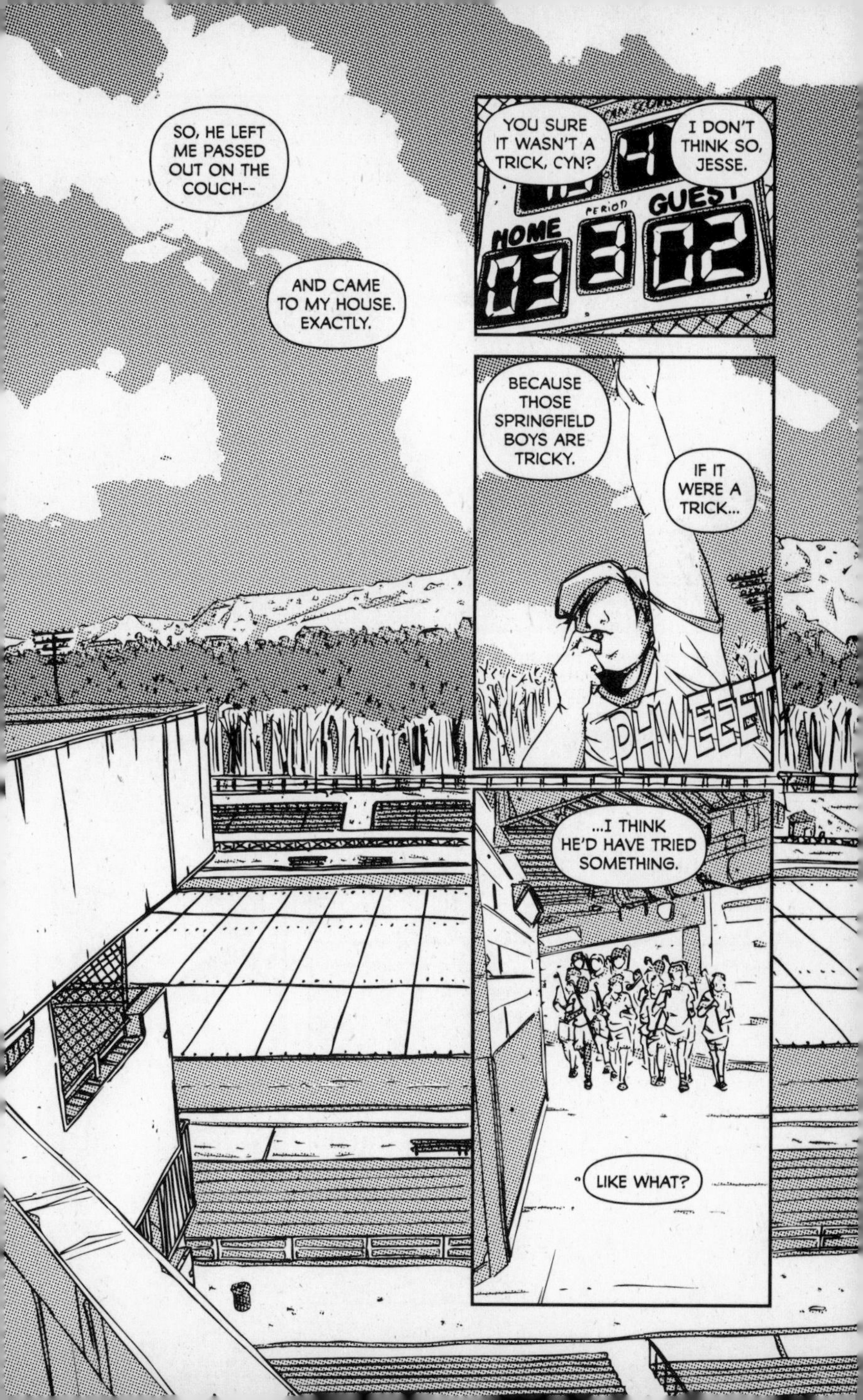
SO, HE LEFT ME PASSED OUT ON THE COUCH--
AND CAME TO MY HOUSE. EXACTLY.
YOU SURE IT WASN'T A TRICK, CYN?
I DON'T THINK SO, JESSE.
HOME
PERIOD
GUEST
13
3
02
BECAUSE THOSE SPRINGFIELD BOYS ARE TRICKY.
IF IT WERE A TRICK...
PHWEEET!
...I THINK HE'D HAVE TRIED SOMETHING.
LIKE WHAT?

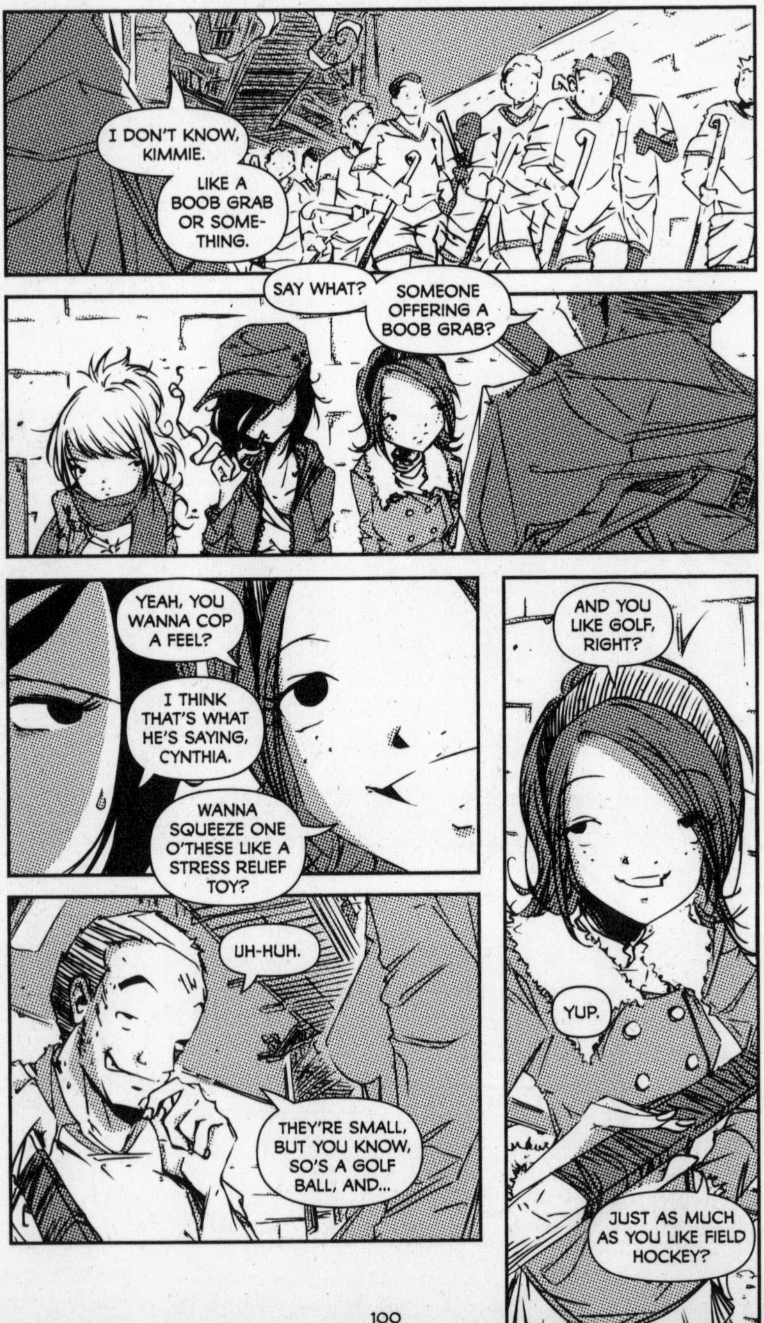
I DON'T KNOW, KIMMIE.
LIKE A BOOB GRAB OR SOME-THING.
SAY WHAT?
SOMEONE OFFERING A BOOB GRAB?
YEAH, YOU WANNA COP A FEEL?
I THINK THAT'S WHAT HE'S SAYING, CYNTHIA.
WANNA SQUEEZE ONE O'THESE LIKE A STRESS RELIEF TOY?
UH-HUH.
THEY'RE SMALL, BUT YOU KNOW, SO'S A GOLF BALL, AND...
AND YOU LIKE GOLF, RIGHT?
YUP.
JUST AS MUCH AS YOU LIKE FIELD HOCKEY?

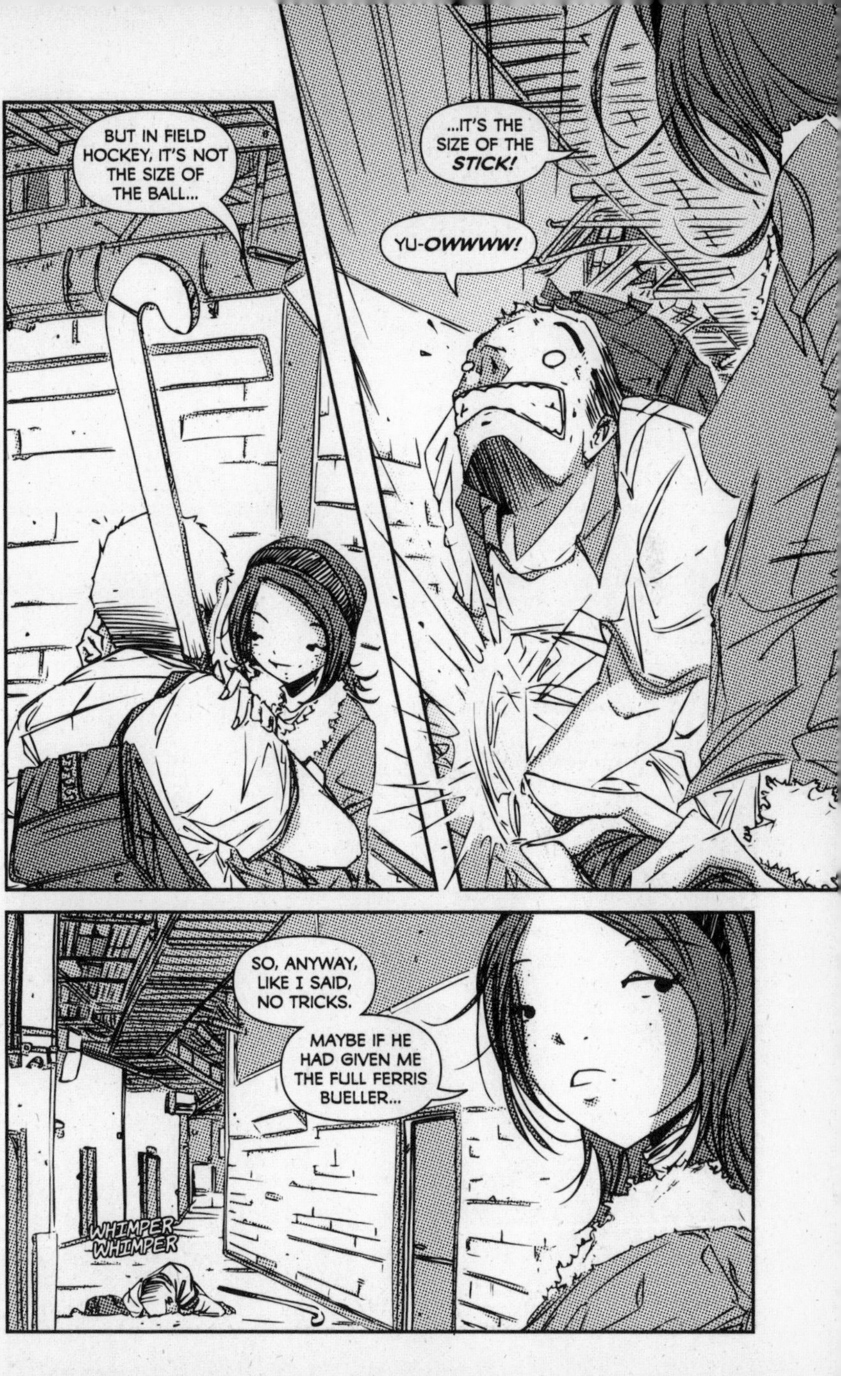
BUT IN FIELD HOCKEY, IT'S NOT THE SIZE OF THE BALL...
...IT'S THE SIZE OF THE *STICK!*
YU-*OWWWW!*
SO, ANYWAY, LIKE I SAID, NO TRICKS.
MAYBE IF HE HAD GIVEN ME THE FULL FERRIS BUELLER...
WHIMPER WHIMPER

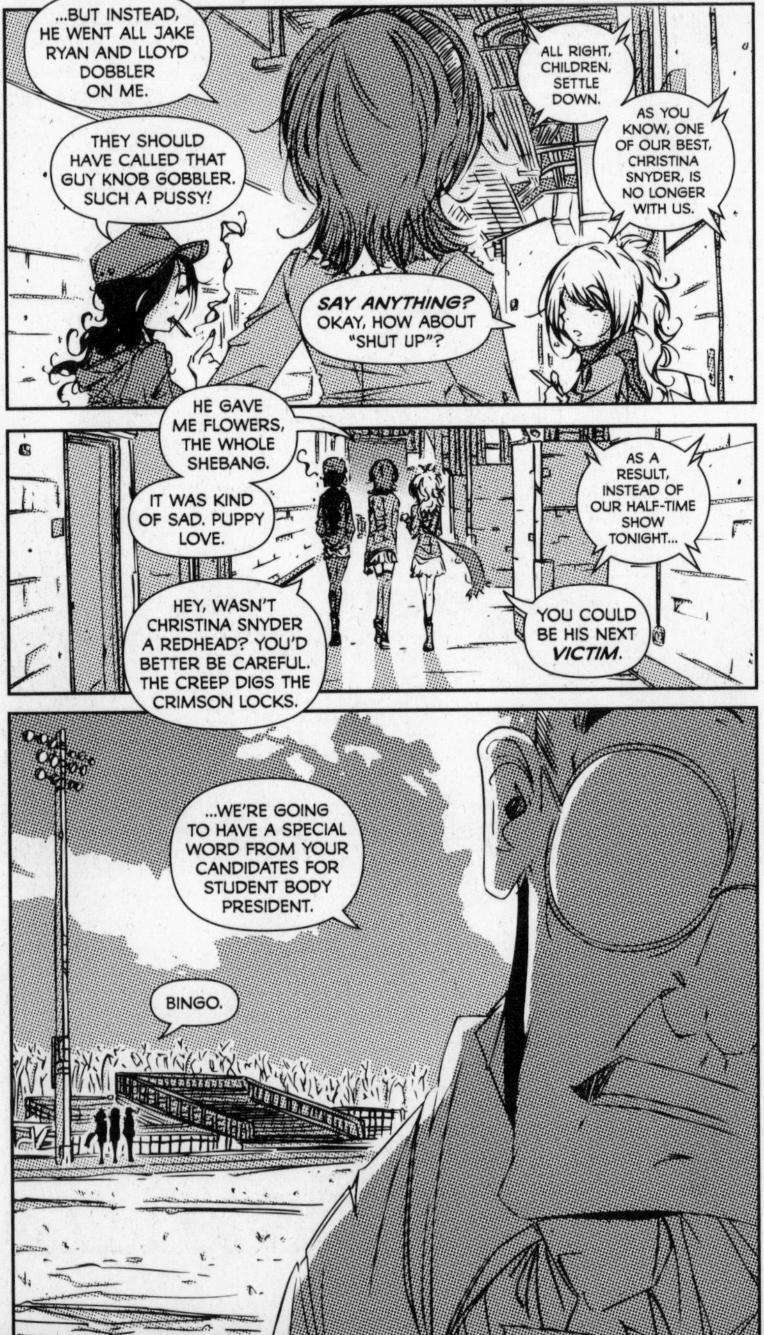
...BUT INSTEAD, HE WENT ALL JAKE RYAN AND LLOYD DOBBLER ON ME.
THEY SHOULD HAVE CALLED THAT GUY KNOB GOBBLER. SUCH A PUSSY!
ALL RIGHT, CHILDREN, SETTLE DOWN.
AS YOU KNOW, ONE OF OUR BEST, CHRISTINA SNYDER, IS NO LONGER WITH US.
SAY ANYTHING? OKAY, HOW ABOUT "SHUT UP"?
HE GAVE ME FLOWERS, THE WHOLE SHEBANG.
IT WAS KIND OF SAD. PUPPY LOVE.
AS A RESULT, INSTEAD OF OUR HALF-TIME SHOW TONIGHT...
HEY, WASN'T CHRISTINA SNYDER A REDHEAD? YOU'D BETTER BE CAREFUL. THE CREEP DIGS THE CRIMSON LOCKS.
YOU COULD BE HIS NEXT VICTIM.
...WE'RE GOING TO HAVE A SPECIAL WORD FROM YOUR CANDIDATES FOR STUDENT BODY PRESIDENT.
BINGO.

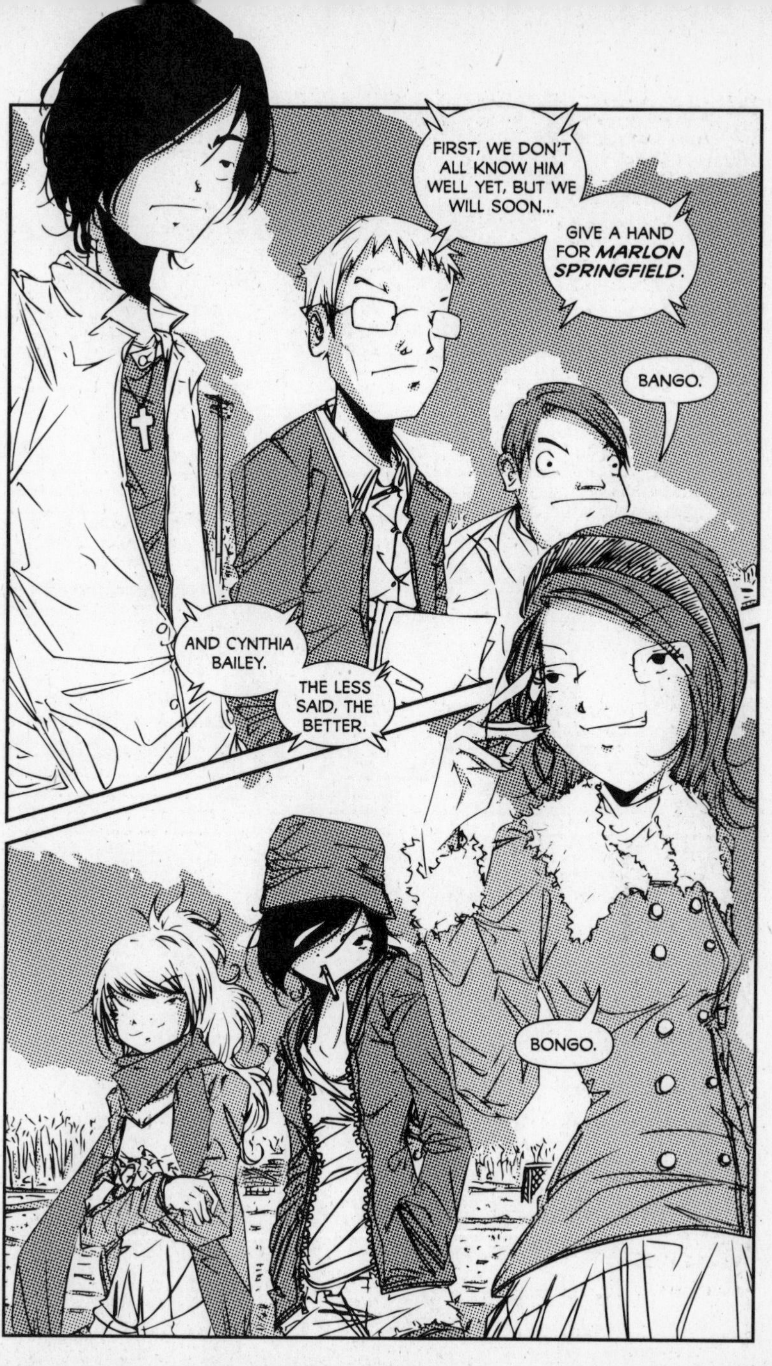
FIRST, WE DON'T ALL KNOW HIM WELL YET, BUT WE WILL SOON...
GIVE A HAND FOR *MARLON SPRINGFIELD*.
BANGO.
AND CYNTHIA BAILEY.
THE LESS SAID, THE BETTER.
BONGO.

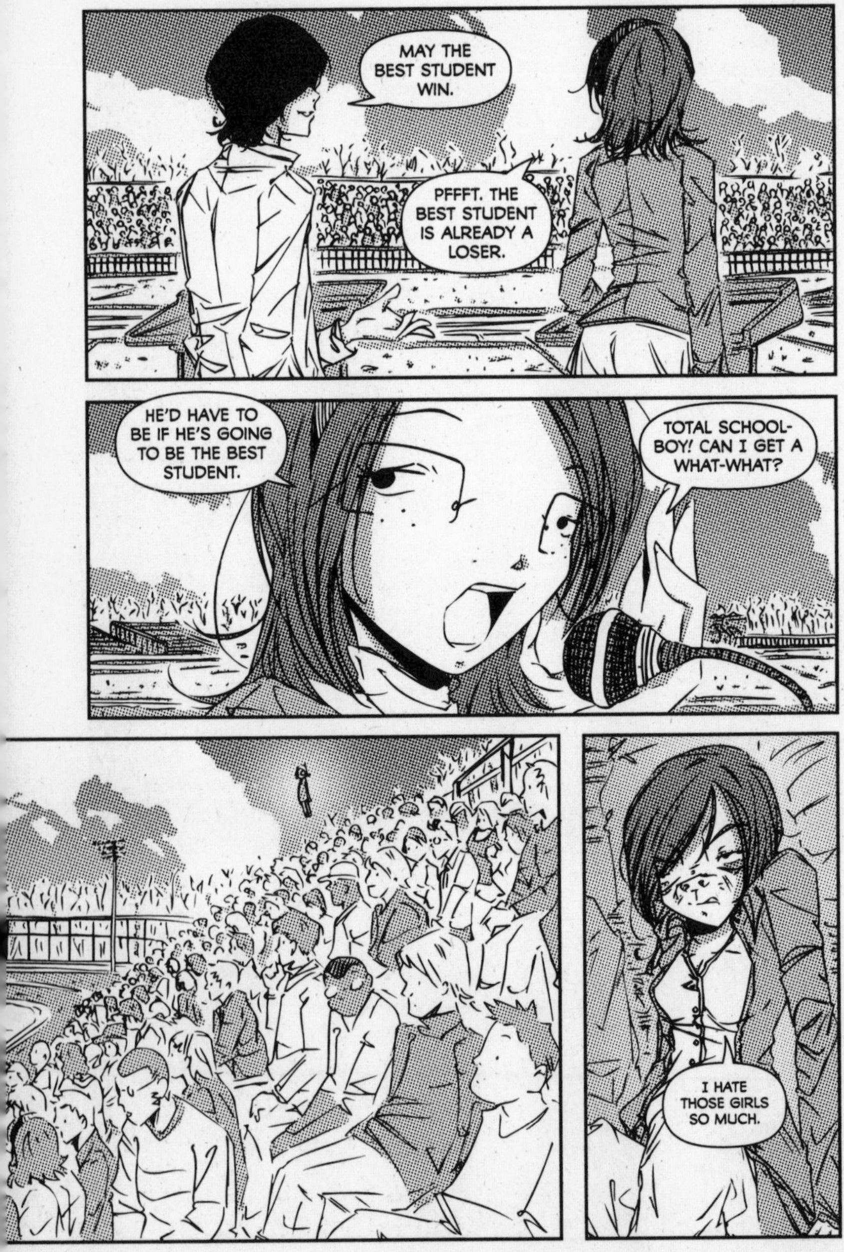
MAY THE BEST STUDENT WIN.
PFFFT. THE BEST STUDENT IS ALREADY A LOSER.
HE'D HAVE TO BE IF HE'S GOING TO BE THE BEST STUDENT.
TOTAL SCHOOL-BOY! CAN I GET A WHAT-WHAT?
I HATE THOSE GIRLS SO MUCH.

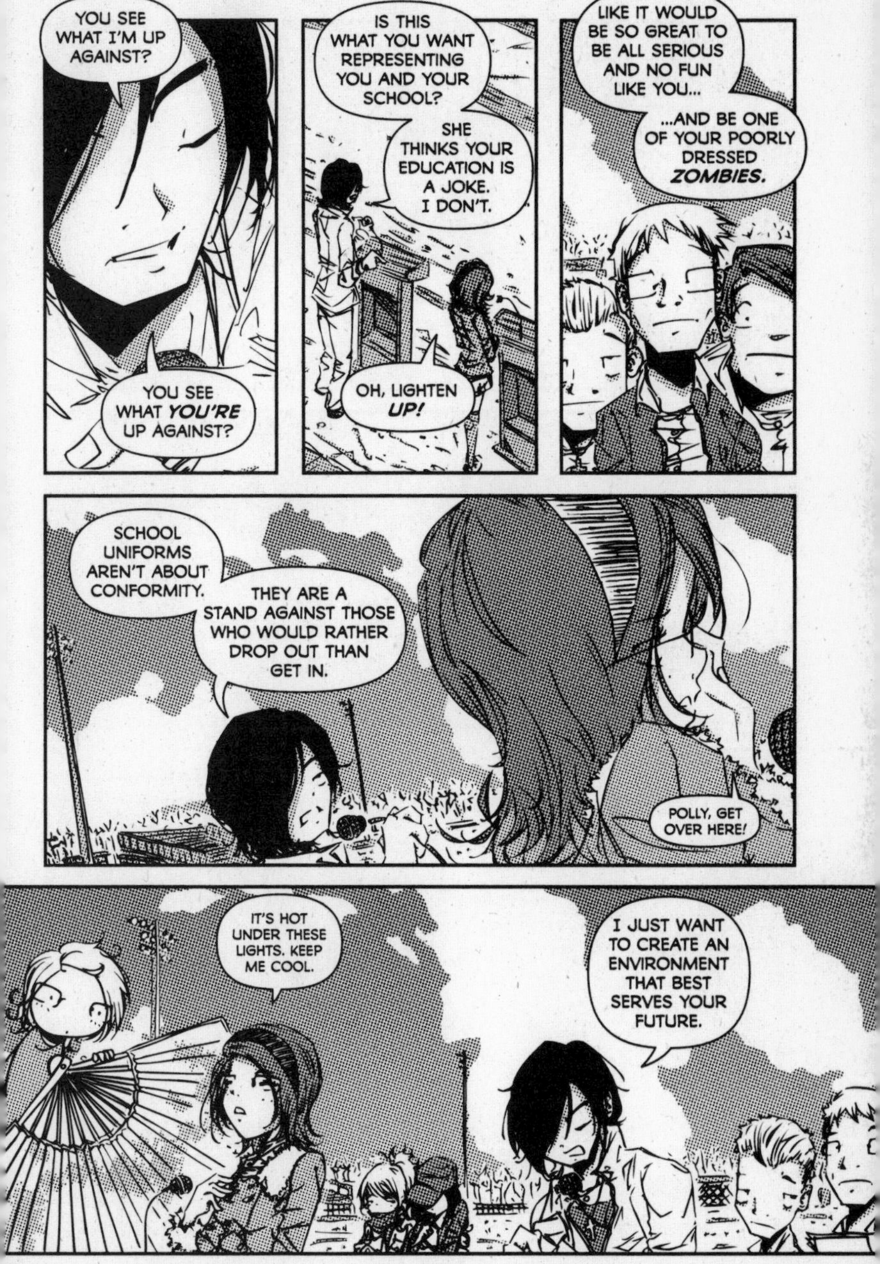
YOU SEE WHAT I'M UP AGAINST?
YOU SEE WHAT *YOU'RE* UP AGAINST?
IS THIS WHAT YOU WANT REPRESENTING YOU AND YOUR SCHOOL?
SHE THINKS YOUR EDUCATION IS A JOKE. I DON'T.
OH, LIGHTEN *UP!*
LIKE IT WOULD BE SO GREAT TO BE ALL SERIOUS AND NO FUN LIKE YOU...
...AND BE ONE OF YOUR POORLY DRESSED ***ZOMBIES.***
SCHOOL UNIFORMS AREN'T ABOUT CONFORMITY.
THEY ARE A STAND AGAINST THOSE WHO WOULD RATHER DROP OUT THAN GET IN.
POLLY, GET OVER HERE!
IT'S HOT UNDER THESE LIGHTS. KEEP ME COOL.
I JUST WANT TO CREATE AN ENVIRONMENT THAT BEST SERVES YOUR FUTURE.

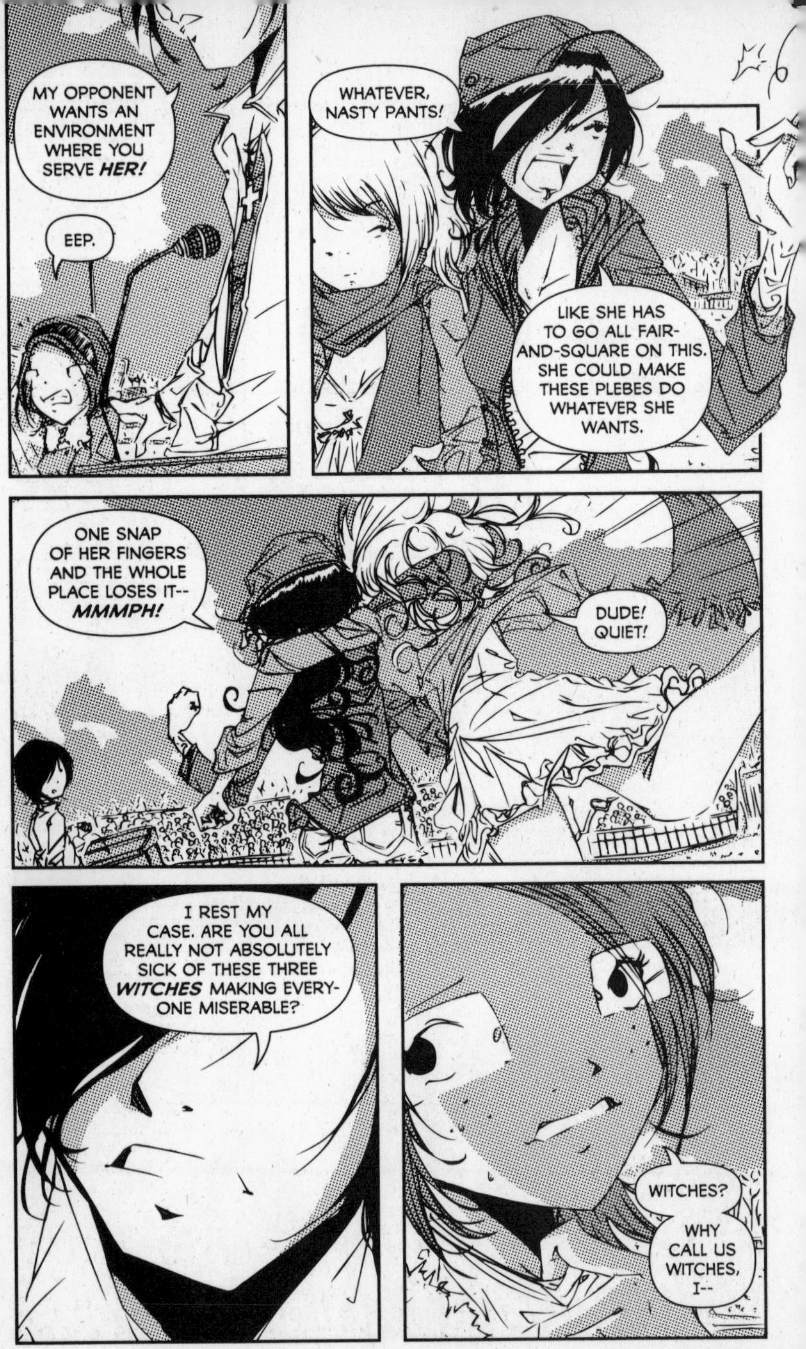
MY OPPONENT WANTS AN ENVIRONMENT WHERE YOU SERVE HER!
EEP.
WHATEVER, NASTY PANTS!
LIKE SHE HAS TO GO ALL FAIR-AND-SQUARE ON THIS. SHE COULD MAKE THESE PLEBES DO WHATEVER SHE WANTS.
ONE SNAP OF HER FINGERS AND THE WHOLE PLACE LOSES IT-- MMMPH!
DUDE! QUIET!
I REST MY CASE. ARE YOU ALL REALLY NOT ABSOLUTELY SICK OF THESE THREE WITCHES MAKING EVERY-ONE MISERABLE?
WITCHES?
WHY CALL US WITCHES, I--

I'M SORRY. YOU'RE RIGHT.

SUCH LANGUAGE IS UNCALLED FOR.

>PHEW<

I DON'T BELIEVE IN POLITICAL RHETORIC OR NAME CALLING.

THERE'S ENOUGH OF THE LATTER IN OUR HALLWAYS AS IT IS.

THE BELITTLED, THE BELEAGURED-- THIS DESCRIBES EACH AND EVERY ONE OF US.

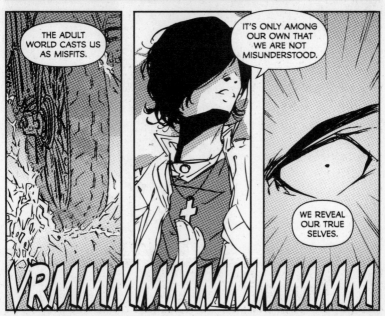

THE ADULT WORLD CASTS US AS MISFITS.

IT'S ONLY AMONG OUR OWN THAT WE ARE NOT MISUNDERSTOOD.

WE REVEAL OUR TRUE SELVES.

VRMMMMMMMMMMMM

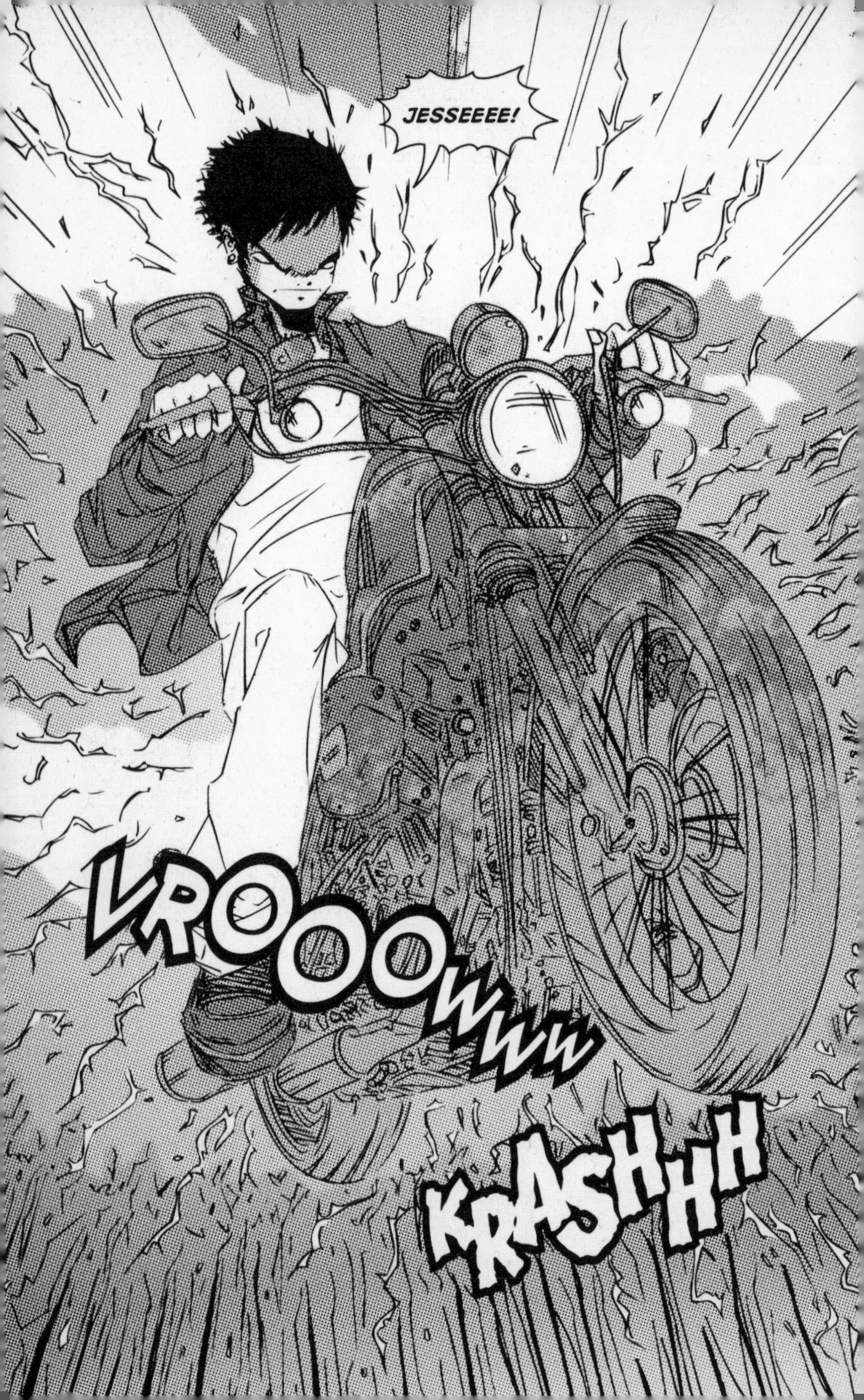
JESSEEEE!
VROOOOWWWW
KRASHHH

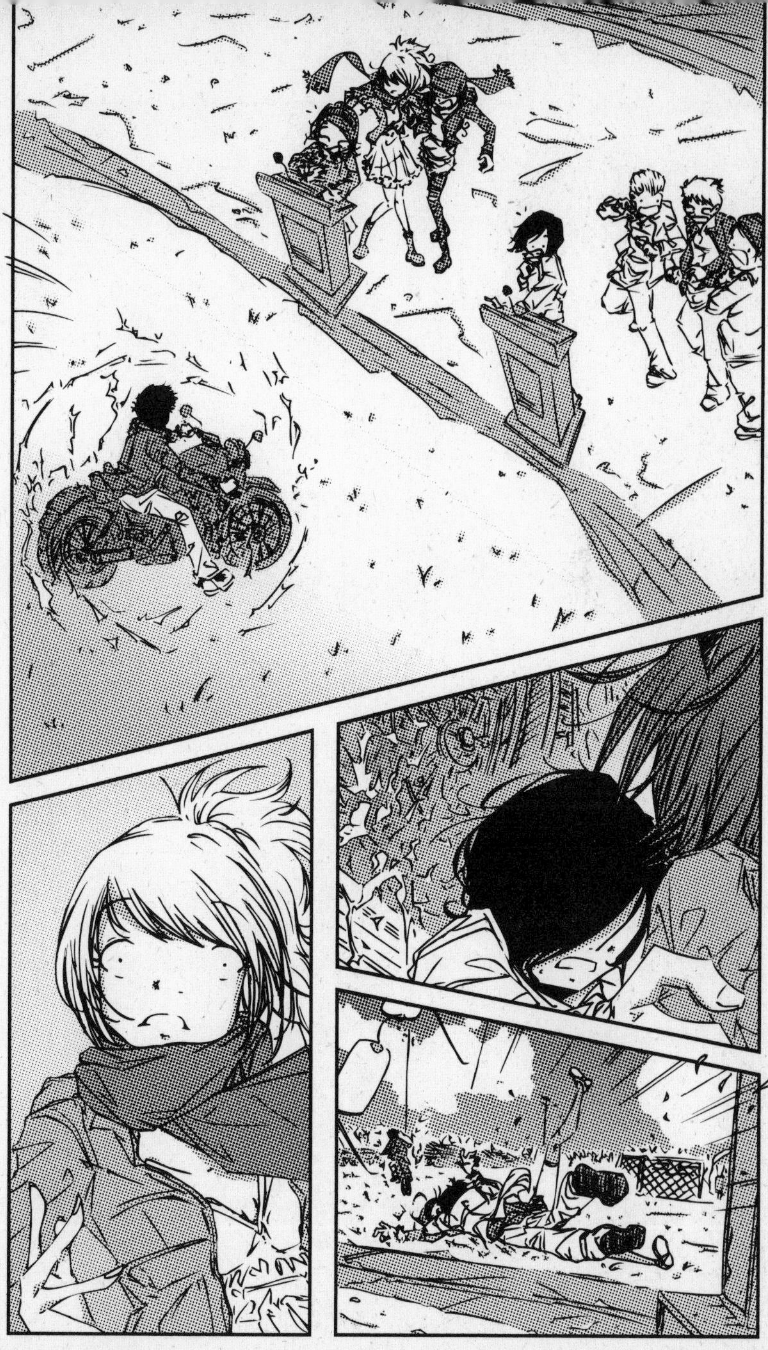

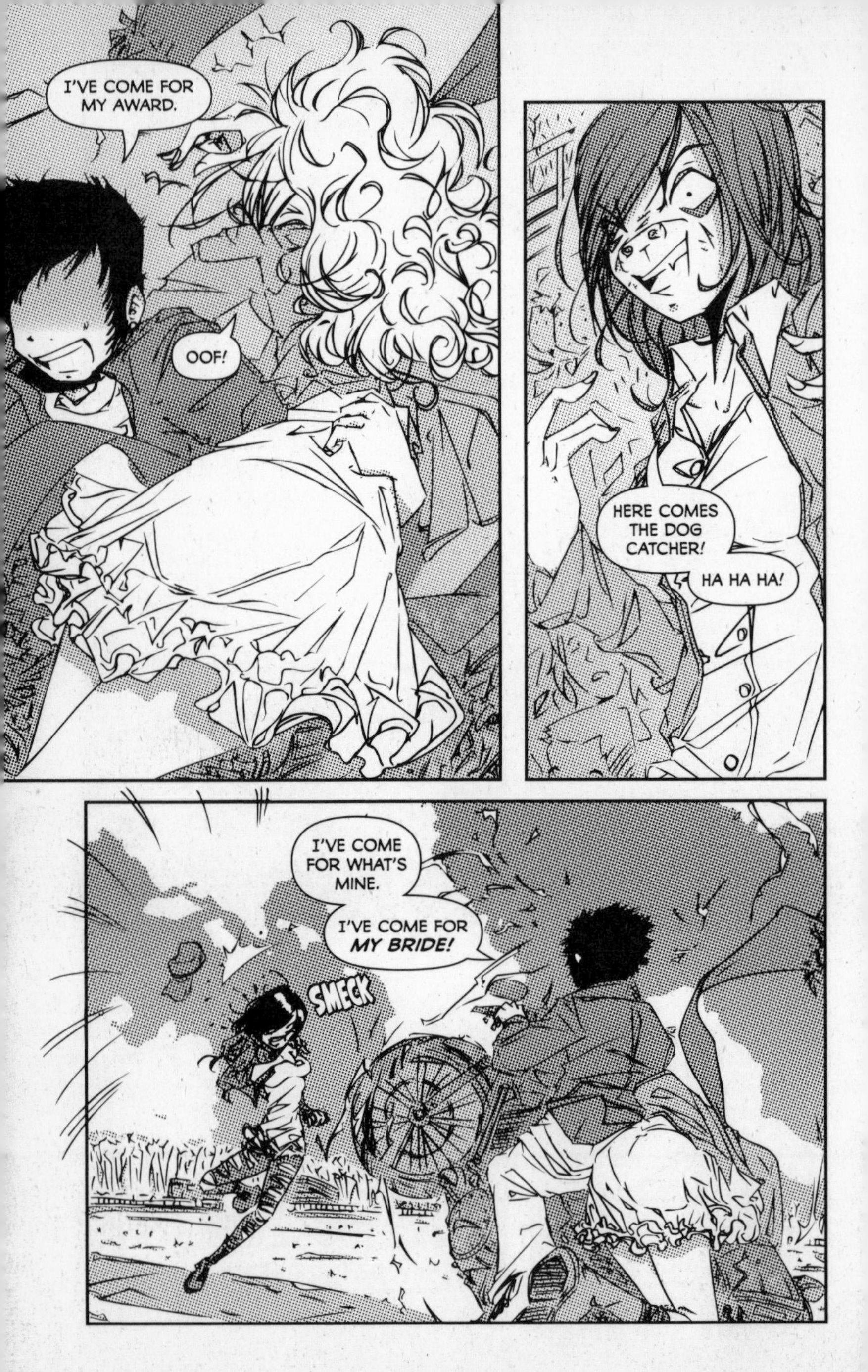
I'VE COME FOR MY AWARD.
OOF!
HERE COMES THE DOG CATCHER!
HA HA HA!
I'VE COME FOR WHAT'S MINE.
I'VE COME FOR *MY BRIDE!*
SMECK

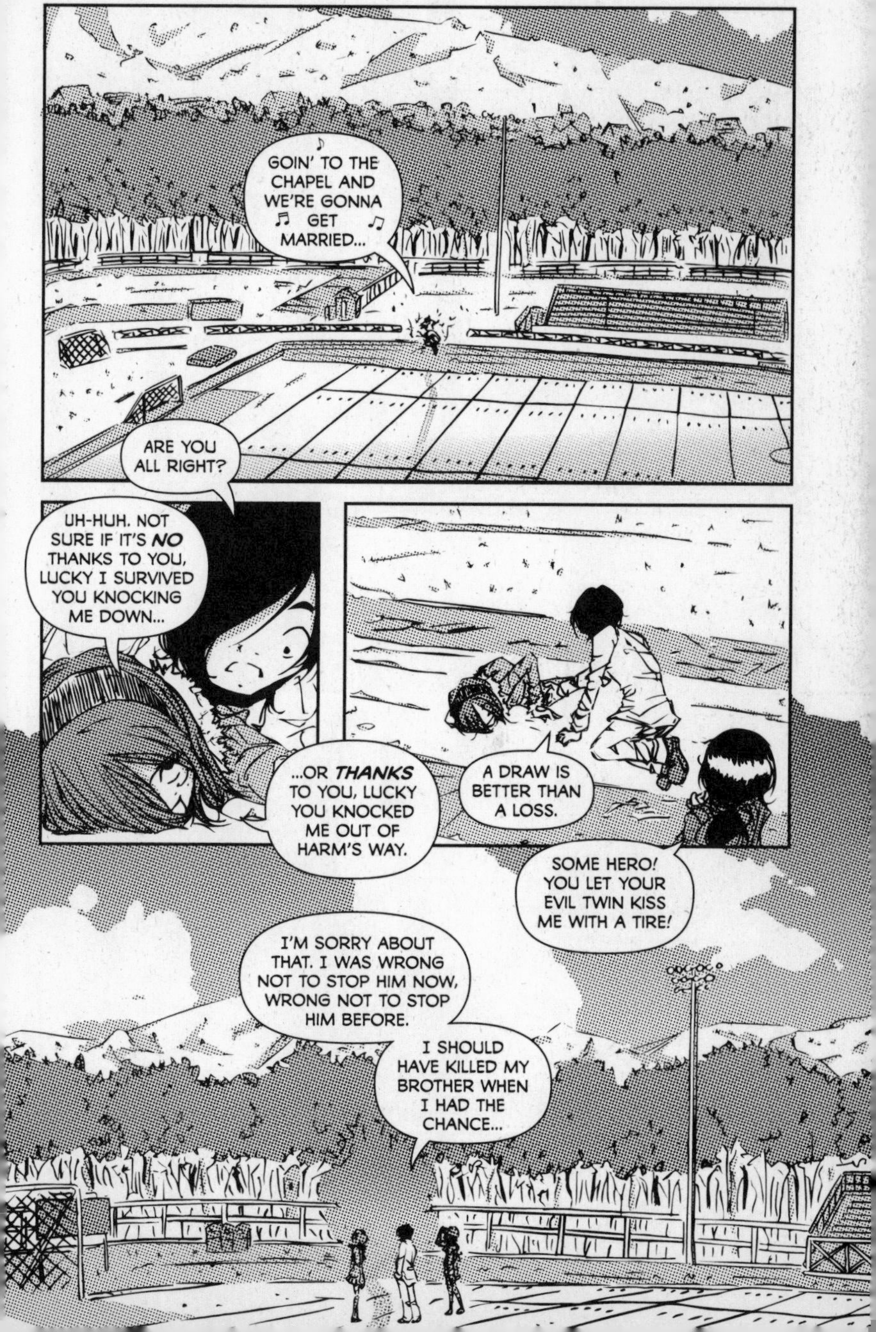
♪ GOIN' TO THE CHAPEL AND WE'RE GONNA ♫ GET ♫ MARRIED...
ARE YOU ALL RIGHT?
UH-HUH. NOT SURE IF IT'S ***NO*** THANKS TO YOU, LUCKY I SURVIVED YOU KNOCKING ME DOWN...
...OR ***THANKS*** TO YOU, LUCKY YOU KNOCKED ME OUT OF HARM'S WAY.
A DRAW IS BETTER THAN A LOSS.
SOME HERO! YOU LET YOUR EVIL TWIN KISS ME WITH A TIRE!
I'M SORRY ABOUT THAT. I WAS WRONG NOT TO STOP HIM NOW, WRONG NOT TO STOP HIM BEFORE.
I SHOULD HAVE KILLED MY BROTHER WHEN I HAD THE CHANCE...

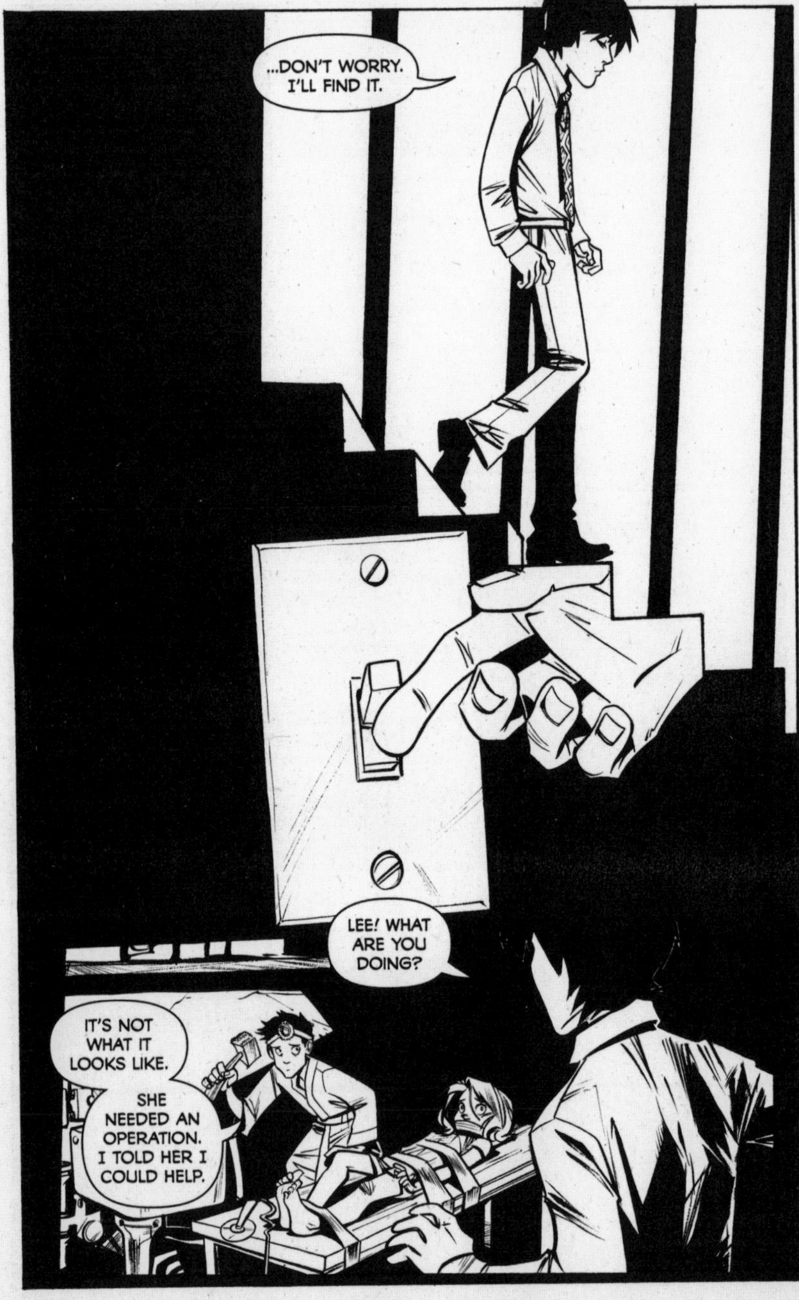
...DON'T WORRY. I'LL FIND IT.
LEE! WHAT ARE YOU DOING?
IT'S NOT WHAT IT LOOKS LIKE.
SHE NEEDED AN OPERATION. I TOLD HER I COULD HELP.

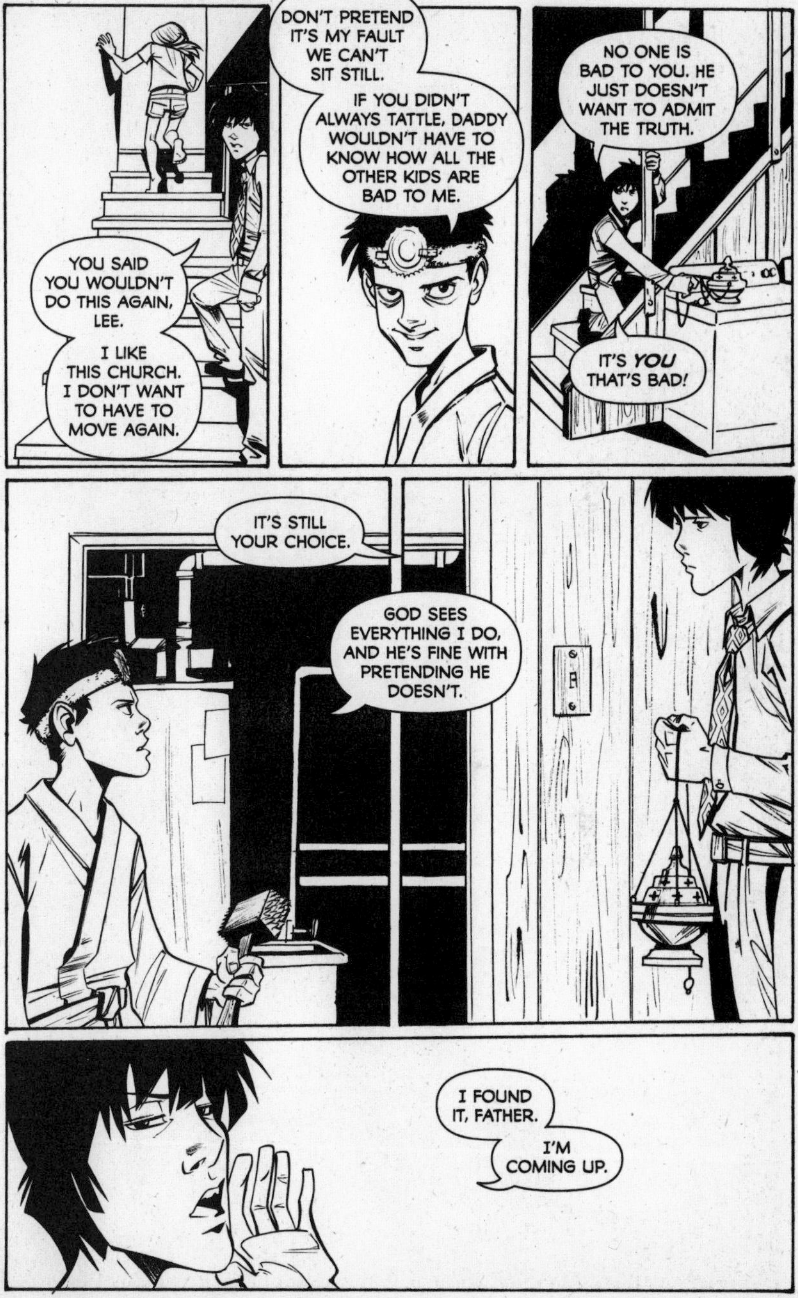
YOU SAID YOU WOULDN'T DO THIS AGAIN, LEE.
I LIKE THIS CHURCH. I DON'T WANT TO HAVE TO MOVE AGAIN.
DON'T PRETEND IT'S MY FAULT WE CAN'T SIT STILL.
IF YOU DIDN'T ALWAYS TATTLE, DADDY WOULDN'T HAVE TO KNOW HOW ALL THE OTHER KIDS ARE BAD TO ME.
NO ONE IS BAD TO YOU. HE JUST DOESN'T WANT TO ADMIT THE TRUTH.
IT'S *YOU* THAT'S BAD!
IT'S STILL YOUR CHOICE.
GOD SEES EVERYTHING I DO, AND HE'S FINE WITH PRETENDING HE DOESN'T.
I FOUND IT, FATHER.
I'M COMING UP.

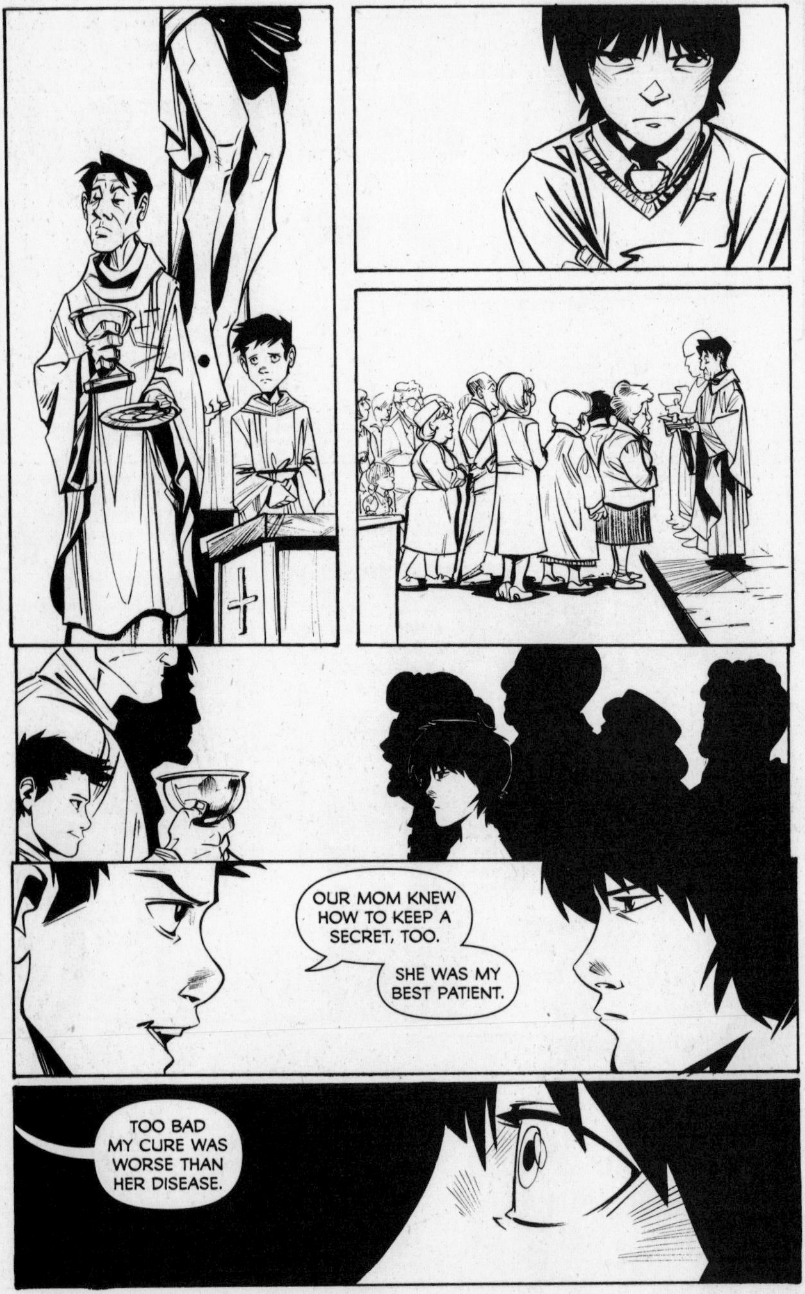
OUR MOM KNEW HOW TO KEEP A SECRET, TOO.
SHE WAS MY BEST PATIENT.
TOO BAD MY CURE WAS WORSE THAN HER DISEASE.

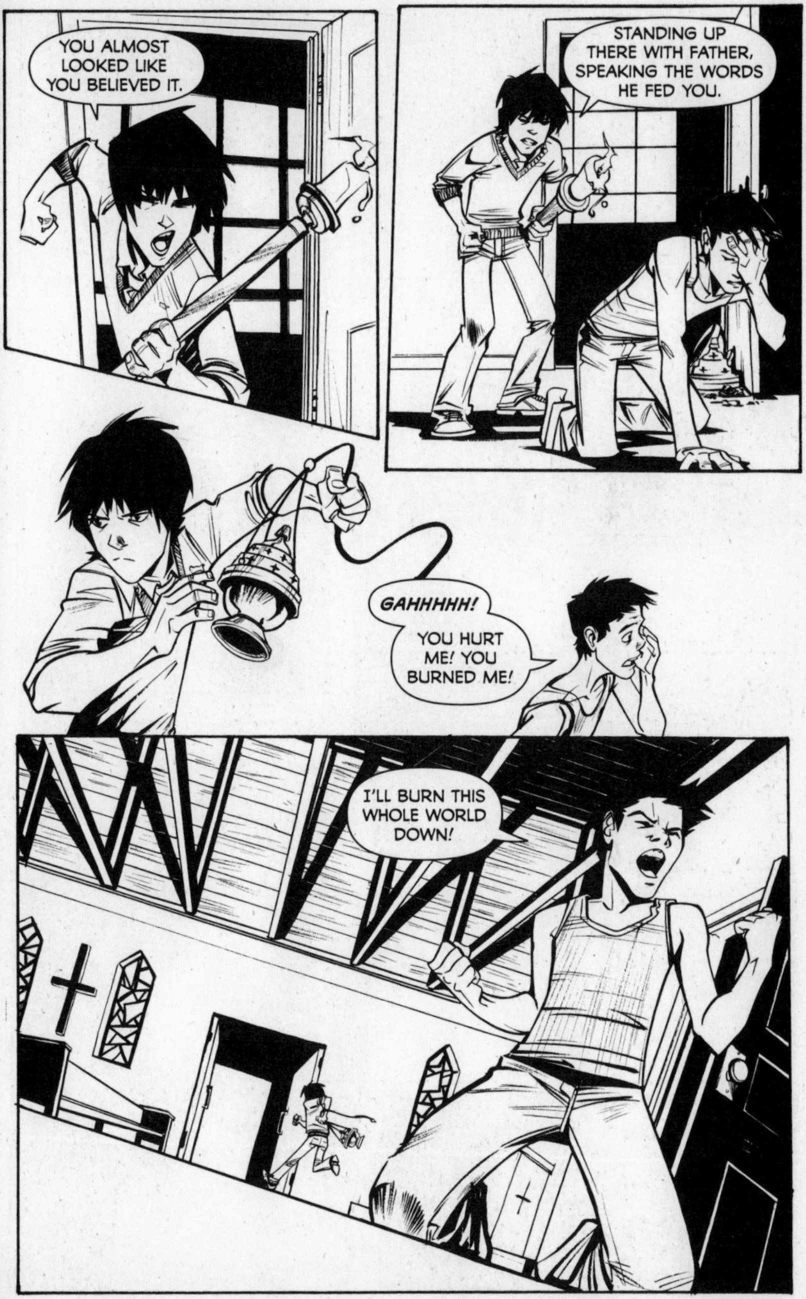
YOU ALMOST LOOKED LIKE YOU BELIEVED IT.
STANDING UP THERE WITH FATHER, SPEAKING THE WORDS HE FED YOU.
GAHHHHH!
YOU HURT ME! YOU BURNED ME!
I'LL BURN THIS WHOLE WORLD DOWN!

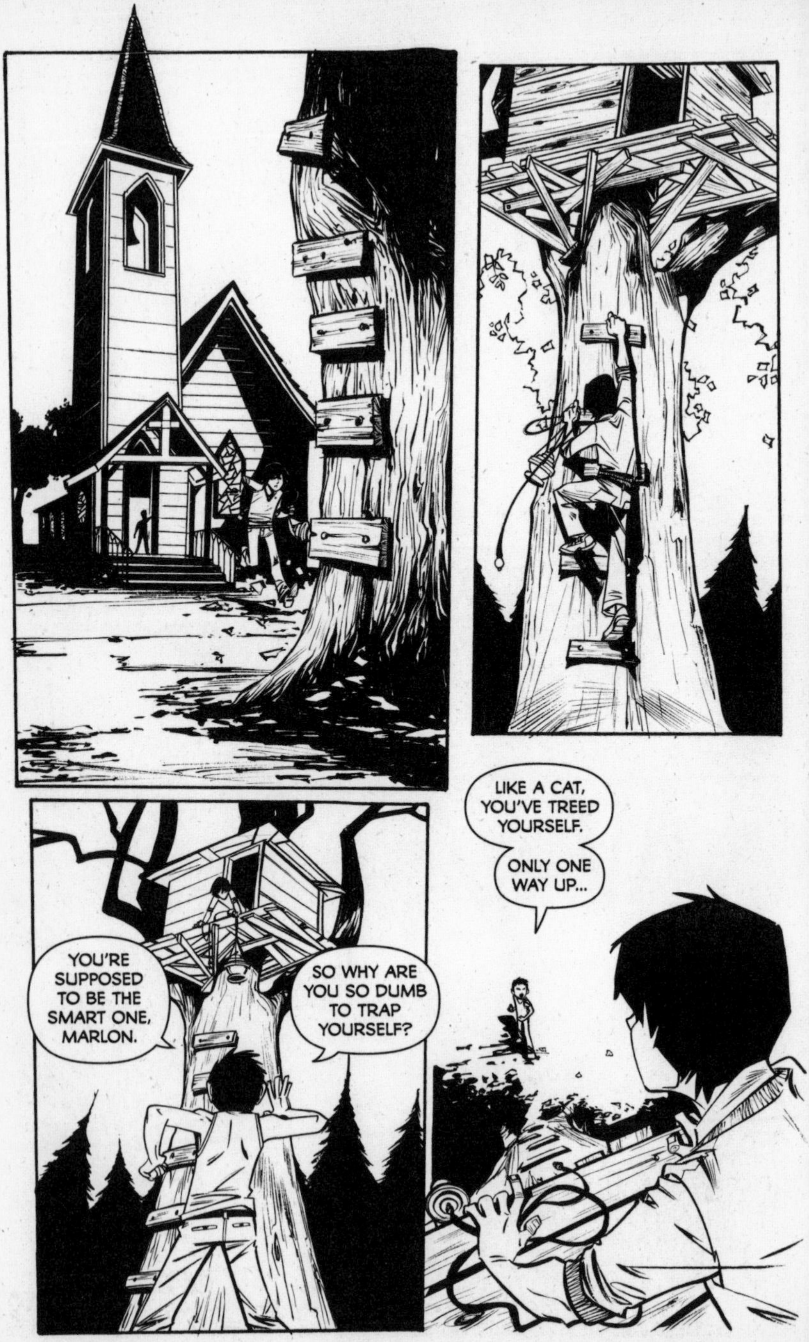
YOU'RE SUPPOSED TO BE THE SMART ONE, MARLON.
SO WHY ARE YOU SO DUMB TO TRAP YOURSELF?
LIKE A CAT, YOU'VE TREED YOURSELF.
ONLY ONE WAY UP...

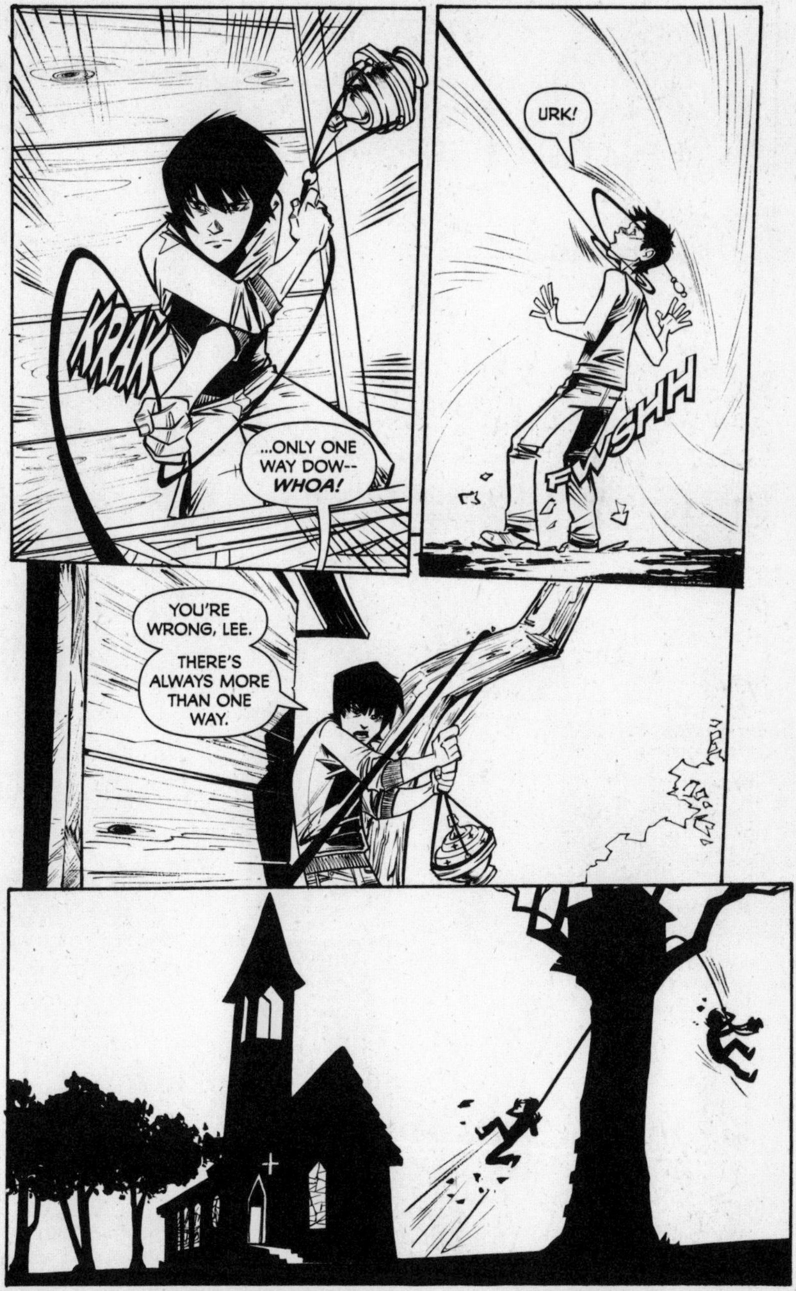
KRAK
...ONLY ONE WAY DOW-- WHOA!
URK!
FWSHH
YOU'RE WRONG, LEE.
THERE'S ALWAYS MORE THAN ONE WAY.

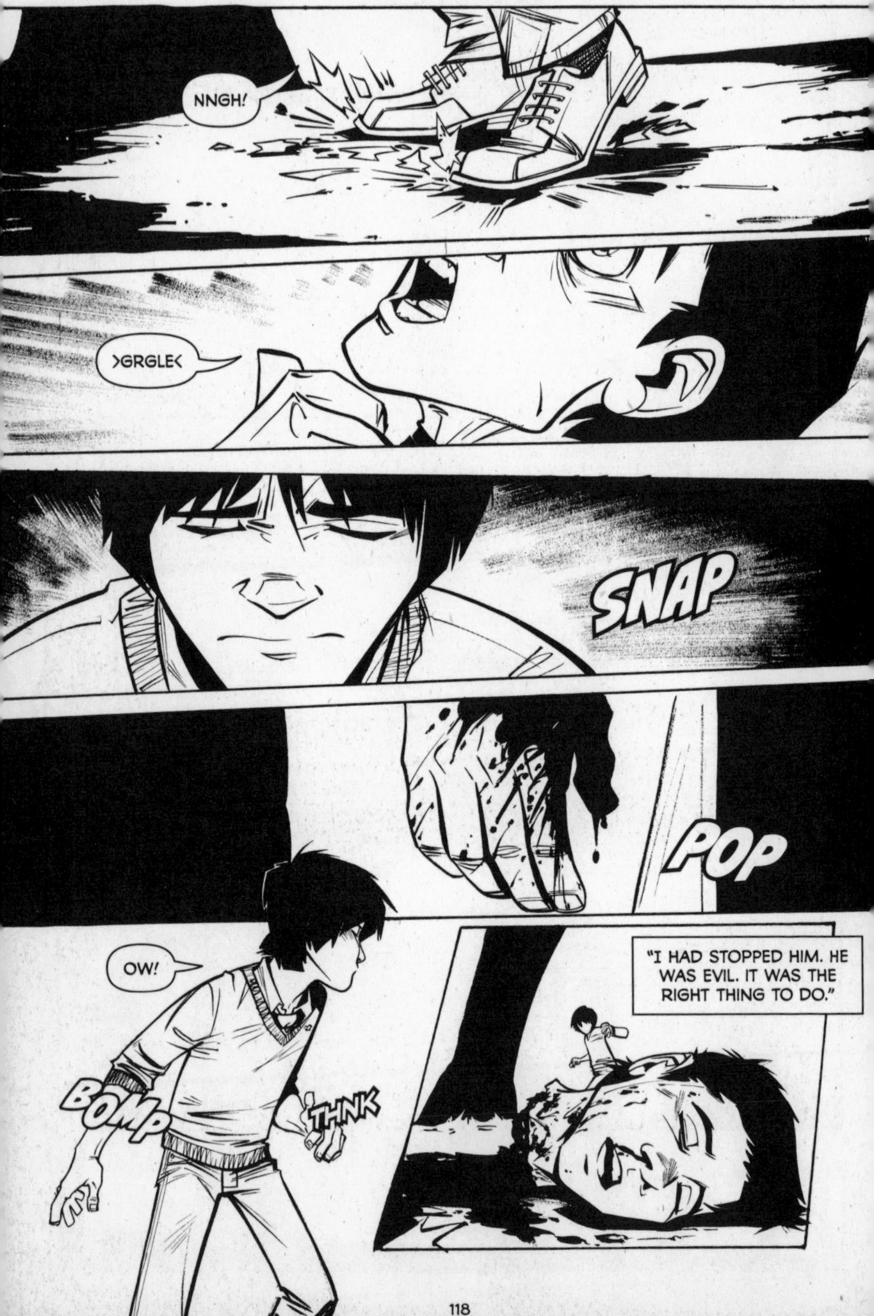
NNGH!
>GRGLE<
SNAP
POP
OW!
BOMP
THNK
"I HAD STOPPED HIM. HE WAS EVIL. IT WAS THE RIGHT THING TO DO."

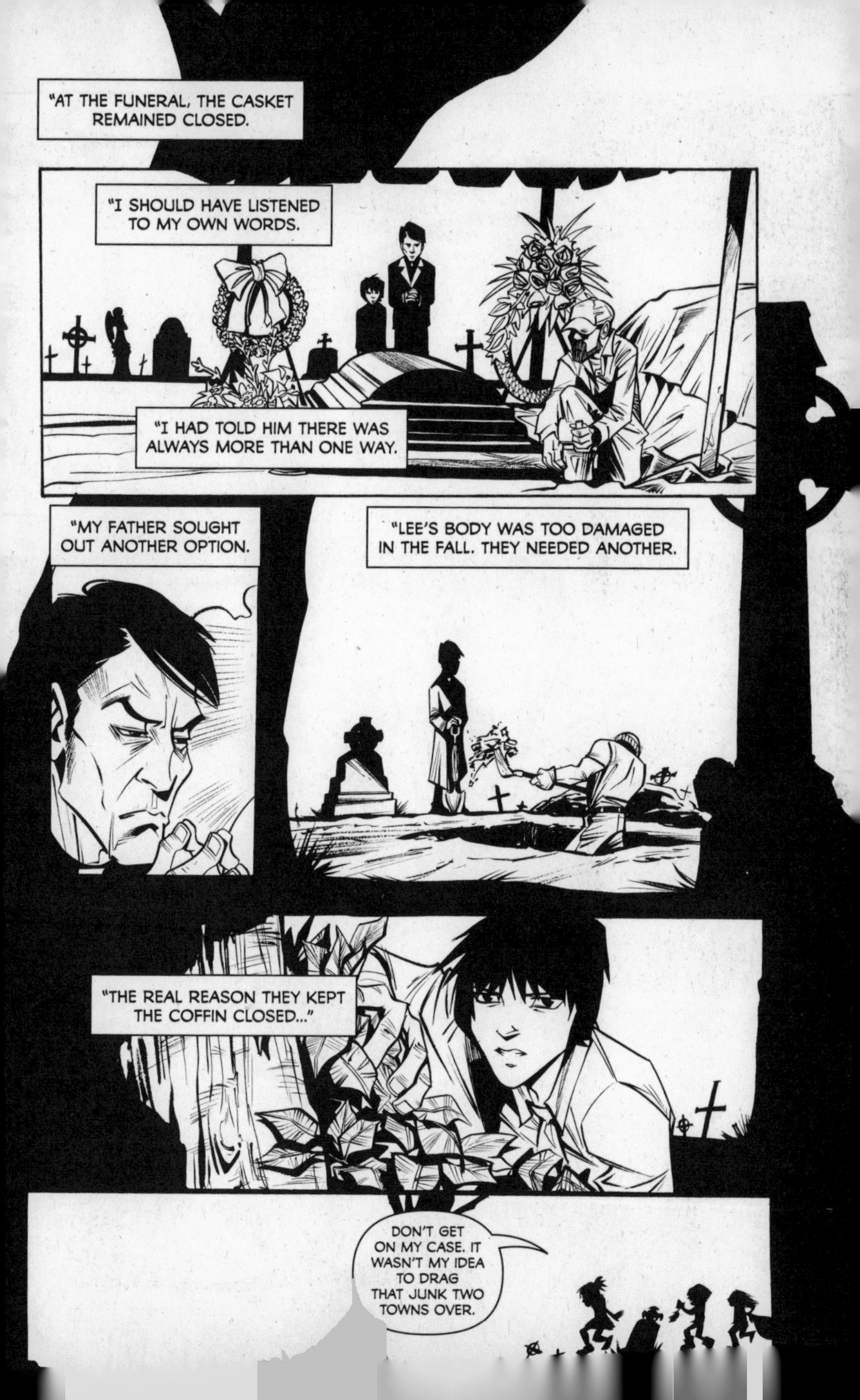
"AT THE FUNERAL, THE CASKET REMAINED CLOSED.
"I SHOULD HAVE LISTENED TO MY OWN WORDS.
"I HAD TOLD HIM THERE WAS ALWAYS MORE THAN ONE WAY.
"MY FATHER SOUGHT OUT ANOTHER OPTION.
"LEE'S BODY WAS TOO DAMAGED IN THE FALL. THEY NEEDED ANOTHER.
"THE REAL REASON THEY KEPT THE COFFIN CLOSED..."
DON'T GET ON MY CASE. IT WASN'T MY IDEA TO DRAG THAT JUNK TWO TOWNS OVER.

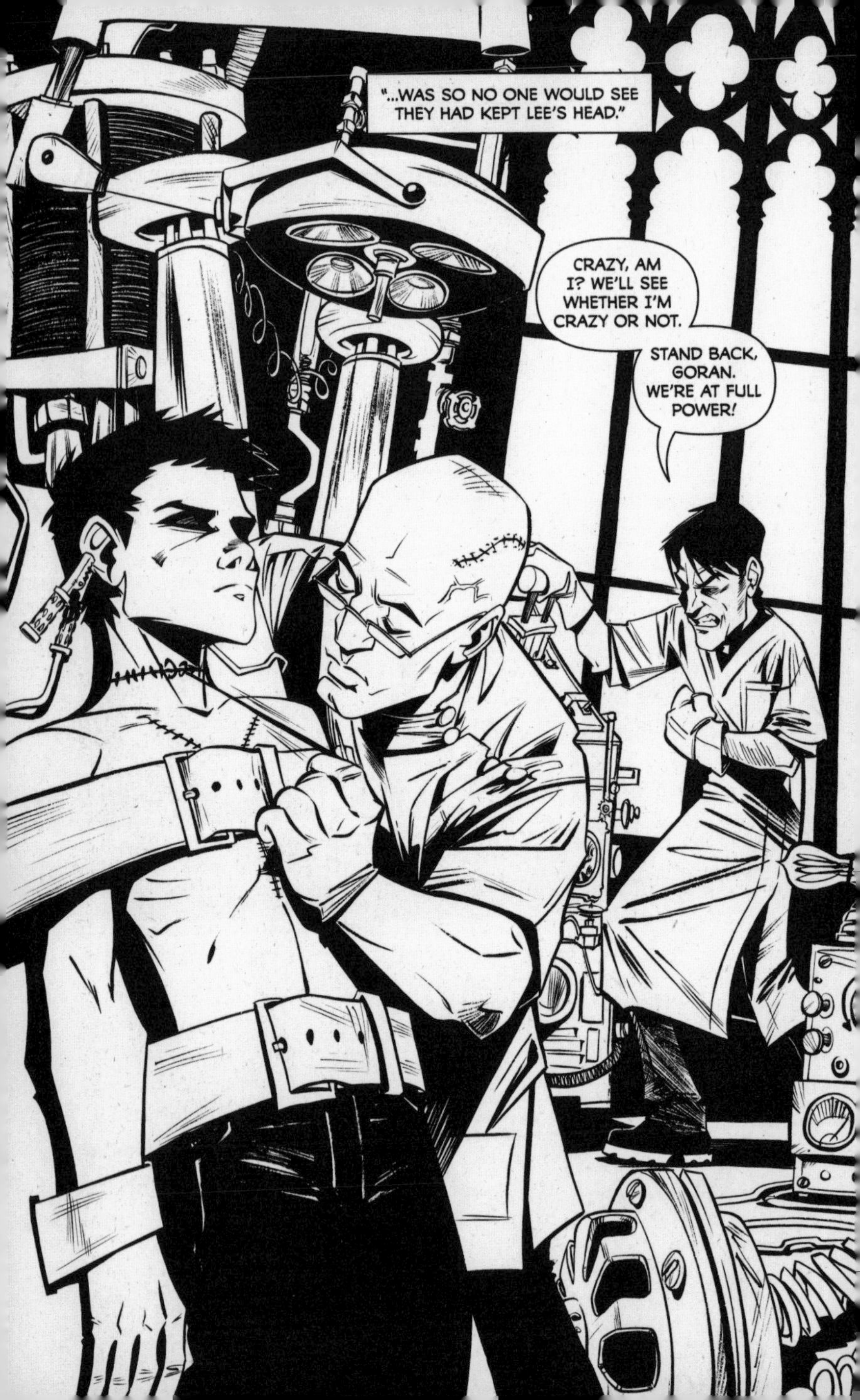
"...WAS SO NO ONE WOULD SEE THEY HAD KEPT LEE'S HEAD."
CRAZY, AM I? WE'LL SEE WHETHER I'M CRAZY OR NOT.
STAND BACK, GORAN. WE'RE AT FULL POWER!

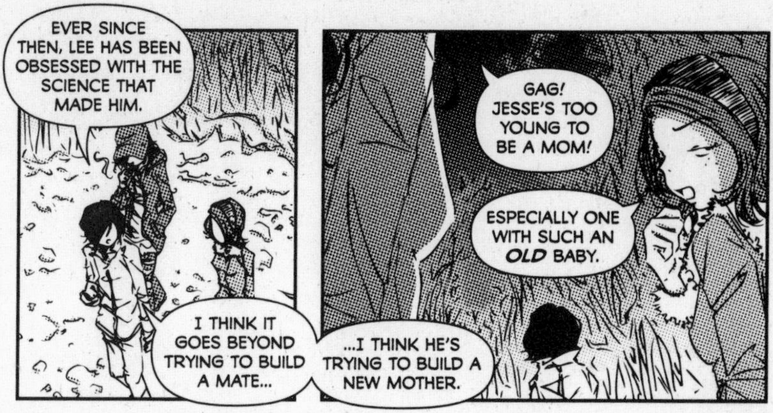
EVER SINCE THEN, LEE HAS BEEN OBSESSED WITH THE SCIENCE THAT MADE HIM.
I THINK IT GOES BEYOND TRYING TO BUILD A MATE...
...I THINK HE'S TRYING TO BUILD A NEW MOTHER.
GAG! JESSE'S TOO YOUNG TO BE A MOM!
ESPECIALLY ONE WITH SUCH AN *OLD* BABY.

"THERE'S NO TIME TO WASTE. WE HAVE TO STOP HIM BEFORE IT'S TOO LATE..."

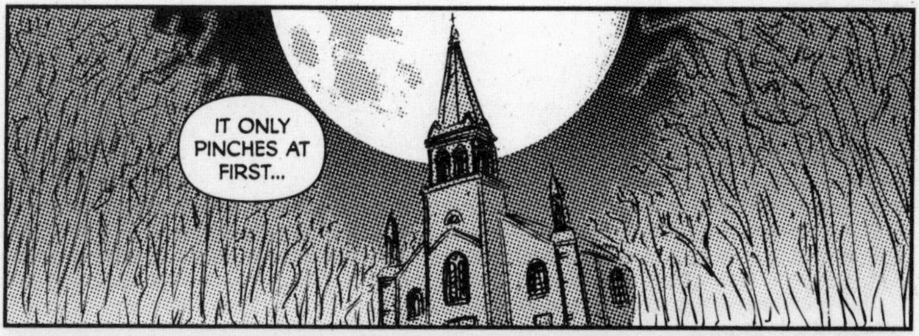
IT ONLY PINCHES AT FIRST...

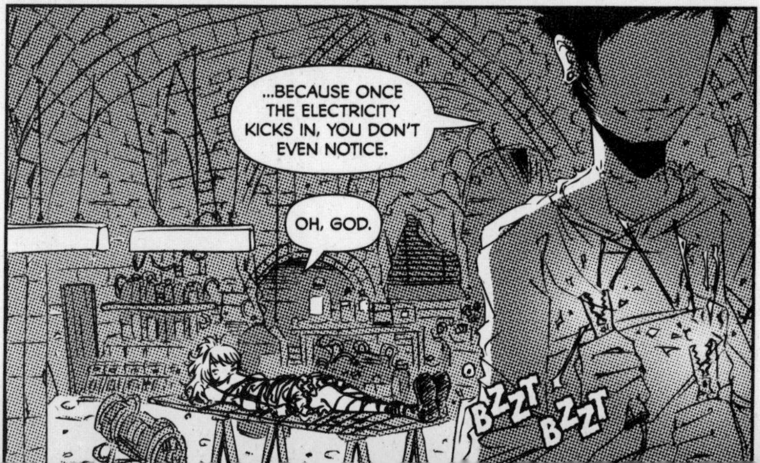
...BECAUSE ONCE THE ELECTRICITY KICKS IN, YOU DON'T EVEN NOTICE.
OH, GOD.
BZZT BZZT

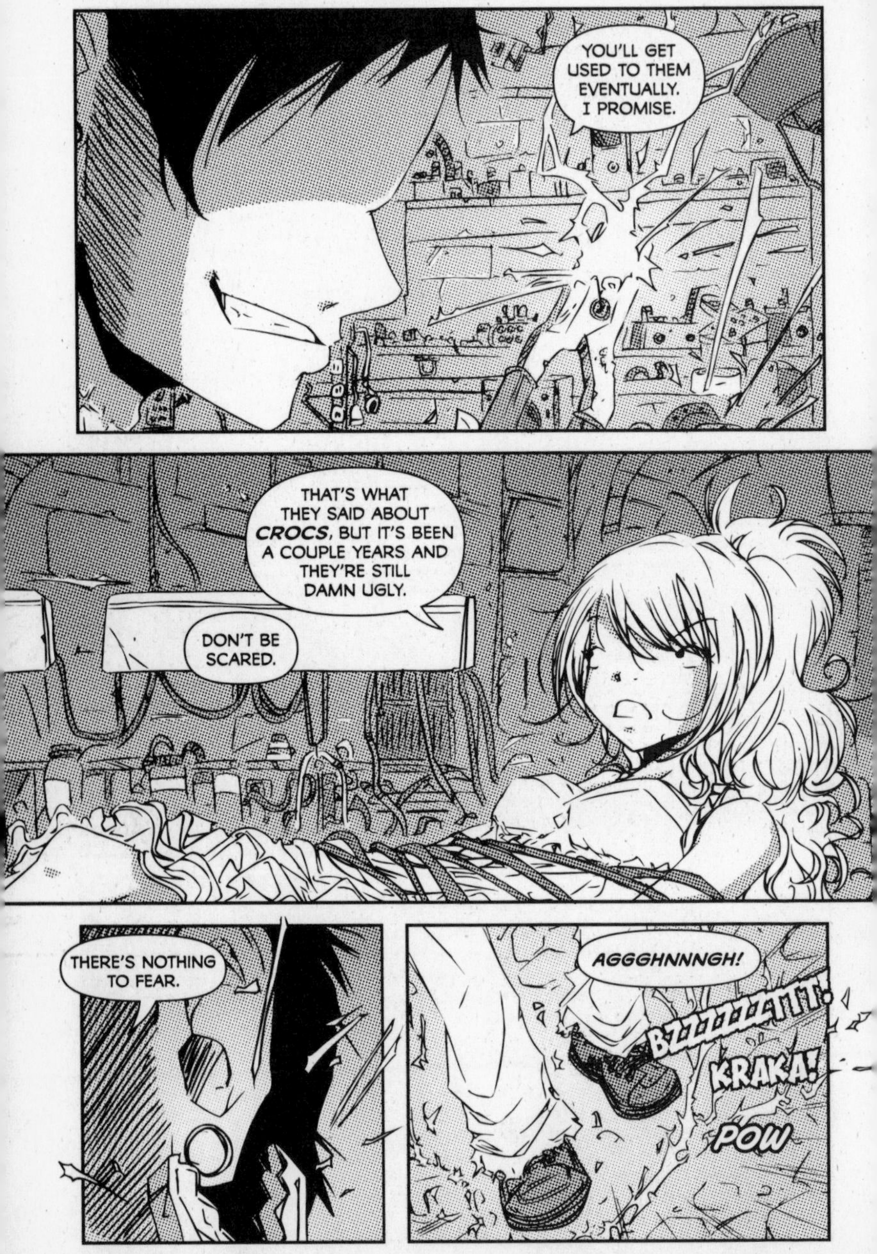
YOU'LL GET USED TO THEM EVENTUALLY. I PROMISE.
THAT'S WHAT THEY SAID ABOUT CROCS, BUT IT'S BEEN A COUPLE YEARS AND THEY'RE STILL DAMN UGLY.
DON'T BE SCARED.
THERE'S NOTHING TO FEAR.
AGGGHNNNGH!
BZZZZZZZTTTT!
KRAKA!
POW

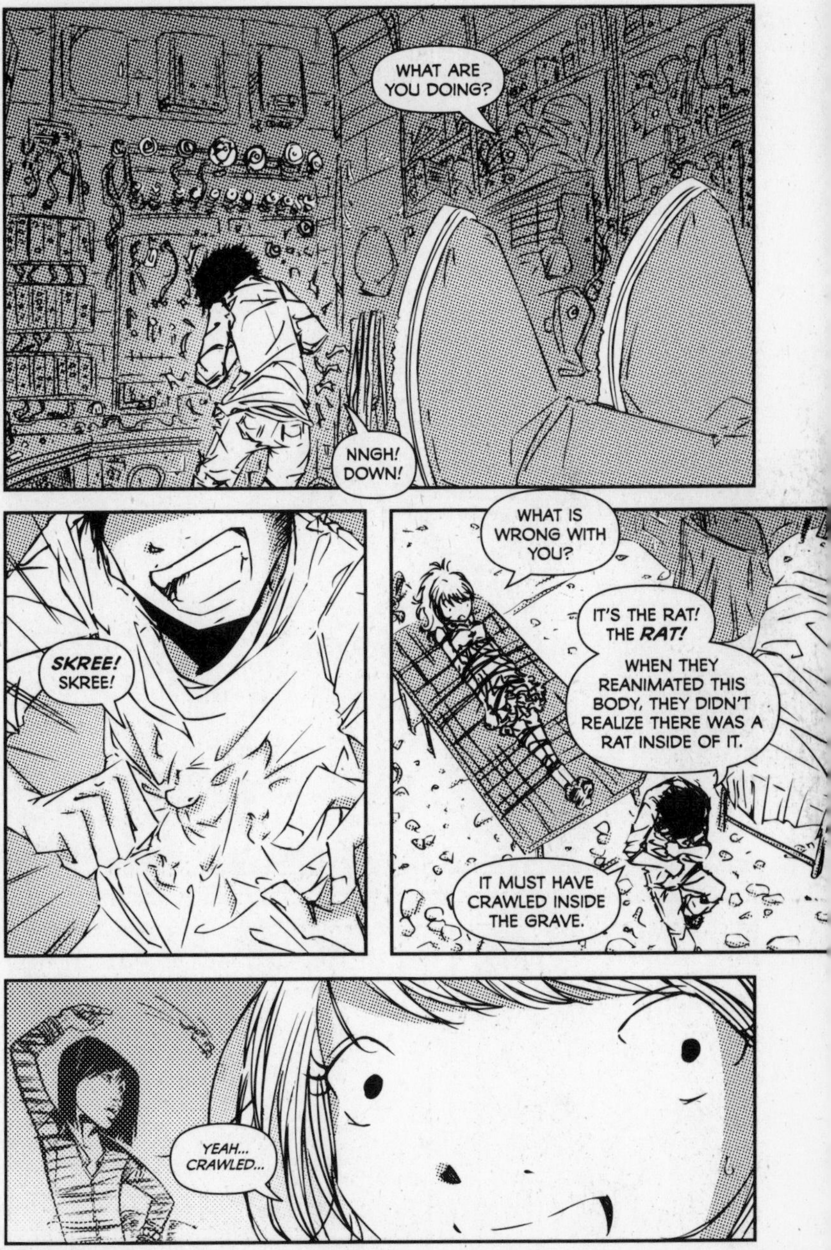
WHAT ARE YOU DOING?
NNGH! DOWN!
SKREE! SKREE!
WHAT IS WRONG WITH YOU?
IT'S THE RAT! THE RAT!
WHEN THEY REANIMATED THIS BODY, THEY DIDN'T REALIZE THERE WAS A RAT INSIDE OF IT.
IT MUST HAVE CRAWLED INSIDE THE GRAVE.
YEAH... CRAWLED...

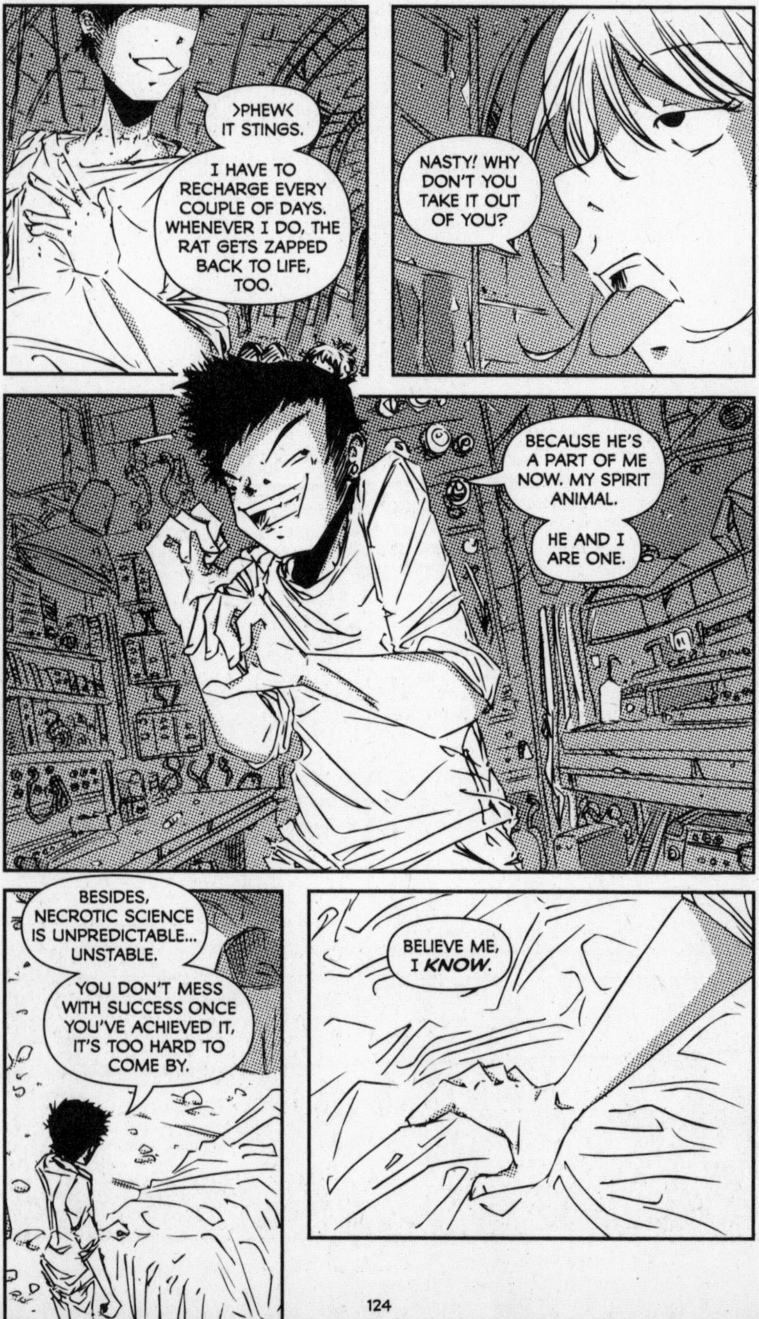
>PHEW< IT STINGS.
I HAVE TO RECHARGE EVERY COUPLE OF DAYS. WHENEVER I DO, THE RAT GETS ZAPPED BACK TO LIFE, TOO.
NASTY! WHY DON'T YOU TAKE IT OUT OF YOU?
BECAUSE HE'S A PART OF ME NOW. MY SPIRIT ANIMAL.
HE AND I ARE ONE.
BESIDES, NECROTIC SCIENCE IS UNPREDICTABLE... UNSTABLE.
YOU DON'T MESS WITH SUCCESS ONCE YOU'VE ACHIEVED IT, IT'S TOO HARD TO COME BY.
BELIEVE ME, I *KNOW*.

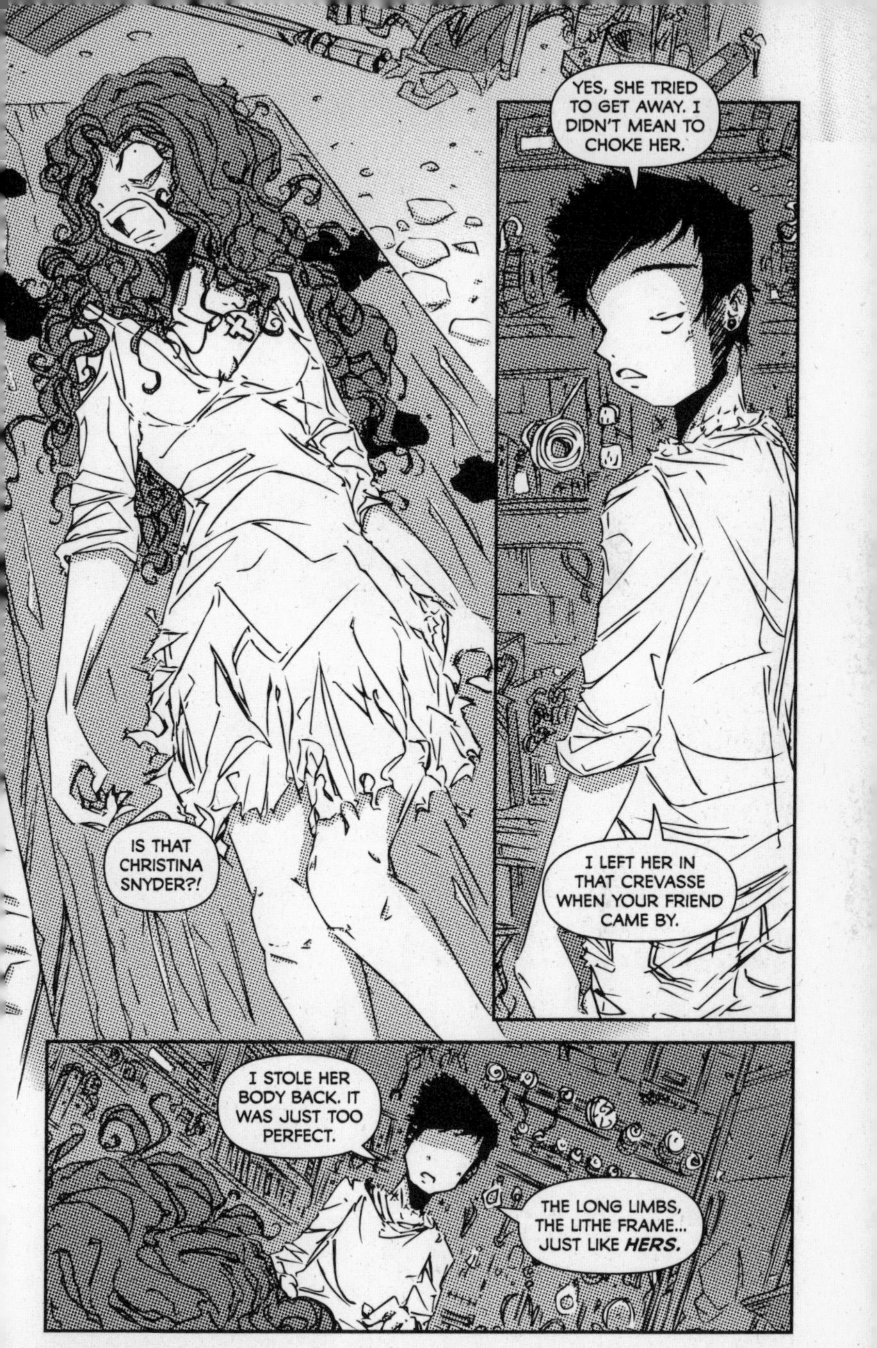
YES, SHE TRIED TO GET AWAY. I DIDN'T MEAN TO CHOKE HER.
IS THAT CHRISTINA SNYDER?!
I LEFT HER IN THAT CREVASSE WHEN YOUR FRIEND CAME BY.
I STOLE HER BODY BACK. IT WAS JUST TOO PERFECT.
THE LONG LIMBS, THE LITHE FRAME... JUST LIKE *HERS.*

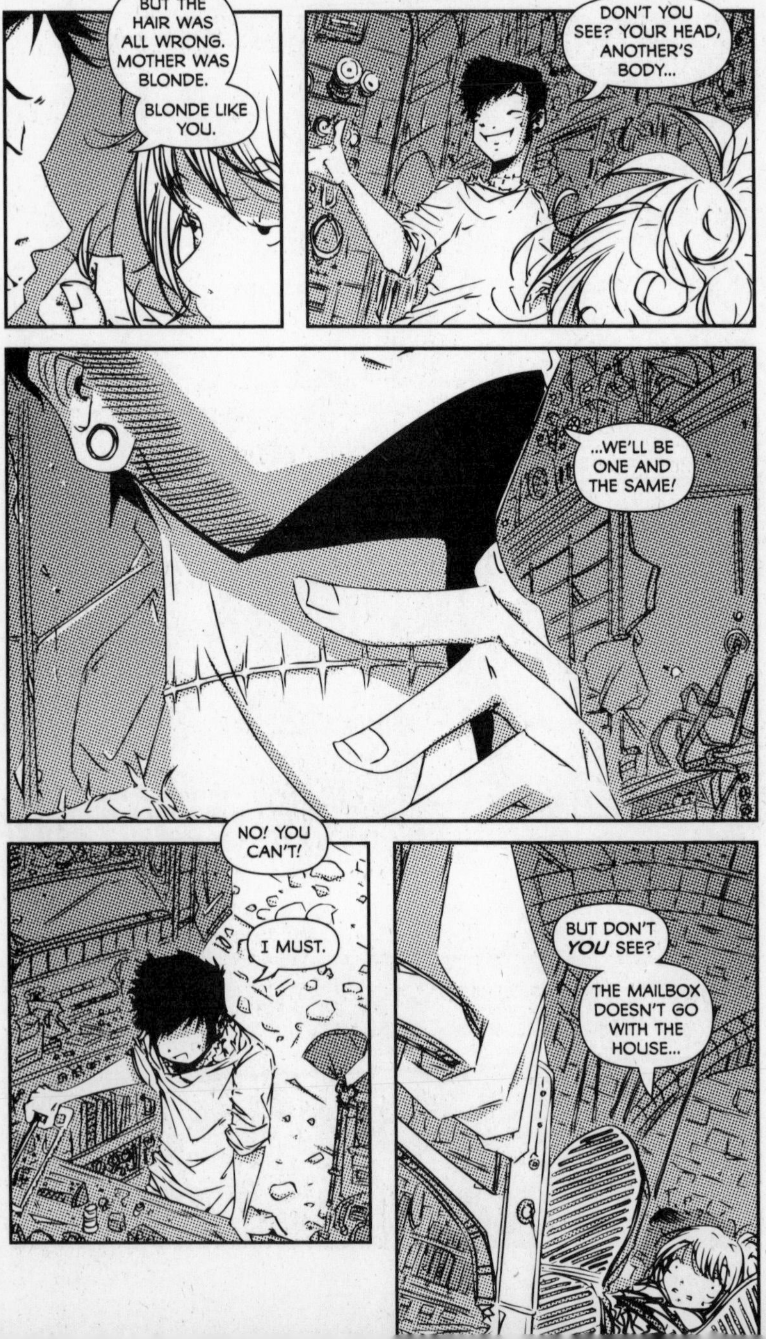
BUT THE HAIR WAS ALL WRONG. MOTHER WAS BLONDE.
BLONDE LIKE YOU.
DON'T YOU SEE? YOUR HEAD, ANOTHER'S BODY...
...WE'LL BE ONE AND THE SAME!
NO! YOU CAN'T!
I MUST.
BUT DON'T *YOU* SEE?
THE MAILBOX DOESN'T GO WITH THE HOUSE...

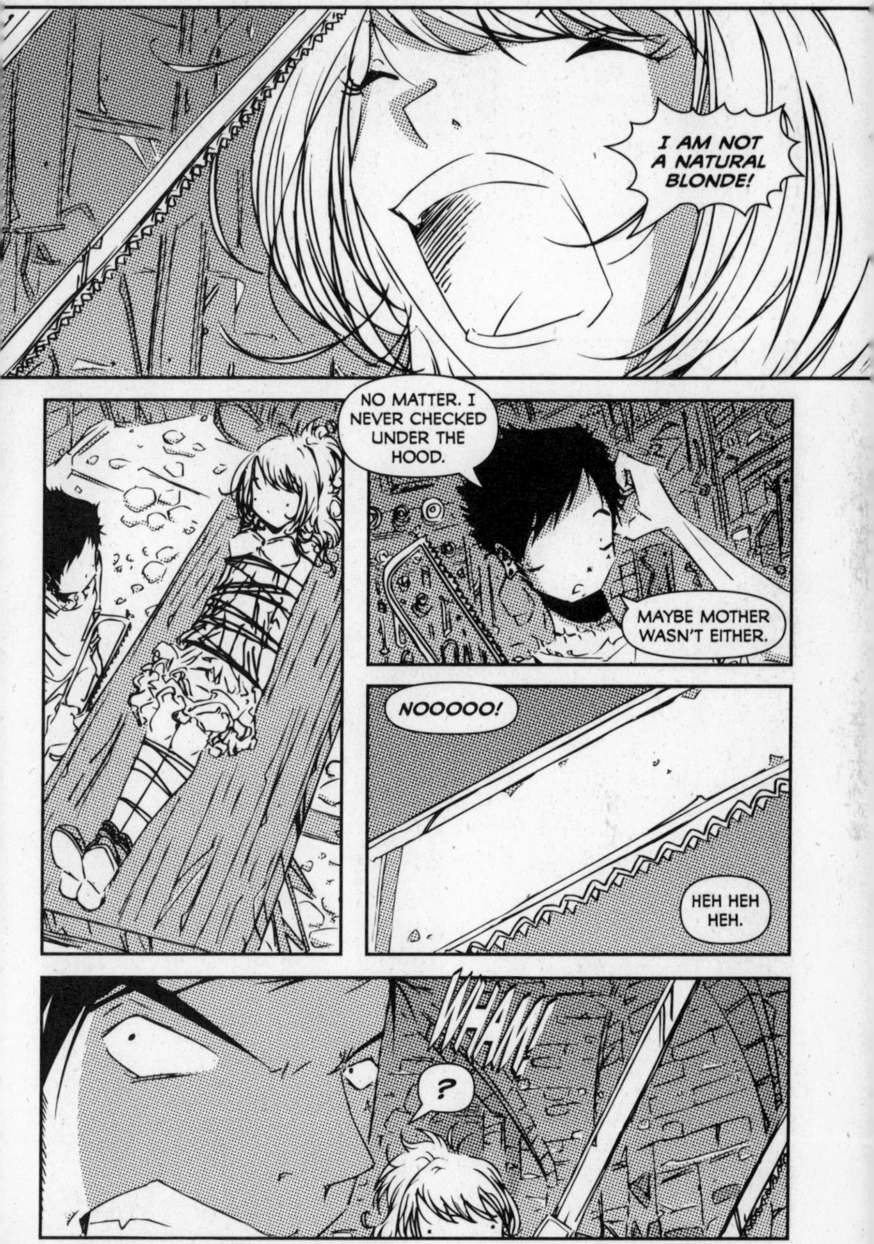
I AM NOT A NATURAL BLONDE!
NO MATTER. I NEVER CHECKED UNDER THE HOOD.
MAYBE MOTHER WASN'T EITHER.
NOOOOO!
HEH HEH HEH.
WHAM
?

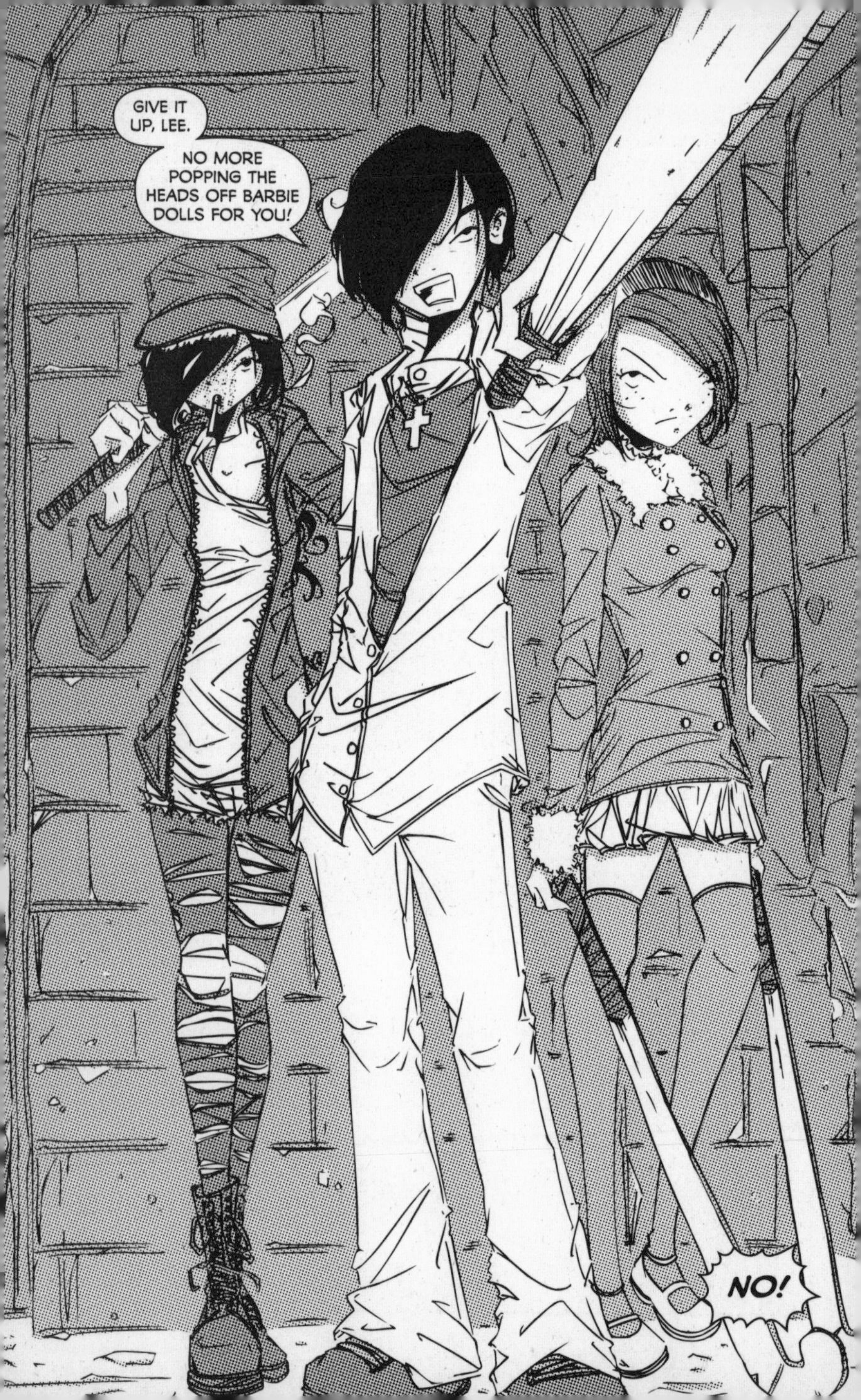
GIVE IT UP, LEE.
NO MORE POPPING THE HEADS OFF BARBIE DOLLS FOR YOU!
NO!

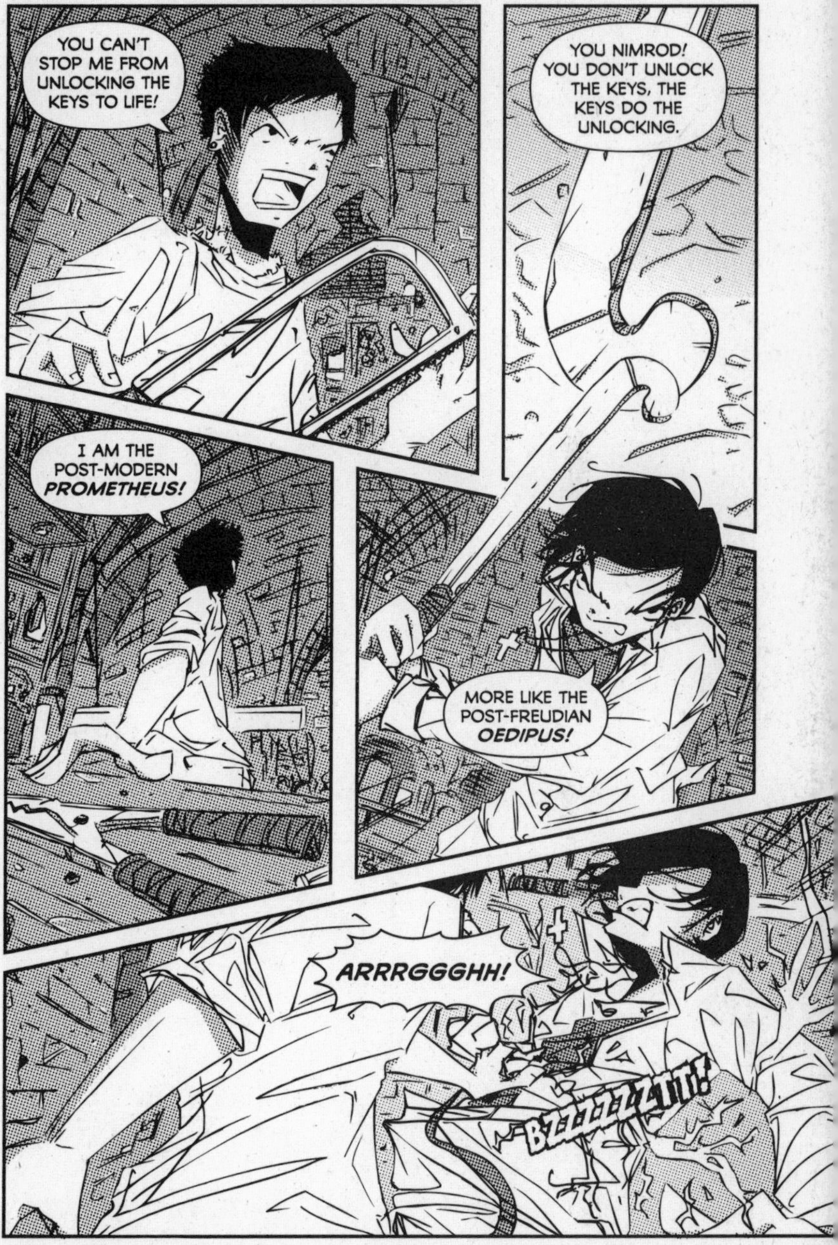
YOU CAN'T STOP ME FROM UNLOCKING THE KEYS TO LIFE!
YOU NIMROD! YOU DON'T UNLOCK THE KEYS, THE KEYS DO THE UNLOCKING.
I AM THE POST-MODERN *PROMETHEUS!*
MORE LIKE THE POST-FREUDIAN *OEDIPUS!*
ARRRGGGHH!
BZZZZZZZTTT!

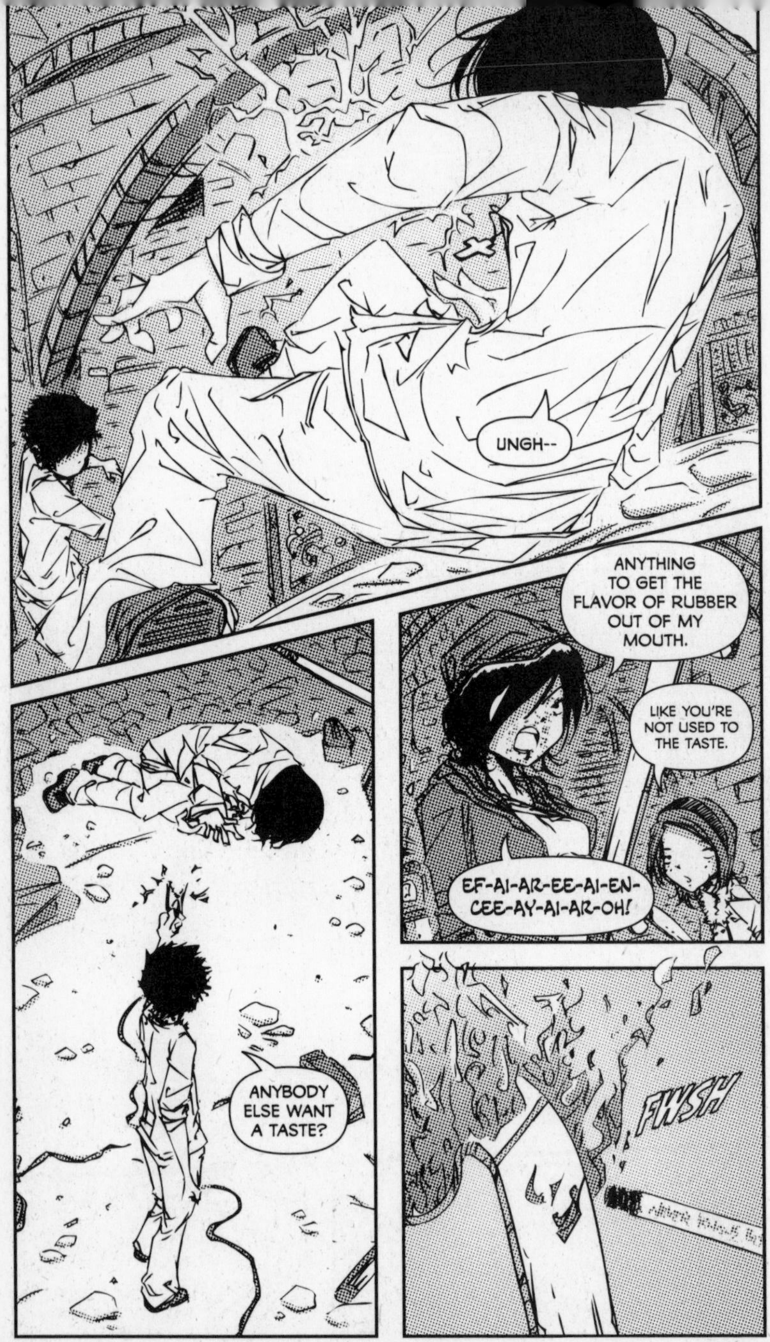
UNGH--
ANYTHING TO GET THE FLAVOR OF RUBBER OUT OF MY MOUTH.
LIKE YOU'RE NOT USED TO THE TASTE.
EF-AI-AR-EE-AI-EN-CEE-AY-AI-AR-OH!
ANYBODY ELSE WANT A TASTE?
FWSH

JOKE FOR THE GOTH KIDS.

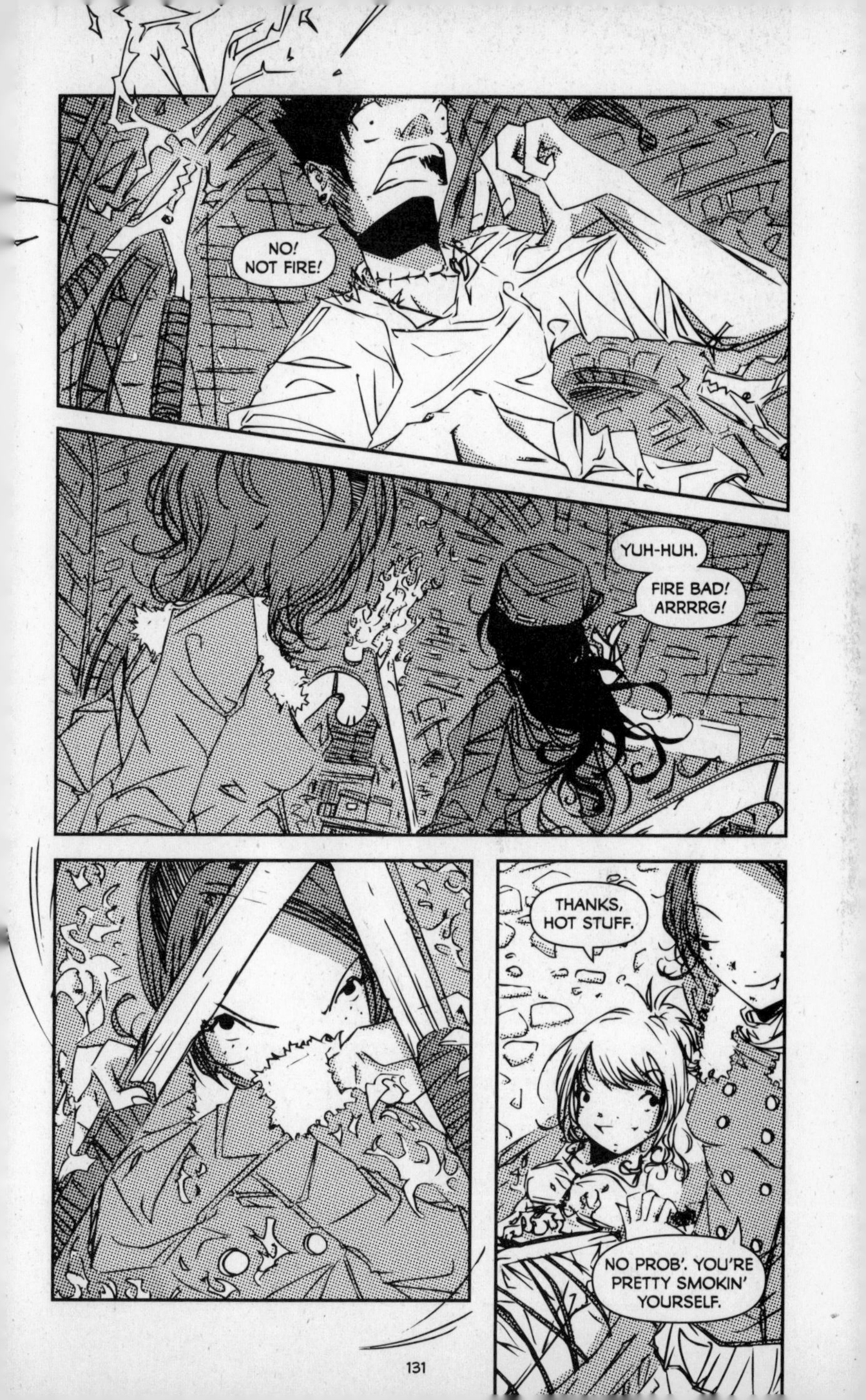
NO!
NOT FIRE!
YUH-HUH.
FIRE BAD!
ARRRRG!
THANKS,
HOT STUFF.
NO PROB'. YOU'RE
PRETTY SMOKIN'
YOURSELF.

TURNS OUT I ***WOULD*** POKE YOU WITH A STICK, DEAD BOY.
IT JUST HAS TO BE ON FIRE FIRST.
I'LL SHOW YOU GIRLS.
I'LL SHOW YOU WHAT YOU'RE MADE OF...
...SHOW YOU WHAT I CAN MAKE OUT OF YOU.
YOUR ARMS, HER FEET...
...THE OTHER ONE'S BUTT--
POP
SZZL

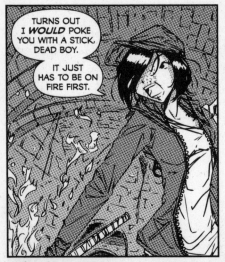

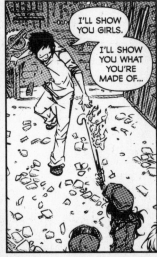

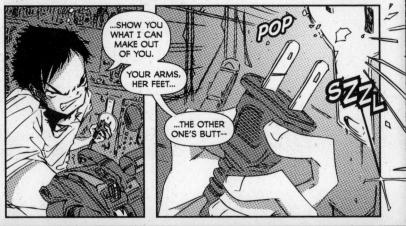

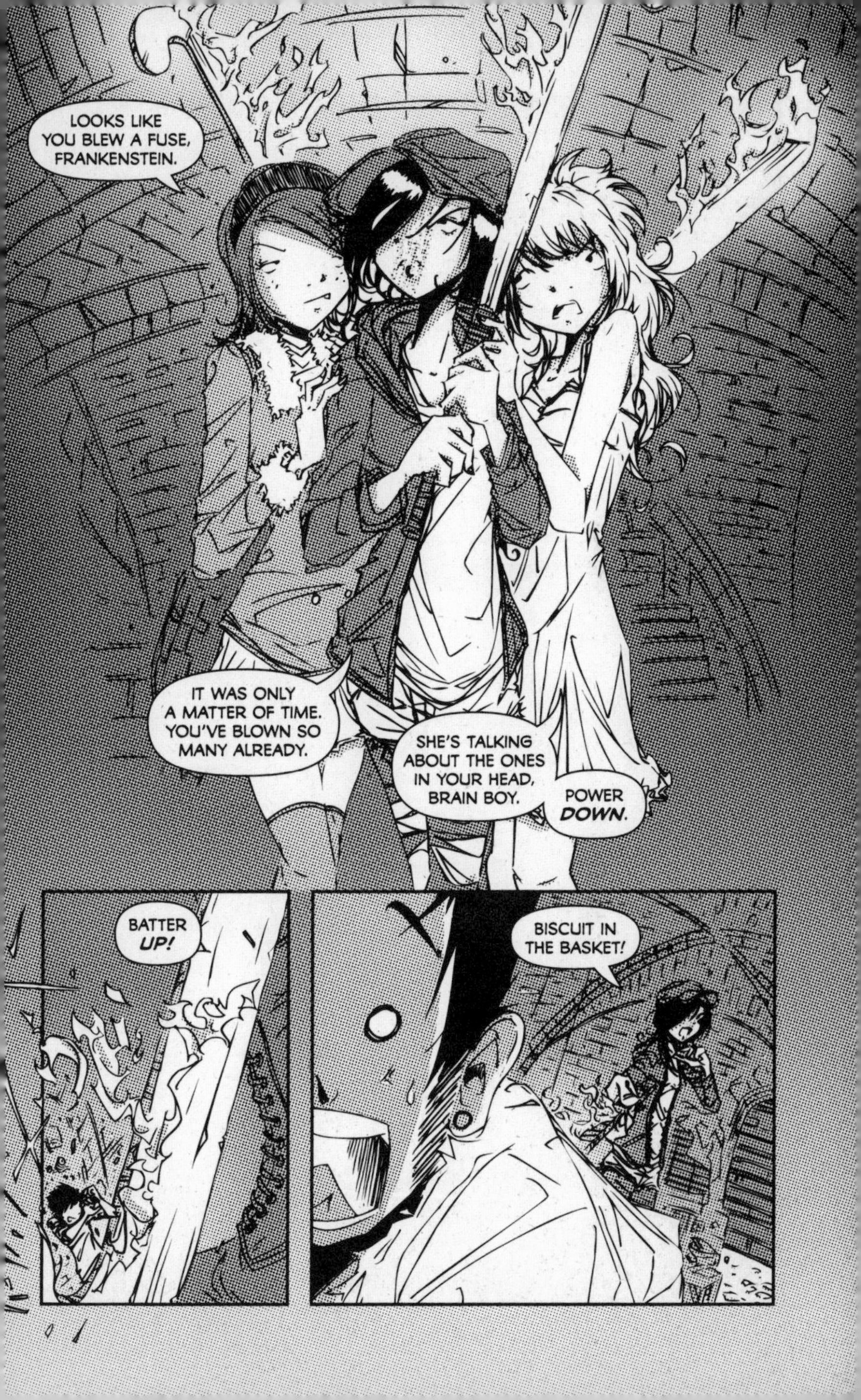
LOOKS LIKE YOU BLEW A FUSE, FRANKENSTEIN.
IT WAS ONLY A MATTER OF TIME. YOU'VE BLOWN SO MANY ALREADY.
SHE'S TALKING ABOUT THE ONES IN YOUR HEAD, BRAIN BOY.
POWER *DOWN*.
BATTER *UP!*
BISCUIT IN THE BASKET!

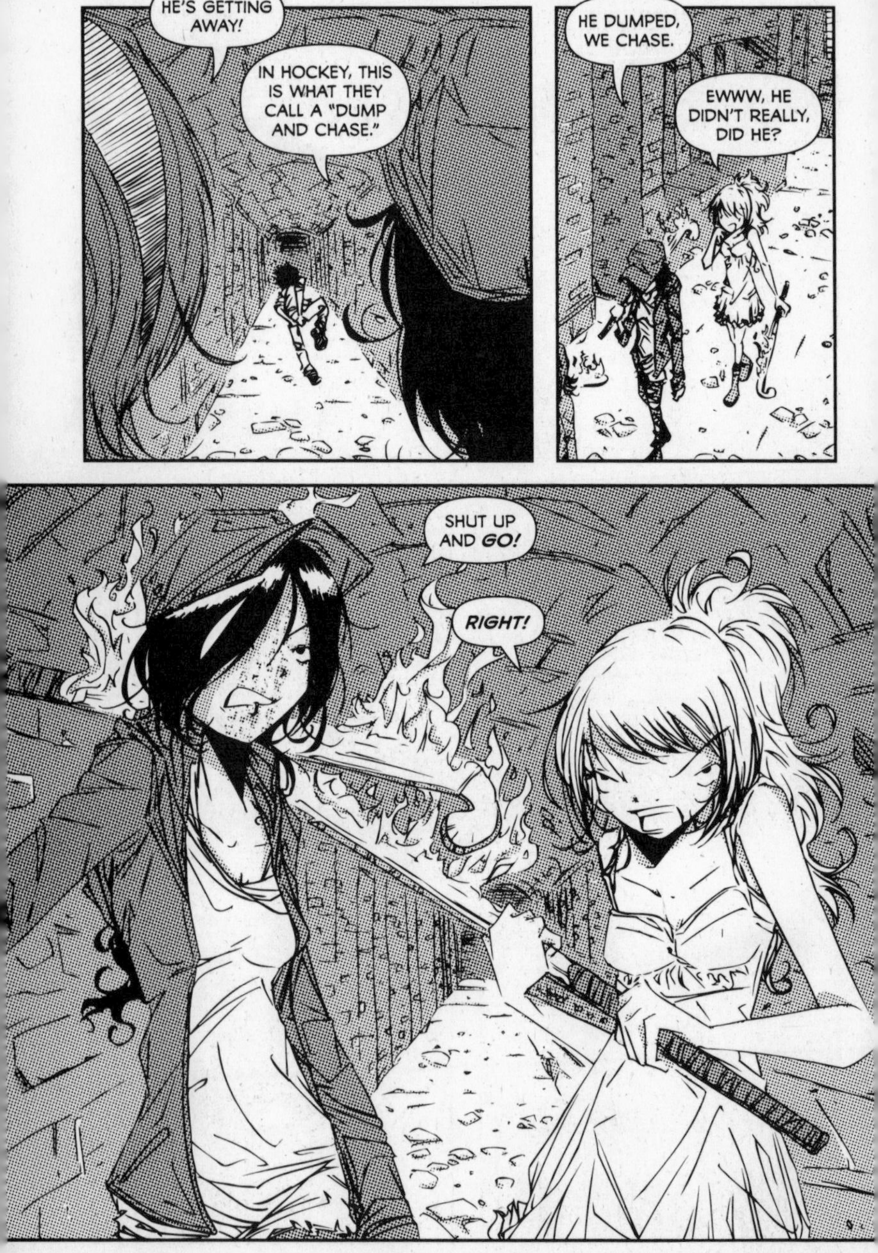
HE'S GETTING AWAY!
IN HOCKEY, THIS IS WHAT THEY CALL A "DUMP AND CHASE."
HE DUMPED, WE CHASE.
EWWW, HE DIDN'T REALLY, DID HE?
SHUT UP AND GO!
RIGHT!

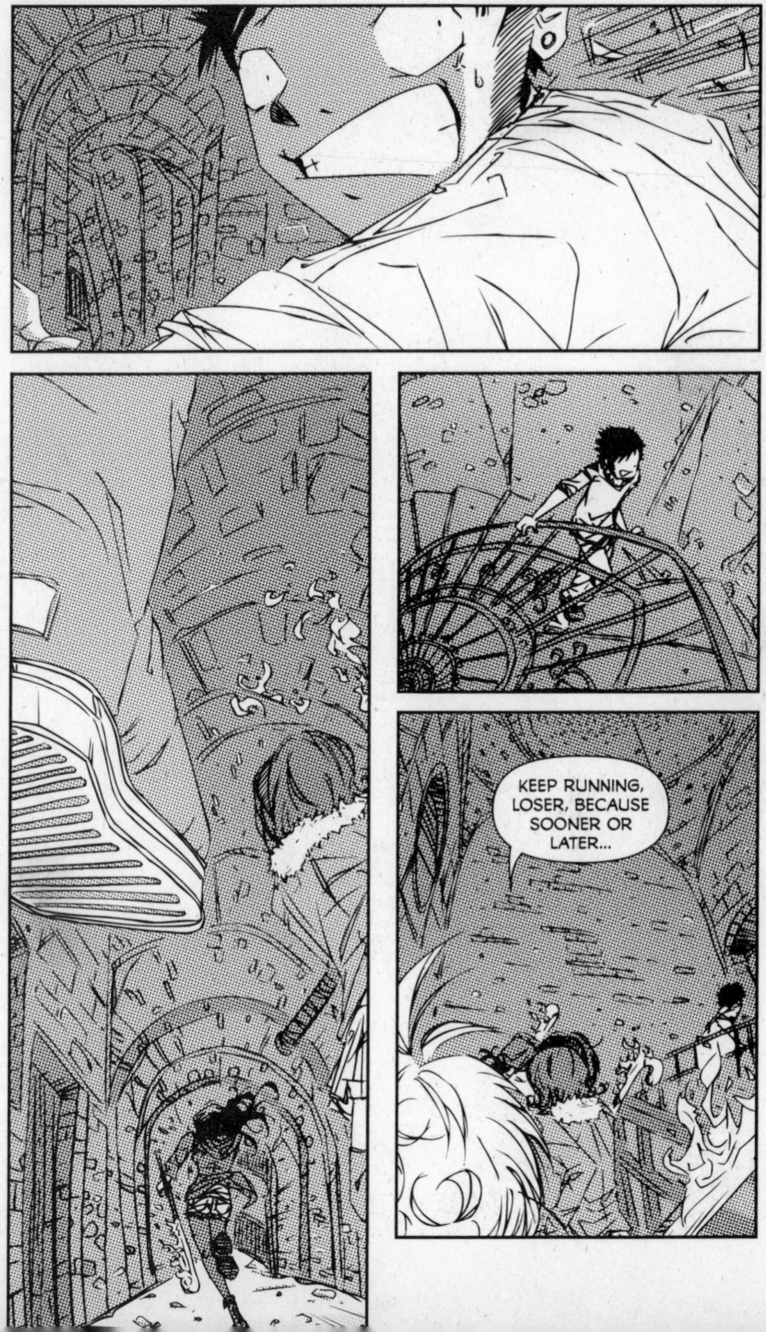
KEEP RUNNING, LOSER, BECAUSE SOONER OR LATER...

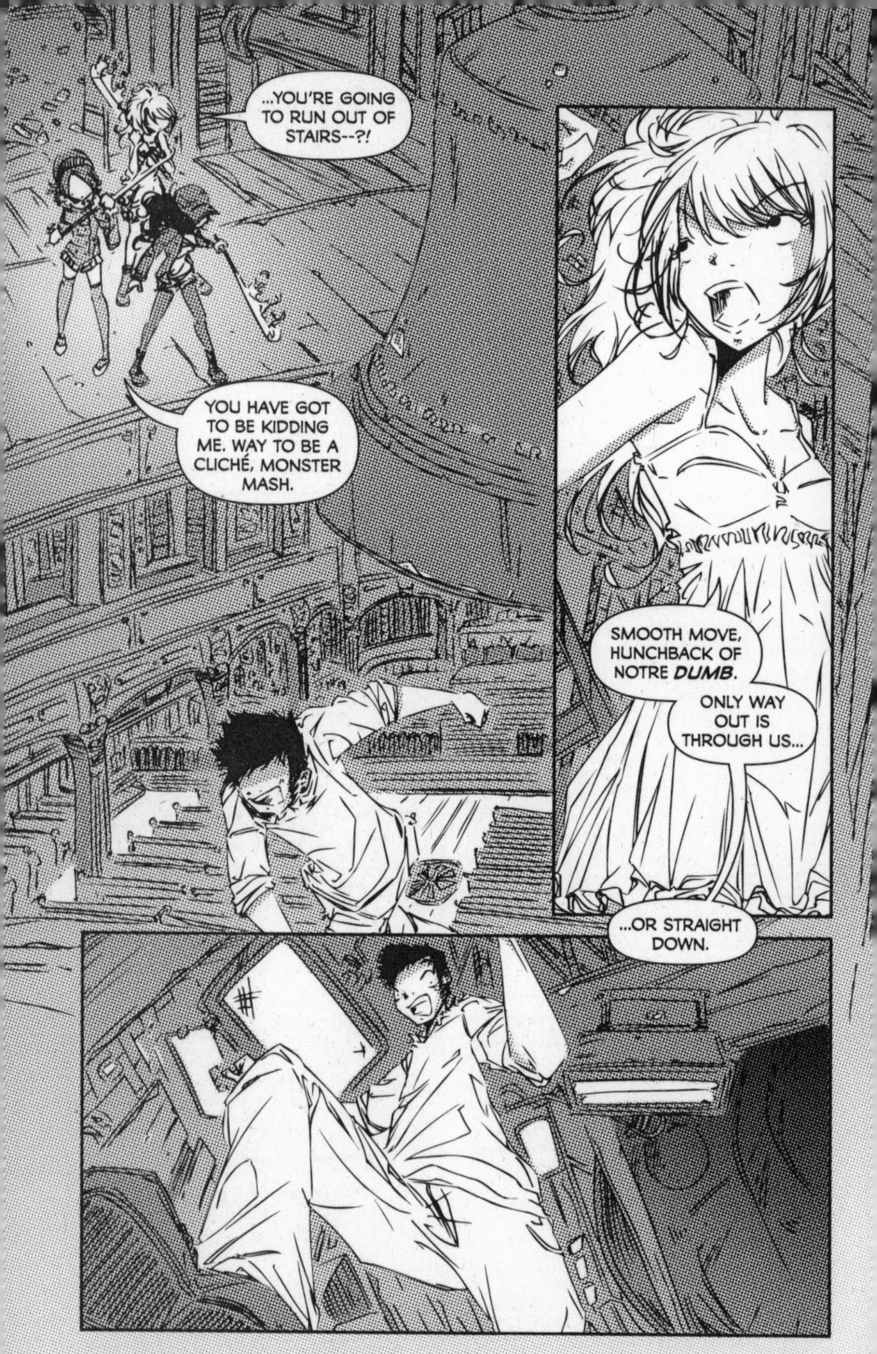
...YOU'RE GOING TO RUN OUT OF STAIRS--?!
YOU HAVE GOT TO BE KIDDING ME. WAY TO BE A CLICHÉ, MONSTER MASH.
SMOOTH MOVE, HUNCHBACK OF NOTRE DUMB.
ONLY WAY OUT IS THROUGH US...
...OR STRAIGHT DOWN.

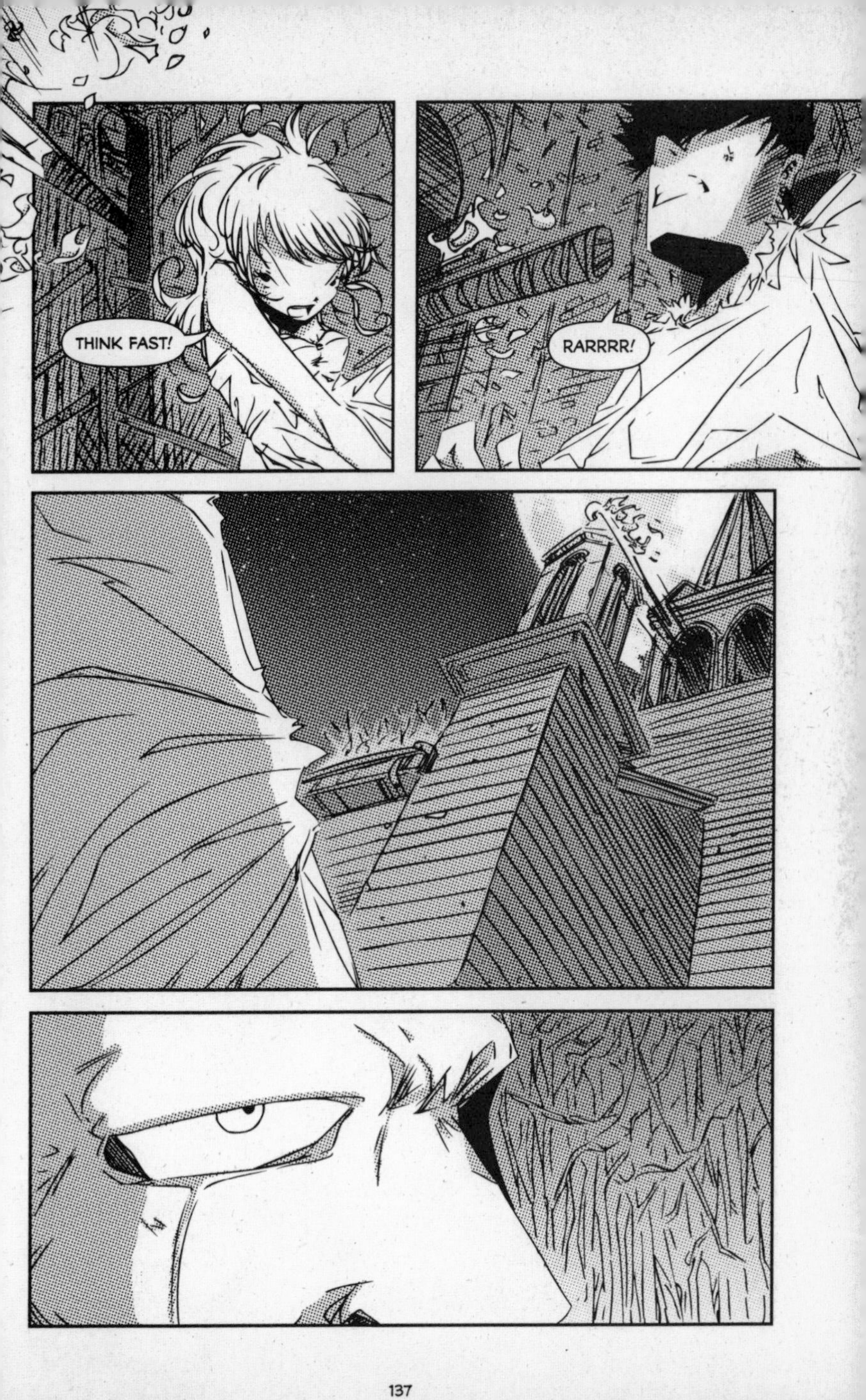
THINK FAST!
RARRRR!

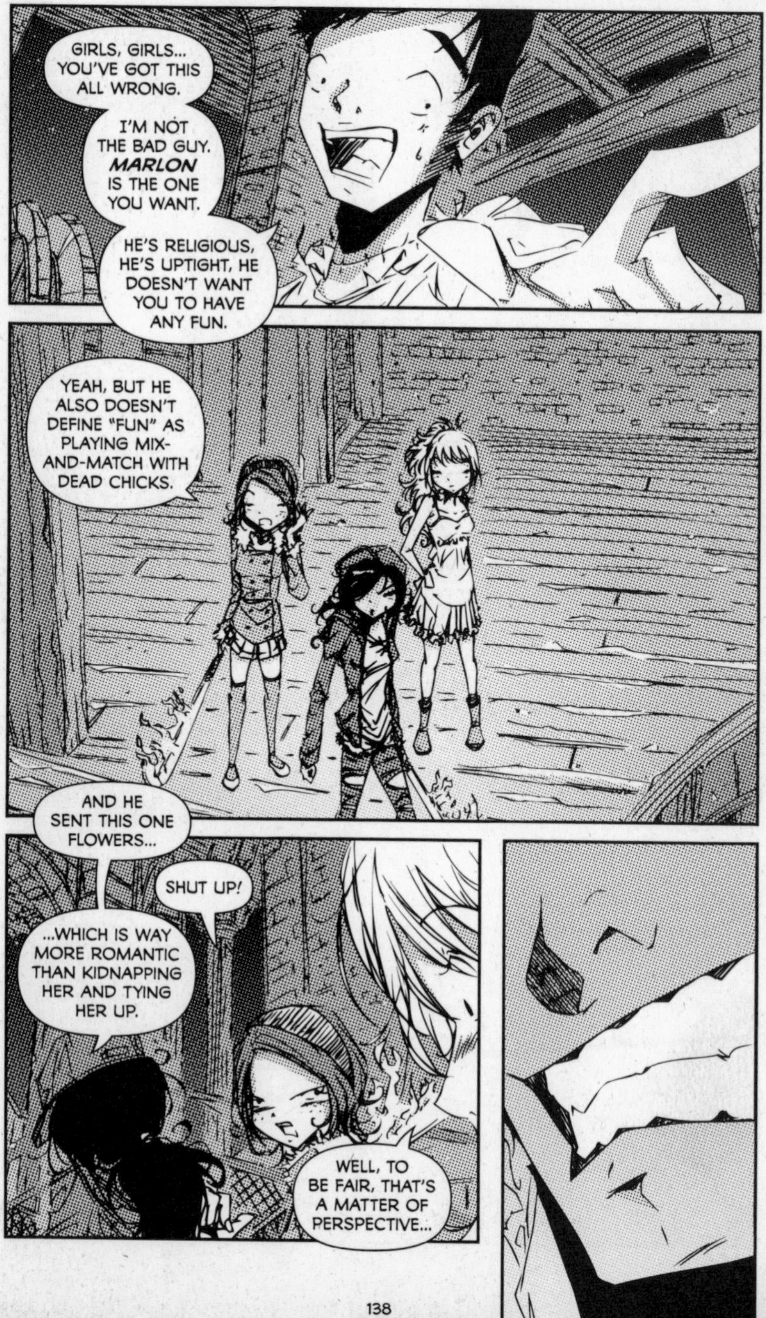
GIRLS, GIRLS... YOU'VE GOT THIS ALL WRONG.
I'M NOT THE BAD GUY. *MARLON* IS THE ONE YOU WANT.
HE'S RELIGIOUS, HE'S UPTIGHT, HE DOESN'T WANT YOU TO HAVE ANY FUN.
YEAH, BUT HE ALSO DOESN'T DEFINE "FUN" AS PLAYING MIX-AND-MATCH WITH DEAD CHICKS.
AND HE SENT THIS ONE FLOWERS...
SHUT UP!
...WHICH IS WAY MORE ROMANTIC THAN KIDNAPPING HER AND TYING HER UP.
WELL, TO BE FAIR, THAT'S A MATTER OF PERSPECTIVE...

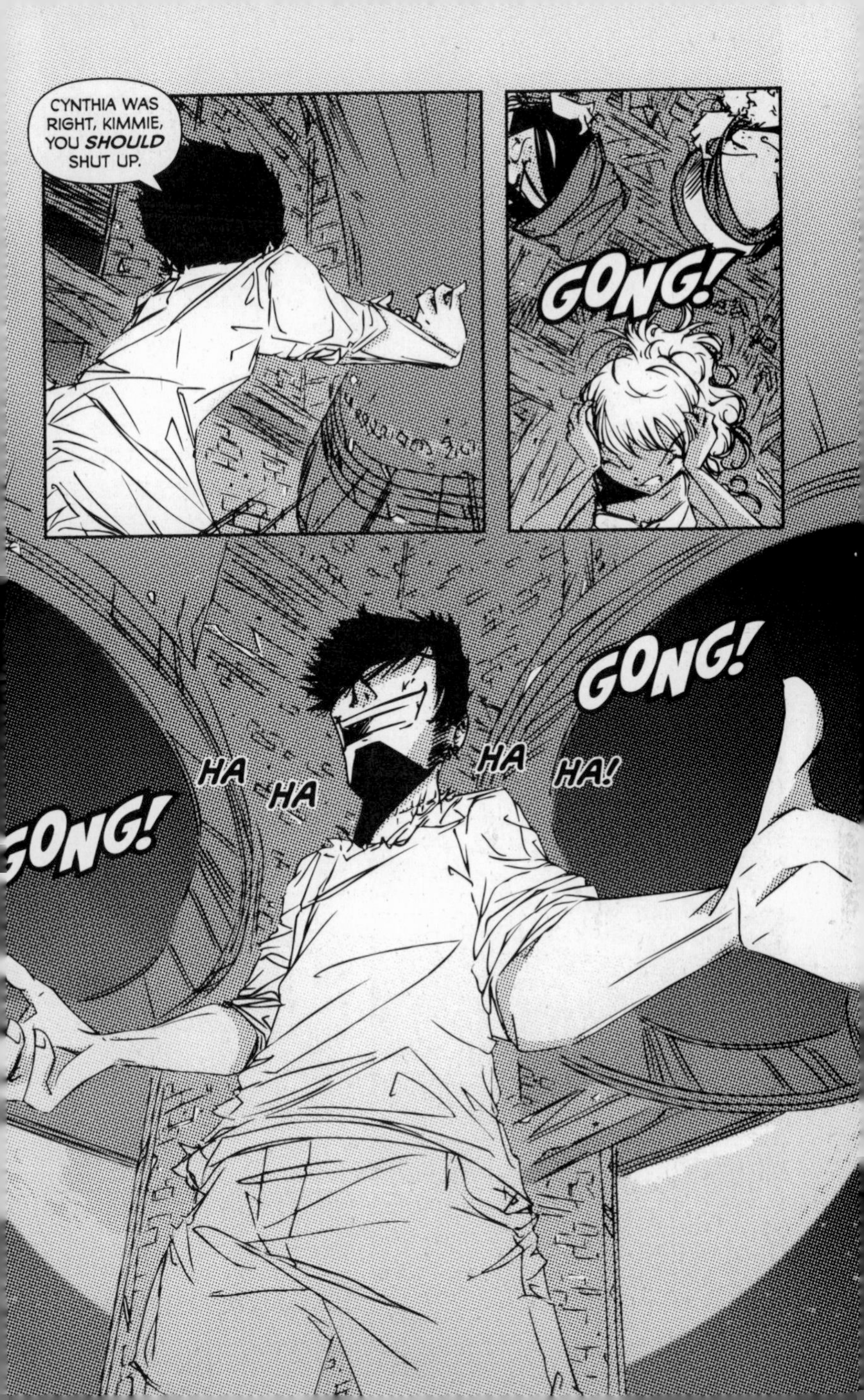
CYNTHIA WAS RIGHT, KIMMIE, YOU *SHOULD* SHUT UP.
GONG!
GONG!
HA HA HA HA!
GONG!

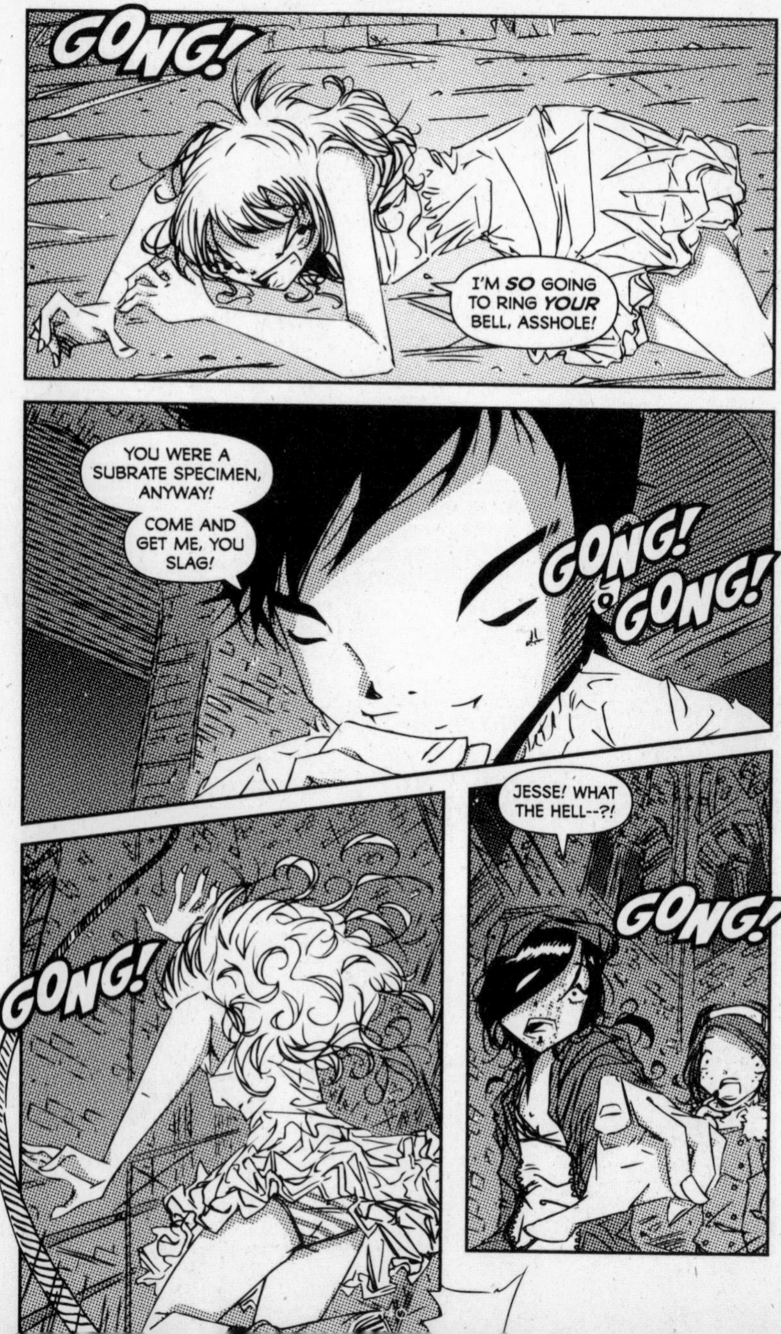
GONG!
I'M SO GOING TO RING YOUR BELL, ASSHOLE!
YOU WERE A SUBRATE SPECIMEN, ANYWAY!
COME AND GET ME, YOU SLAG!
GONG! GONG!
GONG!
JESSE! WHAT THE HELL--?!
GONG!

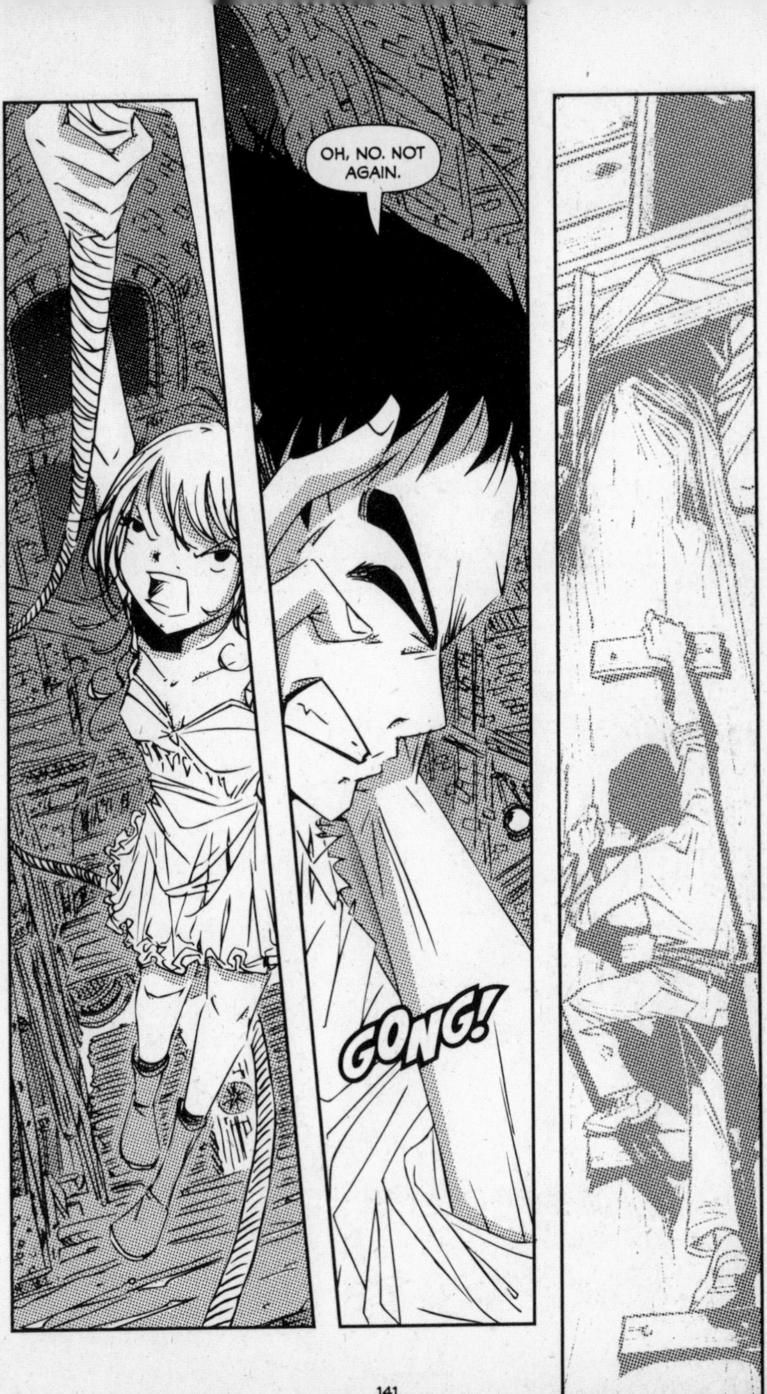
OH, NO. NOT AGAIN.
GONG!

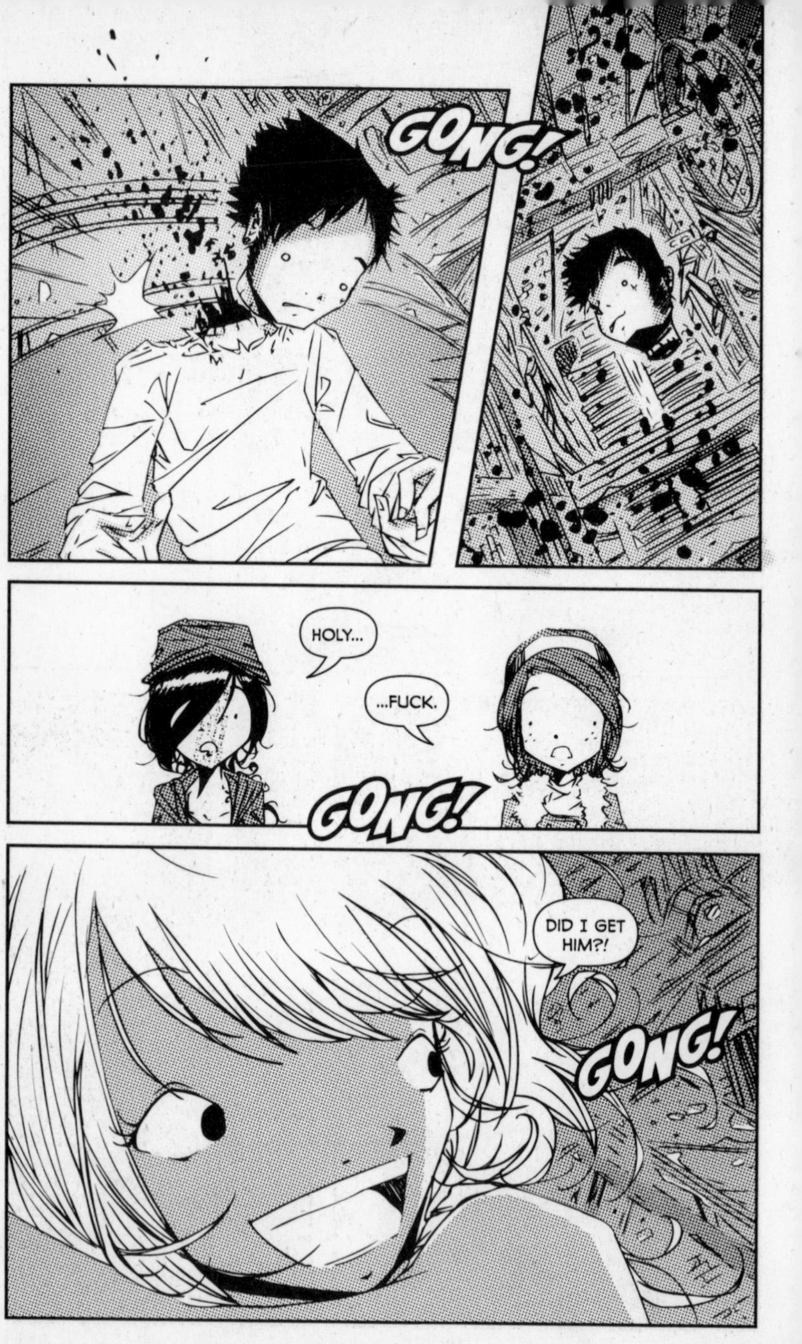
GONG!
HOLY...
...FUCK.
GONG!
DID I GET HIM?!
GONG!

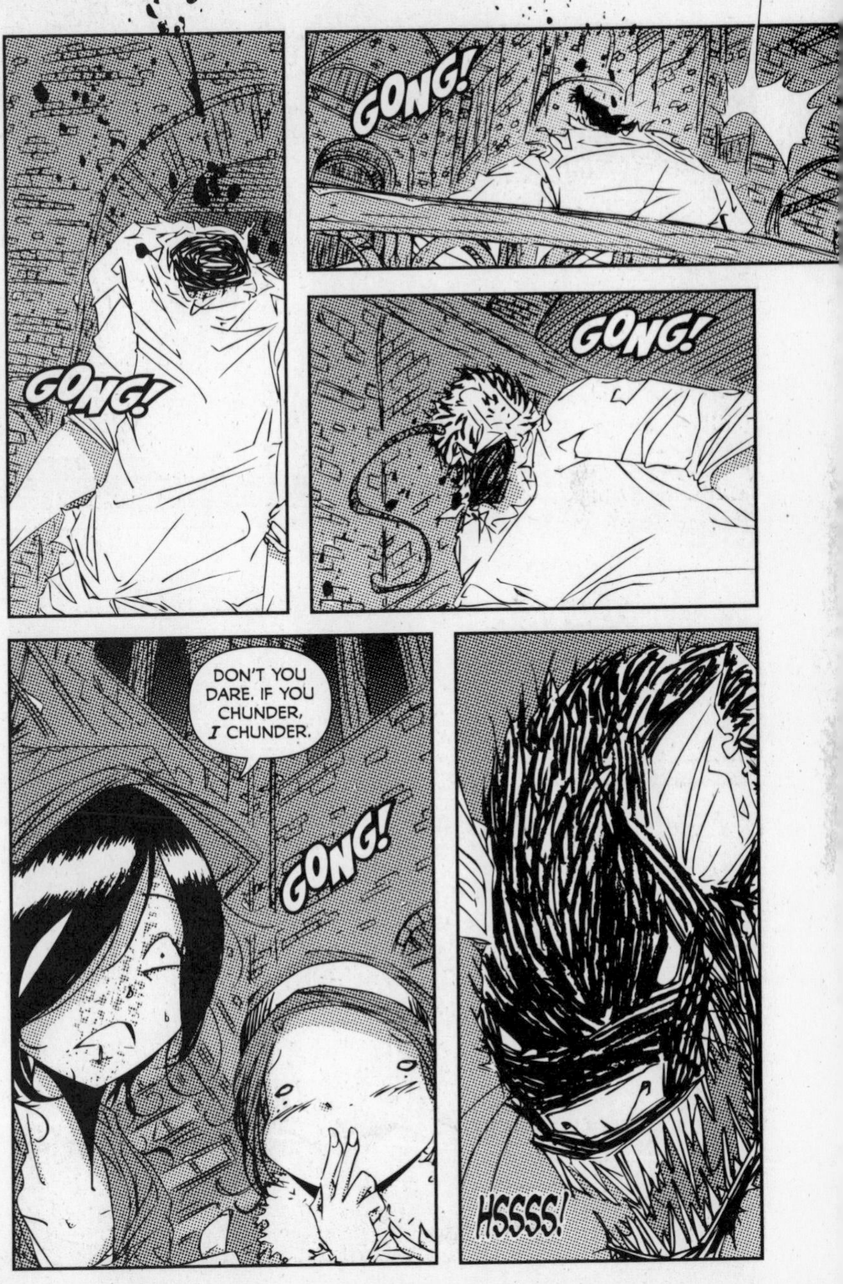
GONG!
GONG!
GONG!
DON'T YOU DARE. IF YOU CHUNDER, I CHUNDER.
GONG!
HSSSS!

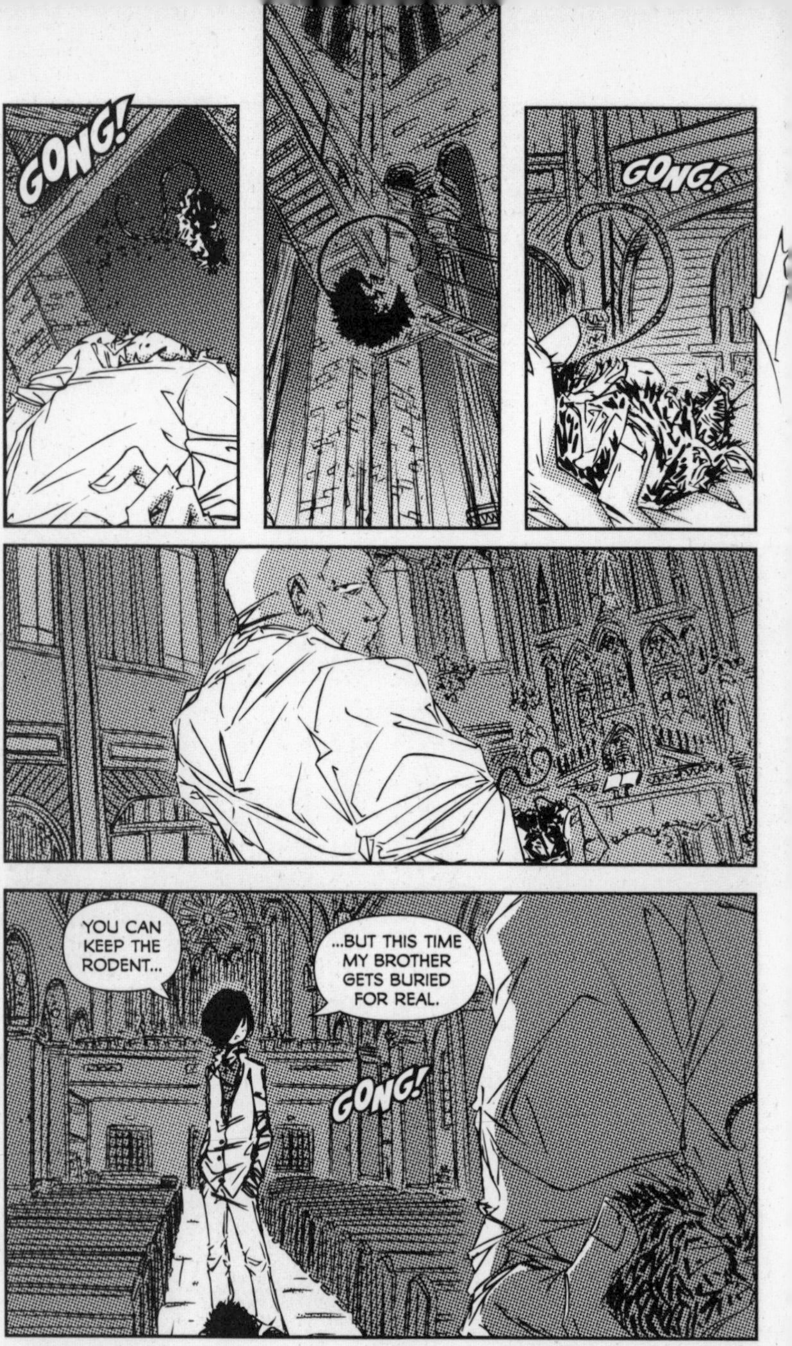
GONG!
GONG!
YOU CAN KEEP THE RODENT...
...BUT THIS TIME MY BROTHER GETS BURIED FOR REAL.
GONG!

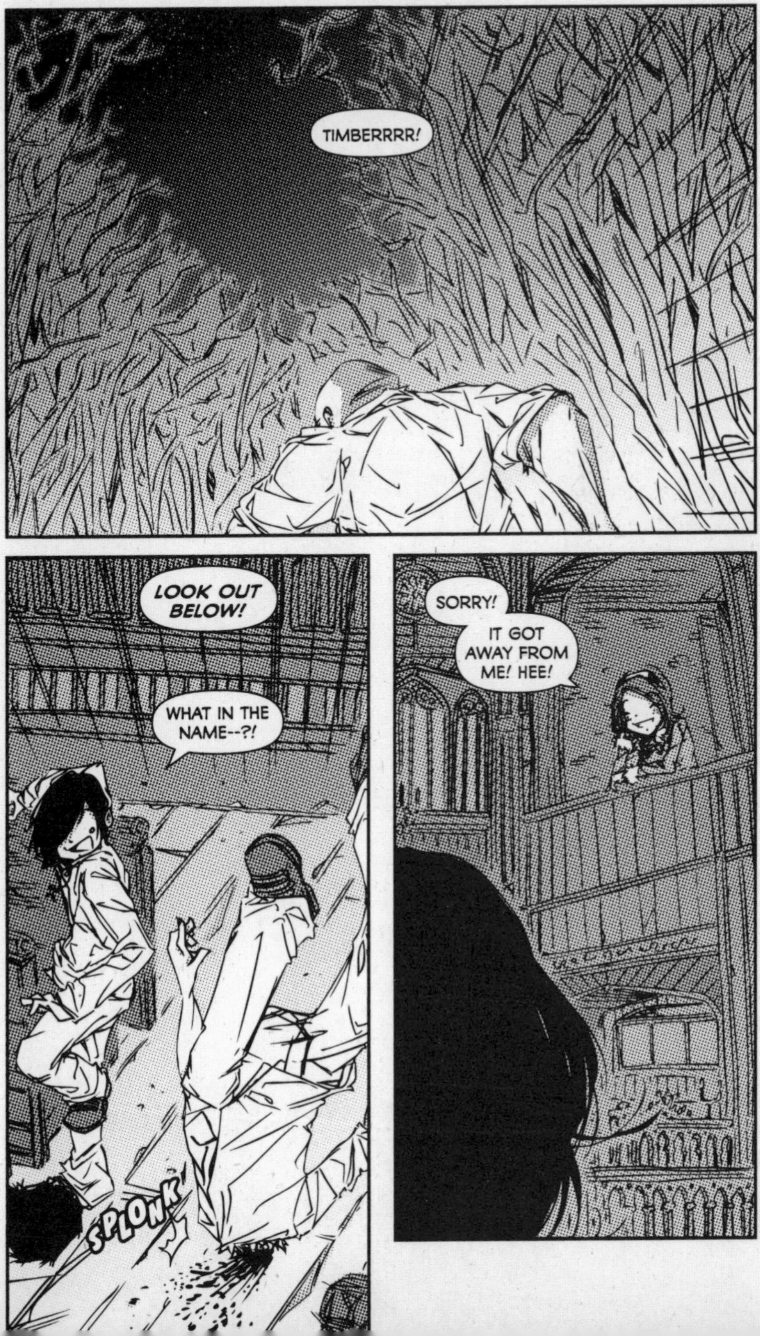
TIMBERRRR!
LOOK OUT BELOW!
WHAT IN THE NAME--?!
SPLONK
SORRY!
IT GOT AWAY FROM ME! HEE!

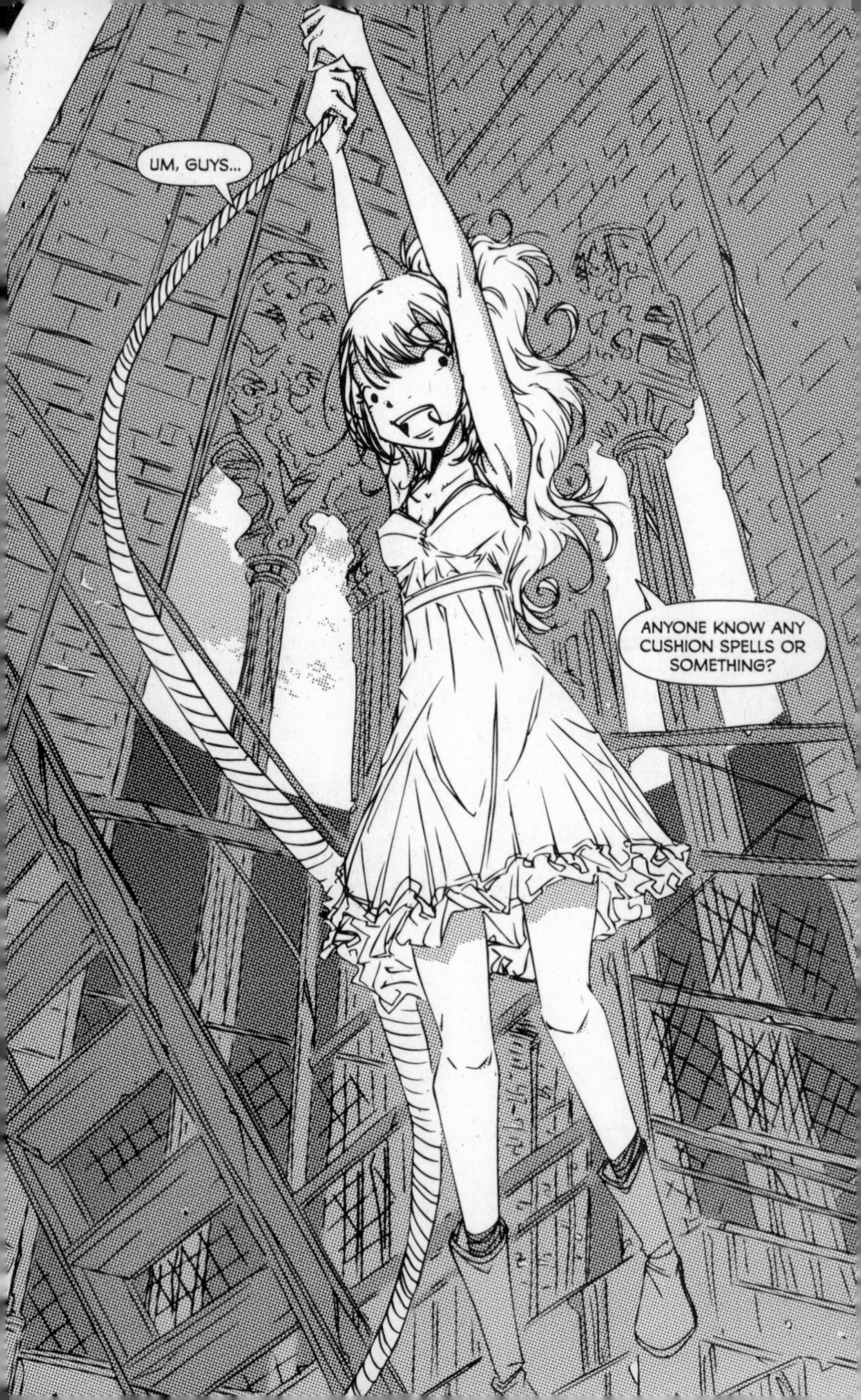
UM, GUYS...
ANYONE KNOW ANY CUSHION SPELLS OR SOMETHING?

Epilogue
"Back to the Start"

I

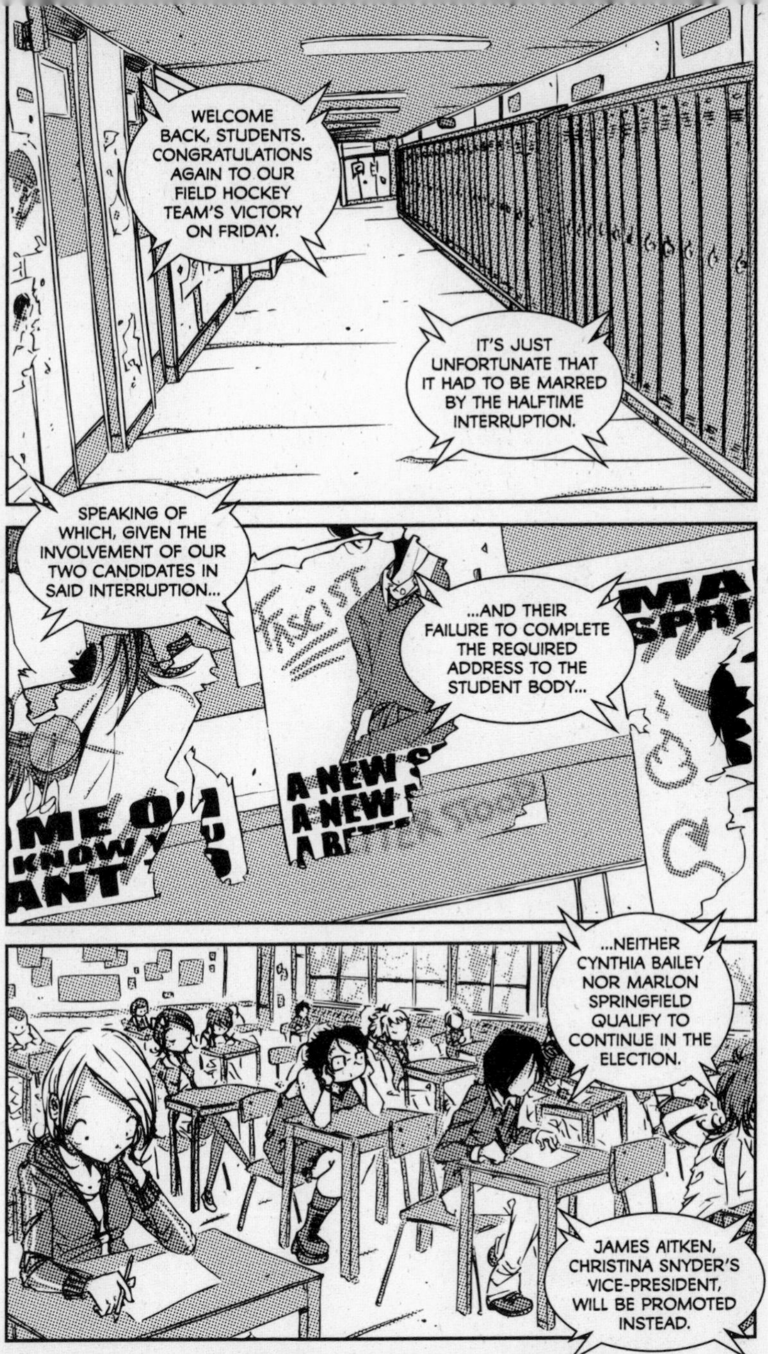
WELCOME BACK, STUDENTS. CONGRATULATIONS AGAIN TO OUR FIELD HOCKEY TEAM'S VICTORY ON FRIDAY.
IT'S JUST UNFORTUNATE THAT IT HAD TO BE MARRED BY THE HALFTIME INTERRUPTION.
SPEAKING OF WHICH, GIVEN THE INVOLVEMENT OF OUR TWO CANDIDATES IN SAID INTERRUPTION...
...AND THEIR FAILURE TO COMPLETE THE REQUIRED ADDRESS TO THE STUDENT BODY...
FASCIST
...NEITHER CYNTHIA BAILEY NOR MARLON SPRINGFIELD QUALIFY TO CONTINUE IN THE ELECTION.
JAMES AITKEN, CHRISTINA SNYDER'S VICE-PRESIDENT, WILL BE PROMOTED INSTEAD.

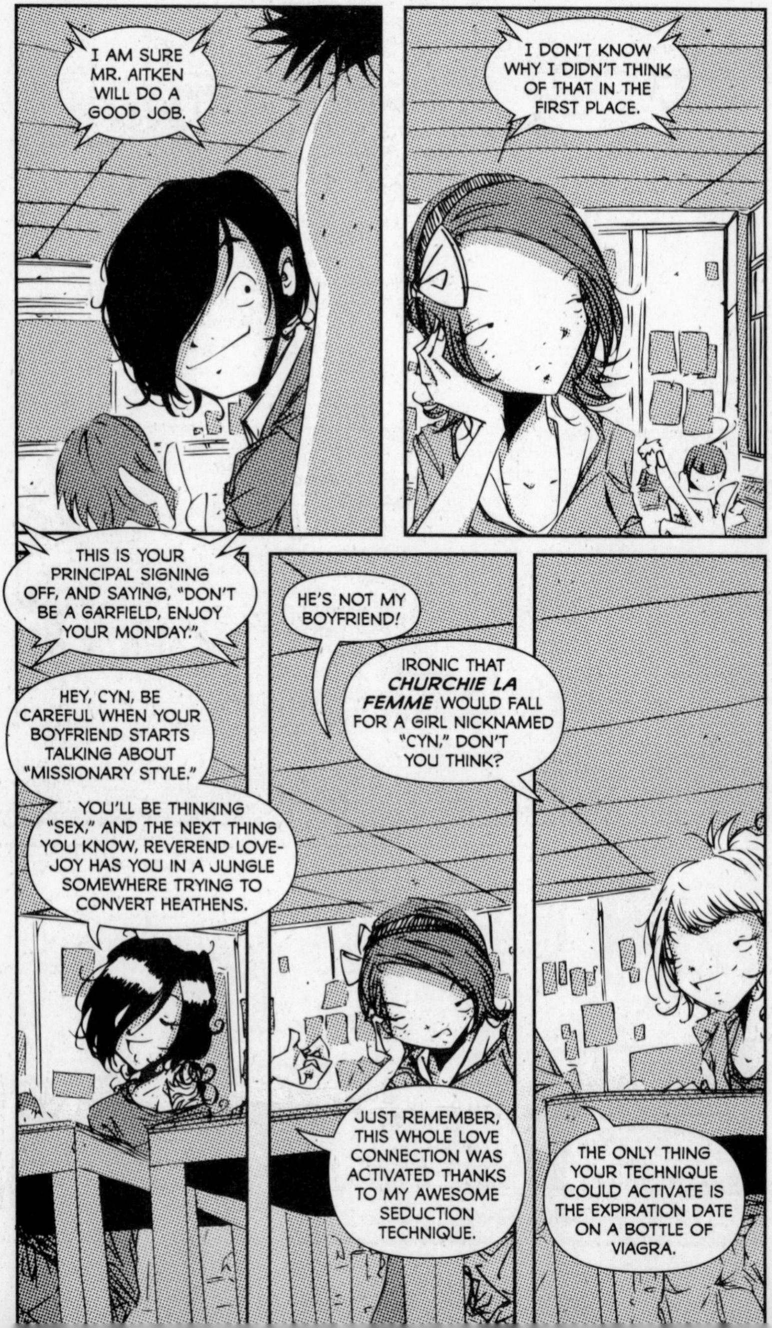
I AM SURE MR. AITKEN WILL DO A GOOD JOB.
I DON'T KNOW WHY I DIDN'T THINK OF THAT IN THE FIRST PLACE.
THIS IS YOUR PRINCIPAL SIGNING OFF, AND SAYING, "DON'T BE A GARFIELD, ENJOY YOUR MONDAY."
HEY, CYN, BE CAREFUL WHEN YOUR BOYFRIEND STARTS TALKING ABOUT "MISSIONARY STYLE."
YOU'LL BE THINKING "SEX," AND THE NEXT THING YOU KNOW, REVEREND LOVE-JOY HAS YOU IN A JUNGLE SOMEWHERE TRYING TO CONVERT HEATHENS.
HE'S NOT MY BOYFRIEND!
IRONIC THAT *CHURCHIE LA FEMME* WOULD FALL FOR A GIRL NICKNAMED "CYN," DON'T YOU THINK?
JUST REMEMBER, THIS WHOLE LOVE CONNECTION WAS ACTIVATED THANKS TO MY AWESOME SEDUCTION TECHNIQUE.
THE ONLY THING YOUR TECHNIQUE COULD ACTIVATE IS THE EXPIRATION DATE ON A BOTTLE OF VIAGRA.

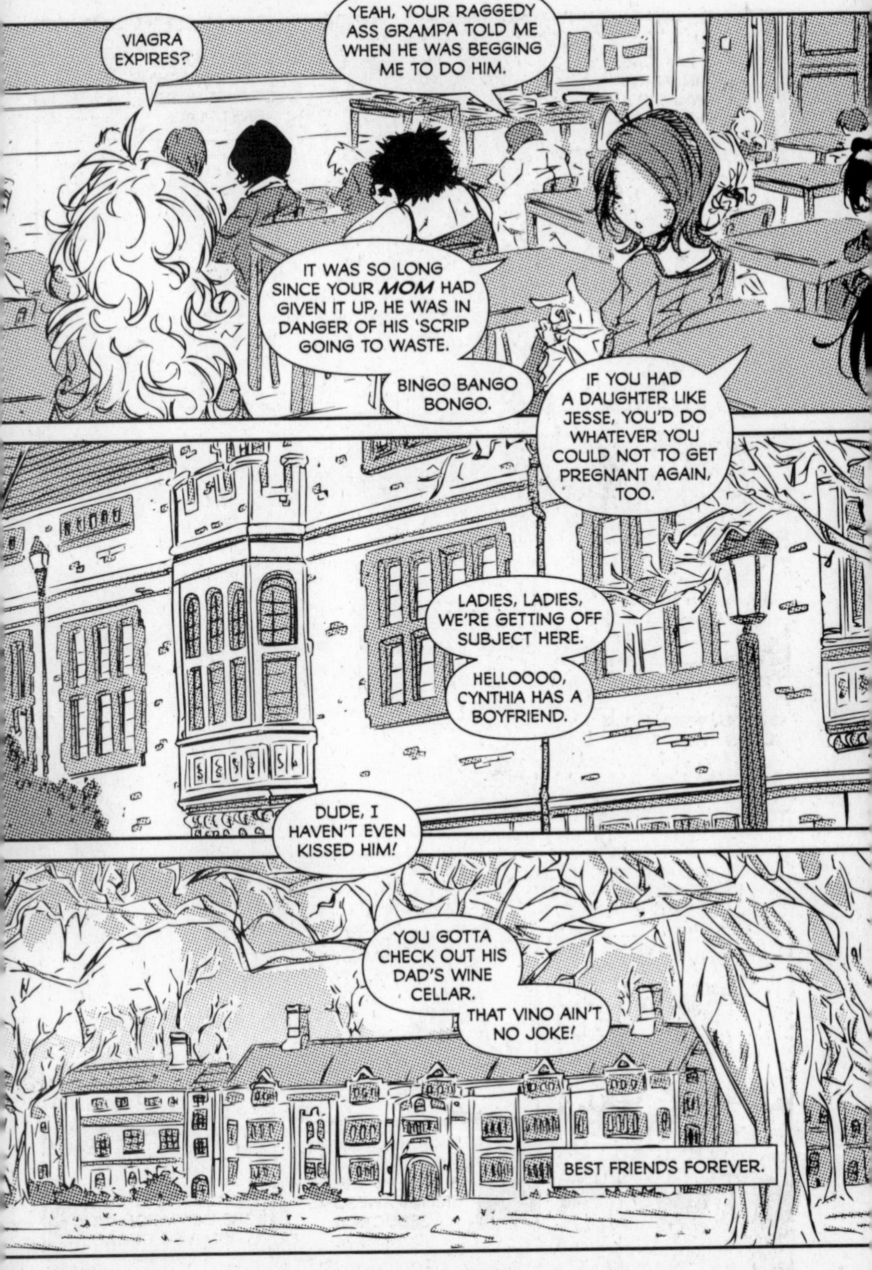
VIAGRA EXPIRES?
YEAH, YOUR RAGGEDY ASS GRAMPA TOLD ME WHEN HE WAS BEGGING ME TO DO HIM.
IT WAS SO LONG SINCE YOUR *MOM* HAD GIVEN IT UP, HE WAS IN DANGER OF HIS 'SCRIP GOING TO WASTE.
BINGO BANGO BONGO.
IF YOU HAD A DAUGHTER LIKE JESSE, YOU'D DO WHATEVER YOU COULD NOT TO GET PREGNANT AGAIN, TOO.
LADIES, LADIES, WE'RE GETTING OFF SUBJECT HERE.
HELLOOOO, CYNTHIA HAS A BOYFRIEND.
DUDE, I HAVEN'T EVEN KISSED HIM!
YOU GOTTA CHECK OUT HIS DAD'S WINE CELLAR.
THAT VINO AIN'T NO JOKE!
BEST FRIENDS FOREVER.

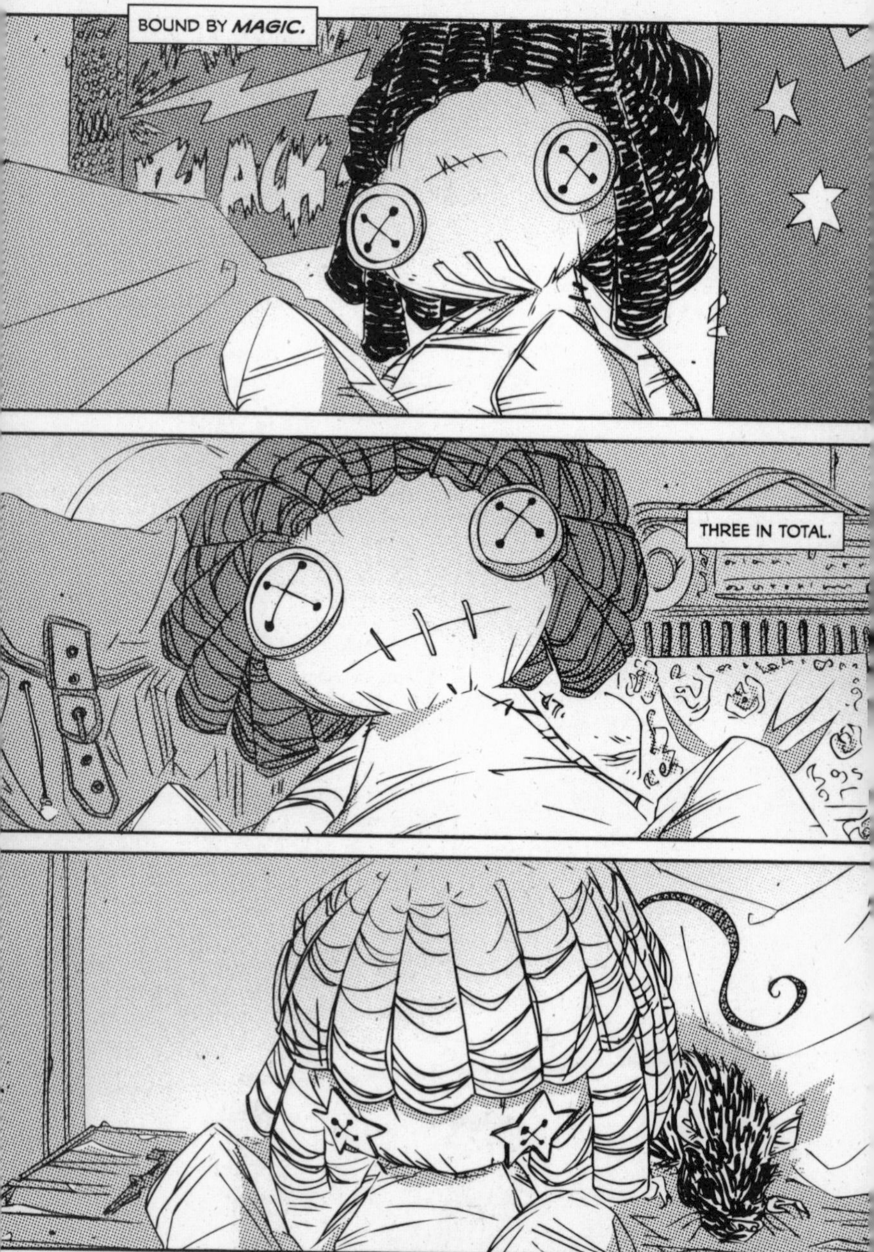
BOUND BY MAGIC.
THREE IN TOTAL.
THREE IN POWER...?

ABOUT THE AUTHORS

JAMIE S. RICH is the author of four prose novels, including *Cut My Hair*, *I Was Someone Dead*, and *The Everlasting*. He wrote the comics series *Love the Way You Love*, which was illustrated by Marc Ellerby. He spends a lot of his time watching movies, which he reviews for DVDTalk.com.

Rich first collaborated with JOËLLE JONES on the acclaimed comic book *12 Reasons Why I Love Her*, and they have since shown up as a team in the pages of *Popgun*, *Portland Noir*, and *Madman Atomic Comics*. Joëlle also did the cover and interior illustrations for Jamie's novel *Have You Seen the Horizon Lately?*, and their most recent full-length effort was the acclaimed crime graphic novel, *You Have Killed Me*. Rich is currently working on new projects with artists Natalie Nourigat and Dan Christensen.

Joëlle Jones has contributed to the long-running comics series *Fables* at DC/Vertigo and *Ultimate Spider-Man* at Marvel Comics, and she drew the Minx young adult graphic novel *Token*, written by Alisa Kwitney. She has drawn two issues of the Eisner-nominated series *Madame Xanadu*, written by Matt Wagner; worked with writer Zack Whedon on a comic book spin-off of the popular *Dr. Horrible* web series; and drew the New York Times best-selling *Troublemaker* graphic novels, a collaboration with author Janet Evanovich that continues the writer's series of Alexandra Barnaby novels. At present, she is putting the finishing touches on long-form books for both Vertigo and Graphic Universe, and she's plotting new creator-owned comics with Rich.

NICOLAS HITORI DE is a comic artist and illustrator living in Amiens, France. Having studied at les ateliers des beaux arts of Paris and Disney Accademia in Milan, he has created works in print (Disney, Milan), publicity, TV (M6, Nolife) and music (Virgin Princesse). After collaborating on Josh Howard's *Dead@17* series, he met Jamie S. Rich on MySpace and has now realized his dream to be published by Oni Press.

confessions123.com • joellejones.com • nicohitoride.com

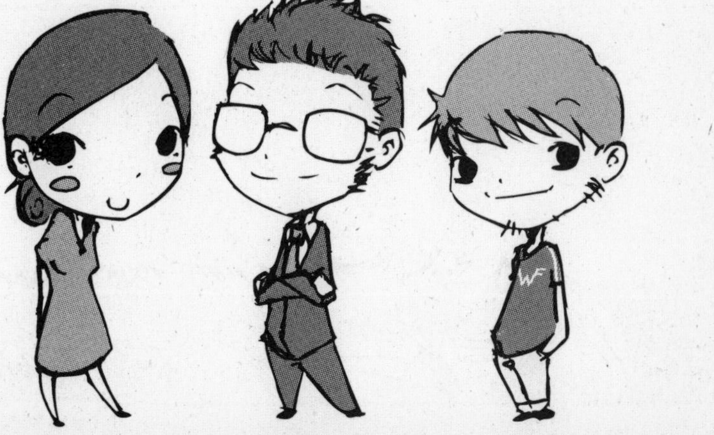
WF